THE NEW MANAGER

Also by Alfred Tack

MARKETING AND MANAGEMENT BOOKS

Executive Development
Building, Training, and Motivating a Sales Force
How to Overcome Nervous Tension and Speak Well in Public
How to Double Your Income in Selling
1000 Ways to Increase your Sales
Sell Better – Live Better
Sell Your Way to Success
How to Train Yourself to Succeed in Selling
How to Increase Sales by Telephone
Profitable Letter Writing
How to Increase Your Sales to Industry
How to Succeed in Selling
How to Sell Successfully Overseas
Professional Salesmanship
Successful Sales Management
Marketing Strategy in Action
Marketing, The Sales Manager's Role
How to Succeed as a Sales Manager
Motivational Leadership
The High Quality Manager

FICTION

The Great Hijack
The Spy Who wasn't Exchanged
The Top Steal
Forecast-Murder
Murder Takes Over
PA to Murder
Death Kicks a Pebble
Selling's Murder
Interviewing's Killing
The Prospect's Dead
The Test Match Murder
A Murder is Staged
Killing Business
Death Takes a Dive
Return of the Assassin

The
New Manager

Alfred Tack

Gower

Published by
Gower Publishing Company Limited,
Gower House,
Croft Road,
Aldershot,
Hants GU11 3HR,
England

Gower Publishing Company,
Old Post Road,
Brookfield,
Vermont 05036,
U.S.A.

British Library Cataloguing in Publication Data
Tack, Alfred
   The new manager.
   1. Management 2. Accounting
   I. Title
658'.0024657   HD31

Library of Congress Cataloguing-in-Publication Data
Tack, Alfred.
   The new manager / Alfred Tack.
   p.   cm.
   1. Executive ability. 2. Management. I. Title.
   HD38.2T34 1988
   658.4--dc19   87-38075

ISBN 0 566 02754 2

Contents

1. The Bombshell   1
2. On Becoming a Manager   8
3. Self-Appraisal   23
4. A Break for Lunch   35
5. People Analysis   42
6. Communications   57
7. Making Plans   75
8. Motivational Forces   80
9. Long-Term Motivation   88
10. Time for Reflection   107
11. More Motivational Forces   111
12. Performance Appraisal   128
13. More Discussions   161
14. Don't Spend – Spend – Spend   165
15. Managing Time   173
16. Decisions Postponed   195
17. Problem-Solving   200
18. Decision-Making   212
19. Staff Training   225
20. Creativity   236
21. Situation-Adaptable Management   252
22. A New Beginning   260

1   The Bombshell

The directors of Management Skills International sat sipping their after-luncheon coffee. Fresh-faced, country-born Mrs Young and her daughter Clare cleared the table after a 'Luncheon Special' – the name coined by Clare for her father's business lunches. George Young had been a director of Management Skills International for 20 years, and was as close as anyone could get to the company's founder, Greg Ryder. Young had invited his co-directors to lunch to discuss a worrying problem.

Sitting around the table were Peter Lewis, in charge of marketing and sales courses; Mary Glynne, concerned with human resources; accountant Philip Cooper, director of financially based courses; and Harvard-trained Nina Westlake, whose sphere of influence was management training in general. When Mrs Young and Clare had left the room, attitudes changed. Foreheads wrinkled – lips tightened – eyes became troubled.

Young said, "We all know why we are here, but since Nina has been in the USA for a month or so she will want to be brought up to date.

"I'm not certain what loyalty means in a business sense, but,

1

whatever the definition, we are all disciples of Greg Ryder – which is not to claim that we could not be head-hunted.

"None of us has a contract; Greg believes that nothing should stand in the way of us leaving if we want to do so, and that nothing should stand in the way of his replacing us if we fail to live up to his high standards. In all my 20 years I have never known him to act unfairly towards anyone – until now, that is."

He paused, and his associates looked expectantly at him, waiting for him to continue.

They saw a slim, fit man of 52, well dressed in a brown birdseye-patterned suit. No leisure wear for him at a business meeting, even if it was being held in his own house. Twice he sipped from the coffee cup, then continued: "I want to remind all of you of your promise; not one word of our discussion must be leaked. If it came to the ears of Greg and he consulted Weinberg's, Sarah Jones would be sacked.

"Nina, the position is this. The daughter of my greatest friend is secretary to the chief executive of Weinberg's, the merchant bankers. For her to break a confidence is almost beyond belief. That she has done so is only because of the great affection she has for my family. She asked her father's advice and he told her that sometimes friendship takes precedence over a wrongful act, provided that act is not criminal.

"The confidence she broke was that Greg Ryder is negotiating through Weinberg's for the sale of our company, Management Skills International, to the electronics group Dysons. Seemingly, they want to enlarge their own training division and offer a training service to industry generally. They think this would turn a non-profit area into a profit centre, and would be very good PR for them."

Young paused again, then added, "I must emphasize that I have great faith in Greg, but we must all consider our future".

Nina Westlake interrupted: "How can we consider the future when we have all made cross-your-heart promises not to reveal the source of our information? Unless we confront Greg, we can't make any decision, and we can't confront Greg because we mustn't let it be known that we have the slightest inkling of what is happening. It's stalemate!"

"I appreciate that", said Young, "but if we approach Greg he will know that something is amiss; and it wouldn't take Weinberg's long to discover the source of the leak. So that can't be an option".

Peter Lewis, his voiced raised, asked, "Then what the hell is the purpose of this meeting? I've been with the company ten years – four of them on the main board. I respect Greg, he's a great man, but if Management Skills International is being sold, we directors should be consulted". Lewis, a slim, fair man whose strength was in initiating courses and teaching, had never become close to the managing director, Greg Ryder, and had often been a discordant voice outside the boardroom.

Nina Westlake had had a brilliant career before joining Management Skills International at the age of 29 and becoming a board member at 32. It was typical of Ryder to promote Nina so quickly, his dictum being: *Only ability counts when considering promotion – not length of service. Long-term loyalty should be rewarded in other ways.* So Nina had bypassed other executives to become a main board director.

She said, "Of course he ought to consult us, of course loyalty is two-way, of course everyone believes in team spirit. In the States, where I spent much of my time, I experienced a great deal of phoney razzamatazz to prove that we all had team spirit.

"I'm very fond of Greg, and I admire him – he's the best chief executive I've met outside the USA. If he sells out, some of us will stay, some will go. That's the nature of things. However, in spite of a general feeling that it is hard luck to be made redundant, it does carry a stigma. There's always a question mark against the person who has been made redundant. If he or she was so good, would they have been cast out? That is the general belief. I don't agree with it, but it is still the belief. Therefore, the reason given for any of us leaving Management Skills wouldn't cut much ice with a future employer – and we are in a very small market. So far as

I'm concerned, I could be particularly vulnerable. Maybe the new chief executive will be a male chauvinist pig!

"My first question is, Why should Greg keep it all so secret? It isn't like him. As we don't know the answer, should we pre-empt his decision, and test out the jobs market now? That seems to make good sense to me."

Young said, "Yes, it does make sense, and no, it doesn't make sense. As I've said, I, personally, have every faith in Greg, but I mustn't let emotion override commonsense. Nina, I've asked myself the question you just raised a hundred times. Why the secrecy, when Greg is usually so open? I can't find the answer.

"It's all very well to pre-empt a decision, but the moment we take any step to consult head-hunters or reply to advertisements, there's the possibility of a leak. Then Greg wouldn't give us two minutes of his time."

"May I butt in?" asked Philip Cooper, thin, 6 foot 2 inches tall, balding at 41. He had wanted to become an actor but had been dissuaded by his parents, and, at their insistence, had qualified as an accountant. His acting ability had turned him into a brilliant, audience-gripping instructor in what could otherwise be some very dull subjects.

Cooper, not waiting for Young's nod, went on: "We must face some facts: Greg holds 95 per cent of the shares and we only hold one qualifying share each. We have become training specialists and are known as training specialists, not line managers.

"Imagine applying for a position as a marketing director or a financial director. I don't think we'd really stand much of a chance against others who have spent their years not teaching, but actually carrying out the marketing or financial functions. We all know the cliché *He who can does — he who can't teaches*. It doesn't refer to us, but will prospective employers appreciate that, especially in view of the very high salaries we are receiving? There is another factor too: no other training group in Europe could pay us anything like the money we're receiving from Greg. Of course, we're worth every penny, but only in our respective spheres of activity.

"Greg has us in a cleft stick. It won't be easy to get jobs elsewhere at anywhere near our current earnings. We've been too long on top, we're too well known, we've all been on television, we've all been interviewed, we're the leaders in the world of training.

"I don't want to return to accountancy, and I'm quite sure that none of you wants to revert to what you were doing before taking up training and consultancy work. From my past experience I know that whatever negotiations have taken place, the merchant bankers, advisers, and the prospective buyers always insist upon secrecy. Buyers, especially, don't want a leak that could affect their shares, their employees, or a trade union's activities, until everything has been settled."

Mary Glynne, tall, slender, with the grace of a ballerina – a legacy from her early days in ballet school – had a degree in personnel management. Before joining Ryder 9 years earlier at the age of 30 she had been personnel manager for Camley Computers. "My views", she said, "coincide with Nina's. Either we should demand the truth from Greg, or call up a few head-hunters and tell them we're in the market. I appreciate that we may not reach our present salaries anywhere else, since we may have to move to a different type of environment, but it's better to take some action than to wait on events."

After some discussion Young said, "This is not a very happy situation"! He repeated, "Not a happy situation at all!"

Peter Lewis snorted. "We're not concerned with happiness, only with our future. Maybe Greg will give us a share of the fortune he'll receive, but that isn't like him. He pays for results; why give us anything if Dyson's insist on employing us?"

Young said, "One thing's for sure: Greg won't work for anyone else. If he sells out he'll walk out."

Lewis said, "I think we're quite capable of carrying on successfully without Greg, provided the new chief executive is someone we can work with, or one of us is made chief executive. After all, Greg is nearly 60!"

"Thank you very much," said Young drily. "I'm 54! Does that mean I couldn't run a company?"

"Of course not," said Lewis, "but it is a fact that everyone slows down after 50."

Young said, "I don't think we need continue on these lines. Let us again consider the options. What steps should we take"?

Philip Cooper, always a calming influence, took over. "We're going round in circles getting nowhere. Because George's friend's daughter is on 3 months' maternity leave, we shan't be able to receive any more information via Weinberg's, and neither can we check out anything at Dyson's; so we shall have to make a decision on the facts as we know them. We can either act collectively or individually. Why should we take the risks which always occur with takeovers, not the least of which is being able to work with the Dyson team? How long should we last there? Some executives are always made redundant in takeovers. To offer our services to a competitor is a non-starter. None of us could work with competitors after the years we've been with Greg. Well, perhaps that's a mistake; we could do so, but none of us would want to, although it may become an option.

"We could check with those clients who have appreciated our worth or made offers to us in the past – we've all had such offers – but there's a difference between negotiating from strength and ringing a client to tell him you've been made redundant!

"Do we confront Greg and tell him that we've learned the news from someone at Dyson's? It's a white lie, but it would take the heat off George's friend. Or do we do nothing, hoping that we'll be offered generous redundancy terms if they are going to make any of us redundant? Some of us are bound to go – they have their own training team.

"At first they may want us all to stay, but never in the history of takeovers have all the old directors stayed on for very long. These facts have to be considered, and we should make up our minds what action to take, within the next 7 days.

"Next week we shall all have to be at Hartley Wintney to finalize our new course, *Welcome to the New Manager*. Next week will be tough going. Greg, as usual, will be at his most difficult, to ensure that the course is as near perfect as possible. But we shall have some spare time each evening, when we can get together and consider the options, over and over again. By Friday night we must come to a decision, and we must all accept a majority decision. Does everyone agree?"

Everyone agreed.

2 On Becoming a Manager

Hartley Lane turns right off the A30 about half a mile short of Hartley Wintney. Some 300 yards along that lane is a gravel area leading to a pair of black wrought-iron gates. Centrally on each gate is entwined an iron girdle of leaves, highlighting MSI in gold lettering. From the gateway an asphalt path twists its way towards the Manor House itself.

Stanton Hall was built for the third Duke of Stanton at the beginning of the century. It then comprised some thirty bedrooms in addition to service quarters. The Duke, a heavy gambler, sold the Hall during one of his losing runs, and it was bought by Cedric Manson, a tycoon who, although wealthy, felt considerable bitterness at not having been awarded a title. He therefore awarded one to himself, calling himself Lord of the Manor, and his home was then referred to as the Manor House.

During the Second World War he decided that there were other places safer than England. He sold the property to an insurance company whose own offices in London had been bombed out. After the war the company, in turn, sold the Manor House to the manager of a five-star hotel, and he formed a consortium to turn it into the Stanton Luxury Hotel.

The manager proved an old dictum correct – that a second-in-command is not necessarily managing director material. The project failed and the liquidators sold the building to Greg Ryder. The Manor House became the headquarters of Management Skills International.

The company had been formed by Ryder some 20 years earlier, with the objective of capturing a large slice of the international training market. Greg had left school at 18, when good jobs were hard to come by. After humping crates of wine for an off-licence for several months, he applied for a straight commission job selling fitted kitchens direct to users. He was successful, and quickly became the company's top salesman. Ryder had found his niche.

His success continued, and at the age of 26 he became sales manager of Carter Rentals, one of the large groups in the TV and home appliance field. Two years later he was appointed managing director, and the next 2 years were record-breaking years for that company.

When asked the secret of his success by a business journalist writing a profile of him, he answered, "A chief executive may be a genius, a great strategist, a fine economist . . . What use are these attributes, however, if his people botch his directives? Greater success could be achieved by a less qualified managing director, one who believed in the continual training of all his personnel. Training is the main reason for our success. Everyone in the group knows he is there to satisfy customer needs."

Ryder had become imbued with training as a means of overcoming recessions and increasing market shares during booms, when he had spent a year in the USA. Later, when he was managing director of Carter Rentals, Ryder would still occasionally take part as an instructor in training courses.

An offer had been made for Carter's by an American company, an offer that could not be refused. But soon after the takeover had been completed, Ryder realized that he did not agree with the policies of the parent company, nor could he carry them out.

Happily married, with two children and a healthy bank
balance from his high earnings and shrewd investments,
Ryder knew exactly what he was going to do. He would set up
a management consultancy that would include a training
services division. The consultancy would help to bring in
leads for training, but the main profit centre would be the
training division. His success was meteoric.

From a small office in Baker Street, with the courses being
held in hotels, his company progressed to an office block
which included three courses and four syndicate rooms. Later
he purchased a building in Slough, which enabled him to have
six course rooms and twelve syndicate rooms.

He changed the name of his company from Ryder
Management Consultancy Ltd to Management Skills
International, so that he could enter the market for
management and financial courses, the emphasis having
previously been on salesmanship. Associate companies were
very quickly set up throughout the world. Ryder was soon able
to make the claim that a multinational could be sure of
employees receiving exactly the same training overseas as in
Britain. His final ambition was realized when he bought the
Stanton Hotel.

After facing many problems concerned with the building of
extensions, he achieved his objective. The main building
housed ten course rooms and thirty syndicate rooms.

Newly built two-storey buildings sprouted from both sides
of the old Manor House, then turned inwards towards the
grounds, forming a quadrangle. There were bedrooms to
accommodate 150 guests, two restaurants, and a leisure
centre. There were also three highly profitable bars. The
health centre contained equipment for stretching limbs,
building muscles, and working off hangovers. In the
quadrangle between the wings were a swimming pool and a
putting green.

Some envious competitors referred to Marketing Skills
International headquarters as a holiday camp rather than a
training centre, but they were wrong. Delegates were worked

extremely hard, and deserved their relaxation. There were of course delegates looking for a good time in mixed company, but the majority were there to improve their management, marketing, and selling skills.

Greg Ryder's office on the first floor of the main building overlooked the swimming pool. The offices housing the registrars, accountants, and sales office staff, and the instructors' quarters were in the annexe. Ryder's office had three television sets – plus videos – each connected to cameras sited in every course room, so that Greg could, if necessary, look in on three courses at a time.

Instructors dreaded a call to Greg's office immediately after they had completed a session. But their fears turned to delight more often than not when, instead of criticism, they received praise.

Ryder was seated in his favourite position, his leather chair tilted back, his feet on the gold-embossed, tooled red leather desk top. It was 8.30 am and he had motored from his home in Cadogan Square, Knightsbridge. Although he had his own bedroom and sitting-room in the annexe for use during his stay at headquarters, and that was often for seven days a week, he went home at weekends whenever he could. To be with his family was his main relaxation, but he was not with them very often.

At that moment Ryder was contemplating the future – *What to do with the rest of his life, if there was to be much of a 'rest' to look forward to.* The cardiologist had told him to take things easy for 6 months and then, after further tests, he would either advise a heart bypass operation or an even more relaxing life. This advice Greg had passed on neither to his wife nor his co-directors. He, Greg Ryder, must always be the strong man – never ill like ordinary mortals. Supermen were not supposed to be affected by standard complaints – coughs and sneezes, aches and pains. He had never taken a day off in 20 years. Fight it off, whatever the 'it' was, by working harder was his creed.

The third factor was exercise. The physician had told him

that he needed to cut out the car travel, walk more, and exercise more. Well he couldn't cut out the car travel, but what he could do was to buy a farm and work on the land over the weekends. A smile spread across his face as he thought of the farm. He knew exactly what he would do. He would work harder than any farmer, and would set out to make the farm the most efficient and profitable farm in the land.

Somehow he didn't feel that that was what the physician had meant by exercise. His mind switched. How would his co-directors and his employees spread around the world react to the news? He shrugged his shoulders, sighed, removed his feet from the desk, and switched his mind to concentrate on course assessments by delegates.

All delegates were invited to rate each session's content and instructor skills, from one to ten. Greg Ryder was not the type of man to be palmed off by generalities. His courses had to be the best, and the only way to discover whether they were the best was to obtain delegates' views.

At 8.50 the intercom light flashed and his secretary's voice announced that all the directors were in the rehearsal room. Ryder stood up, took a practice golf swing without a club, straightened his tie and left the room.

Rehearsal rooms were in fact any syndicate room which happened to be vacant at the time. All were furnished in the same style — in the centre a round table, while alongside the wall facing the window were ranged the computers and TV video recorders.

In the rehearsal room George Young looked at his watch. "Two minutes to go," he said, knowing that Ryder always arrived on the stroke of the appointed time, a gimmick which had led to many stories, mostly apocryphal.

Ryder, in the meantime, had left his office, walked along the oak-lined corridor, still intact from the original Manor House, down the curving staircase to the lobby. Opposite the front entrance hall was a door opening on to a corridor that led to the annexe. Arriving at the course room sector, he smilingly acknowledged the instructors and delegates who were arriving to attend the courses beginning that day.

He walked up the stairs to the syndicate rooms lining another corridor, opened the second door on the left, to be greeted by his team. The first step was about to be taken in launching a new course for new managers.

Automatically, Ryder glanced at his watch. Exactly 9 am.

After the usual chorus of good mornings, Ryder sat down at the table, to be joined by his associates. There came the opening of expensive briefcases, papers placed on the table, a flick back of hair by Mary Glynne, a straightening of the back by George Young, who did not want to be dwarfed by his neighbour, Philip Cooper . . .

Peter Lewis thought the opening words were typical of Ryder. The man had to be punctilious about everything, and boring repetition meant little to him if he wanted to emphasize a message. For weeks he had been driving home the need for a course for new managers, and had set objectives for each of the instructors.

Ryder, unaware of Lewis's thoughts, began: "We are all aware that most new managers are fearful – fearful of the unknown, fearful of not measuring up to expectations, fearful of the reactions of old friends now under their control . . . Overcoming these fears can be a difficult problem . . ."

Peter Lewis, immaculate in a grey flannel suit, pink shirt with white attached collar, and a carefully knotted multicoloured tie, went into a comatose state. Usually, when Ryder spoke everyone became alert, listening carefully to his words of wisdom, but not when Ryder wanted only to dot every i and cross every t. Ryder would argue that it was his insistence on perfection in every detail which had played a large part in his success. On other occasions he would use this strategy of repetition to wear down the opposition.

Lewis came to and once more focused his mind on Ryder's voice as he heard his chief saying, "Let me emphasize the need to keep to a schedule. This week we must decide on our controllers. As you know, the controllers are responsible for appointing their understudies, who will, later, take over the sessions. Sometimes the rehearsing of substitutes is unnecessarily delayed. Although you are all hard-pushed for time, I would ask you to learn the sessions delegated to you within 4 weeks. You will also complete the scripts for each session within 6 weeks. You will complete plans for syndicates, workshops, films, videos and games within 8 weeks — and at each step there will be checks, which I shall control personally.

"Rehearsals will be in 10 weeks, and a dress rehearsal 2 weeks after that, that is, 12 weeks from now. Peter, you will arrange for the sales brochures and the changes in programmes. You will also brief your sales people immediately we know the exact date for the first course."

Ryder paused, then went on: "The first session will begin as usual, with names of instructors, standard introductions, background of our group and administrative details, etc."

He smiled broadly, deepening the furrows in his cheeks. "Then I'll begin by telling the delegates that while mind-reading is not scientifically proven, I shall try to read their minds."

At this stage even George Young thought that Ryder was taking repetition too far. He was merely reiterating the standard opening for every course; but Ryder continued with his theme. "I shall paint a word picture of their thoughts subsequent to being told about their promotion. First you will have feelings of elation — 'I've got the job!' Friends and family will be telephoning, perhaps about some entirely different matter, and the promotion will be introduced casually. You'll probably use words such as 'Oh, by the way, I've just been made manager of the supplies division', or whatever. There is all-round pleasure and pride over your achievement. Possibly the immediate question from your wife will be 'How much?' This can cause a minor setback. The fact is, whatever the reward, it never seems to come up to expectations. But remember, ultimately your remuneration will depend upon how successful you are. Your being here is an important step towards that success.

"Of course, if you have applied for an advertised post, that is different. But I think I am right in saying that most of you here have been promoted from within your own companies."

Glancing around at his co-directors, Ryder added, "Any comments?"

There were none.

Mary Glynne moved her chair back so that she could not only stretch her long, shapely legs, but cross them as well. Nina Westlake thought *Mary always does that!*, while noticing Greg's glance at the glimpse of shapely thigh as Mary smoothed the slits in her skirt. Nina always wore long skirts to hide her own rather chubby legs.

Ryder continued as if addressing the delegates, not his co-directors: "After that initial high you may come down to earth and find that from time to time there are uncomfortable spasms working their way across your stomach and back again. Fear may take over, but don't worry about that. It is really fear of change, and although you have every confidence in yourself, the dreadful thought may cross your mind that now you have to make the decisions, some of which could be wrong.

"By the end of this week all your fears will have disappeared completely. This whole course is based on facts that have been verified by research. We shall not mislead you, and you must not mislead us. But most of all, you must not mislead yourselves."

Ryder switched his address to his associates, saying, "I shall then give them encouragement by explaining that there is a dearth of dedicated managers – managers who want to improve their knowledge and skills, managers who can innovate and motivate, managers who do not disappear at the slightest sign of trouble. Then I'll continue: "That old tag *A price has to be paid for success* is true, and being an old tag does not make it any less true. If you are not willing to pay a price you cannot succeed.

"Possibly the first price to be paid is that you can no longer be 'one of the boys' or one of the girls. If, in the past, you have made it a practice to have the odd beer after working hours with a colleague, that may have been fine. It can continue, but not as a regular habit. Now and again is enough. Such after-hours meetings, as you all know, become gossip times. The outcome invariably is criticism of higher authority. As a manager therefore you can no longer take part in such discussions. You must be friendly and helpful and also allow subordinates to let their hair down and complain if they wish to about you or higher authority, but when that happens, you have to take the side of higher authority.

"This does not mean that you are subservient to such authority, only that you do not agree with the subordinate until you have cleared the matter with the executive concerned. When you discuss the matter with the executive, you may well take the subordinate's side – you may argue his case strongly and, if you wish, you can then return to the subordinate and explain to him the changes which are to be made.

"So remember, you are to be friendly, helpful, and have the occasional drink together, but, I repeat, you are no longer 'one of the boys'. You may perhaps have to change their attitudes or your own. You know all their tricks – personal use of the firm's telephones, untrue excuses for absenteeism, that day off because of some feigned illness . . . You can no longer condone even minor offences. It may be that on occasion you will turn a blind eye to them, but you cannot agree that they are right."

George Young interrupted: "Don't you think, Greg, that you are giving home truths too early? Shouldn't we try to win them over first? Mightn't they be squirming a little when you hit them so hard, and that squirming could turn to antagonism."

Ryder shrugged his shoulders. "I disagree," he said, without giving any reason for his disagreement.

Nina Westlake said, "My session is built around the new manager seeing himself as others will see him. The first step, surely, is for him to understand himself."

George Young said, "Fair enough, Nina, but the question I am posing is, *Is it wise to stress fears so early in the day?* Not all managers are fearful."

Ryder interrupted. "Our research proved otherwise, George. Even the most bombastic, arrogant, and supposedly very strong characters, under controlled questioning, still had to admit that they were perhaps putting on a bit of an act to cover up some of their fears."

"I'm not sure," said Young, "But . . ."

Nina interrupted again. "You're too kind, George. You don't like to feel that you may be upsetting anyone."

"I could be wrong", Ryder admitted. "I'm not always right you know . . ."

"But you are!" said Mary Glynne with a look of mock innocence. "You are always right, Greg."

"How about when I disagreed with you," said Ryder with a smile, "about wearing trouser suits at courses?"

"Oh well, you were wrong about that, and still are. But that wasn't a mistake on your part. You still remember the mini-skirt, and would like to see it come back."

Everyone laughed except Nina.

Pausing for the laughter to subside, Ryder continued: "Let's change the subject and continue with the session."

Peter Lewis said, "If you don't mind my saying so, Greg, I feel you should mention, even at this early stage, that we believe in situation-adaptable management."

Mary Glynne cut in: "I have that down as my session to close the course. If a manager can't adapt to various situations he will never be a top class manager."

Everyone agreed, and Mary continued: "It would help my session if, quite early, we profiled the successful manager, as we do with leadership." She looked down at her notes and said, "This is a list from my last supervisors' course, but with a little guidance it would be quite applicable to this course:

- Get work done on time
- Keep costs down

- Motivate people to give of their best
- Communicate clearly
- Make good decisions
- Solve problems
- Be willing to delegate
- Use experience and knowledge to help subordinates
- Be dependable, loyal and tactful
- Behave consistently
- Ensure that working areas are kept clean and tidy
- Maintain control at all times
- Plan and organize efficiently
- Influence people by cheerfulness, integrity, patience, and enthusiasm
- Train people for promotion
- Create a good working atmosphere
- Correct people's mistakes constructively
- Be approachable and understanding
- Listen well
- Recognize priorities, and make good use of time
- Be flexible
- Be keen to improve own performance
- Be co-operative and helpful to colleagues and seniors
- Establish and maintain good working relations with everyone
- Do not pass the buck
- Have no favourites, and be fair to everyone
- Treat people as individuals
- Do not be easily deceived
- Encourage and help people to progress
- Praise good work
- Set standards of behaviour by example
- Know company policies, objectives, rules, agreements, procedures, standards, systems, accepted customs and practices."

When Mary had finished reading from her notes, Nina Westlake spoke: "Although I agree wholeheartedly with allowing delegates to set objectives, the delegates of course won't recognize their own weaknesses. I only mention this because, as you have gathered, my session will be based on interpersonal comparison tests. That's why I think it is right to profile early. I can build on that, and also, the sooner we can bring about participation the better."

"Good for you!" said Mary, again unnecessarily recrossing her legs, just to irritate Nina.

Greg looked at his two lady directors. He greatly admired Mary's abilities, but recognized her feminine wiles. She was obviously on the lookout for a worthwhile husband. Nina was happily married to an export director.

"We're going ahead too fast," Ryder said.

"We're covering future sessions. Let me return to the session after I've given Mary's list of objectives. I'll say something like this. Irrespective therefore of your title and skills and duties; irrespective of whether you are a shop foreman, a ward sister, a superintendent or a milk depot manager; whether you have charge of a hundred salesmen, eight operatives, twenty riggers, or fifty miners; you all have one thing in common: you have to work through people.

"A manager may have his own specific tasks, but if the people he manages are not effective, he cannot be a success as a manager. While a manager must never be so emotionally linked with any of his staff as to affect his clear thinking, he should still have a high regard for them, and this should be brought out in the training and help he gives them. A manager is judged by the results of his team.

"Too many managers are thrown in at the deep end and allowed to muddle through, so that they believe too much in skills instead of people management."

Ryder paused to look at some notes and, at that moment, there was a timid knock on the door, which opened to reveal a white-coated lady about to wheel in a coffee trolley. "Have your coffee," said Ryder. "I've some 'phone calls to make. We'll start again" — he looked at his watch — "at 10.30."

When the cups had been filled Lewis said, "He seems

subdued this morning. Maybe the fire has gone from his belly at last."

George Young disagreed: "Not on your life! I've known him for many years and his enthusiasm is unquenchable; at times he quietens down a little, but only to allow him time to have his next dynamic burst of innovative thinking." Young paused, then said, "I've booked a table at the Cricketers' Arms for 8 o'clock. I think we should leave our personal discussions until then."

Nina Westlake said, "I may possibly have the solution to our problems — in fact, I'm sure I have."

Young didn't like the sound of that. Ryder himself, while acknowledging that Nina could think clearly, also knew that she could be most difficult at times. When she made up her mind, it was almost impossible to dissuade her from implementing her decisions.

Peter Lewis said, "I'm sure we've all developed our own ideas as to how to tackle the situation. May I suggest that rather than have heated arguments, we each state our case on different evenings. Then on Friday we can all vote on the best solution."

Young agreed, but with a proviso. "As I mentioned before, I don't want us to get too involved now while we're in the middle of a rehearsal. I am in a difficult position. On the one hand I trust my old friend Greg implicitly, but on the other hand I know that sometimes he has strange ideas as to what is, and what is not, generous.

"He has told me so many times that we're all paid for the work we do, and if our appointment is terminated at the end of any week we have been paid right up to that time for our services, and should not expect anything extra. On the other hand, in spite of these views he is, as we all know, most generous on occasions to those who have either been dismissed or made redundant. I think you all know that I'm not a spendthrift, but because of my wife's asthma I've bought a flat in Fort Lauderdale, Florida, so that we can retire and live there during the winter months. I've also invested some of my savings in my son, and set him up as a computer consultant. At this stage, therefore, I can't take any risks, not for anyone, but I must apologize, because now I'm talking about the very subject that I said we should leave until this evening. So let's call off this discussion."

Cooper held up his hand, "But I must make my point," he said. "You're right about Greg – he's either wholly generous or positively mean. He's quite likely to offer us standard redundancy money plus a small golden handshake if we decide not to join the new company. On the other hand, he might give us a slice of what he receives from MSI."

That ended the matter of their future for the time being, and the discussion continued on a more general level.

Punctual as ever, Ryder returned, seeming more tense than earlier. The reason for this was that his cardiologist had telephoned him to confirm an appointment for Friday of that week. He explained to the directors that he had had a telephone call which necessitated him attending a meeting of some importantce and he would therefore be leaving early on the Friday. They all guessed, incorrectly, that the meeting was with Weinberg's, the merchant bankers, and the Dyson board.

Like Ryder, they were all capable of switching their minds and concentrating on the business on hand. They settled down and listened carefully to Ryder, who said, "Continuing with the ground to be covered in the opening session, I shall tell the new managers that they must ask for a full job description if there is not one already available. Without a job description, I'll explain, they will not know the parameters of their authority, and the objectives they will be expected to achieve. If there is no such description available, they should set themselves the task of listing every conceivable action they will be expected to take – the longer the list, the better. That list can then be pruned and they will be left with their key activities.

"After that we'll have another participation session, with each delegate drawing up his own job specification. These will be studied during the interval, and advice given individually, later on.

"And that, I think," Ryder concluded, "will cover most of the opening session."

Cooper asked, "Shall we be including a session on finance for the non-financial manager?"

"That's a point worth discussion," said Ryder. "Now it's over to you, Nina, for your session on self-appraisal; and before you begin, Peter, will you check that the recording is OK."

3 Self-Appraisal

Nina Westlake stood up. "I'll begin," she said, "as if I am addressing the class.

"Your purpose in being here is to become not just good managers but excellent managers, which will inevitably lead you to further promotion at some time in the future. However, at this stage your minds, I am sure, are already filled with plans and ideas for change: how you will tell Mr Z or Mrs Y that socks must be pulled up and shoulders put with an extra heave to the wheel. There will be a new layout to the office. You will give thought to how to appraise others, and how to motivate your team, possibly by holding a series of meetings to tell them what they should do, or should not do."

Nina paused, looked around at the supposed class, then said, "But have you asked yourselves the question you would surely put to a subordinate during an appraisal interview? What do you consider your strengths and what do you consider your weaknesses? Quite a futile question really, as you will learn during our version of performance appraisal.

"Why futile? Because it is not given to us mortals to see ourselves as others see us. We may be reasonably sure of our strengths, although maybe we haven't realized that we have other, hidden strengths; but we are rarely aware of our weaknesses, except in specific skills.

"At this course we are not considering skills as such, but mostly people management. What I am seeking in this session is for you to have a better understanding of yourself, so that you can add to your strengths and overcome any weaknesses."

Mary Glynne interrupted. "You're attempting to change people in one hour − that's a gimmick. You can't change people anyway."

"Nonsense!" Nina snapped back.

Mary laughed. "Sorry, Nina, I must apologize. I was only reacting as a delegate might."

Lewis said, "But people do change, all the time. People serving a prison sentence for armed robbery can become pillars of society. Many a coward has become a hero, and many an alcoholic has become a great advocate for abstinence".

Ryder said, "Yes, we are all changing continually. These are changes that come from within. The inner voice can inspire the greatest change.

"But that isn't the question. The question is, Can we change people's attitudes, their way of thinking, their actions, when no inner voice urges them to change and they see no reason to change?"

Nina could hold herself back no longer. She knew exactly what Greg Ryder was doing, although he was agreeing with her views. He wanted to introduce discussion. He did so enjoy discussions.

"Greg," she said, "you know full well the direction of my talk. You know that my objective is to implant in the minds of delegates the fact that only by allowing the truth to reach that inner voice can there be any change to enable them to become better managers. You know, Greg, that we do change people, but only if they believe they are making up their own mind and are not being directly criticised."

Nina, who had sat down during the discussion, stood up once more and continued, "Commonsense should influence change, but, as they say, how common is commonsense?"

Cooper said, "You can't teach people commonsense."

"That's not quite right, Philip, as I shall now try to prove." Then, as if once more addressing the new managers, she added, "Commonsense can be derived from a self-assessment plan by the use of interpersonal comparison tests.

"On the assumption that you all want to improve yourselves, your objective, as I said earlier, can only be achieved when you know what weaknesses to eradicate and what strengths to strengthen. But how are you to recognize these weaknesses? We are rarely able to accept criticism from others, since we generally believe that we are right and they are wrong.

"If someone complains that there is not enough output from your department, do you agree? Surely not! You have so many excuses − the quality of the staff is bad, staff you took over would not be those whom you would have engaged yourself − or expenses have been cut, thus not allowing you to do as you wish in buying new typewriters, computers, etc. If output from a department is bad, it is always the manager who is at fault; but if I were directly to accuse one of you of this fault, you might, metaphorically, walk out of the room, disagreeing strongly with me.

"The cure lies within yourself, and I am going to show you a way in which you will find criticism acceptable. The answer of course is self-criticism.

"If you have the strength of character to admit that you are erring in one direction or another, you will find this quite acceptable − in fact, praiseworthy. No one can read your thoughts; no one knows your views except yourself, when you have only expressed them to yourself. If I were now to ask each one of you if you are proficient at writing winning sales letters, always provided you are in a sales department, you would probably answer, 'I'm not too bad!', insinuating that in reality you were quite good. But is this true? You would not accept my judgment on your skills as a letter writer, but if that inner voice were to tell you that you were wrong, you would listen, and possibly take action.

"Do those awful after-dinner speakers ever listen to their inner voices? I doubt it! Possibly one in fifty is outstanding, and another two might be reasonable. The rest are bores — awful, terrible bores. The tragedy is that they believe themselves to be good, even those who stutter and stammer, ah and hmm, cover their plates with their voluminous notes, tell ghastly funny stories, and seem to go on for ever and ever. But who dares tell a managing director that he is not impressive as a speaker? Worse than that, after his address those nearest to him, i.e. his executive team, or associates, will say something like 'Well done, A.J.!' or 'As usual, sir, perfect!' But when these same flatterers speak to their friends or family later on, they will tell the truth with such expressions as 'Oh God, he was so bad tonight, and he thinks he's so good!'

"When that managing director returns home and his wife asks if he was pleased with his address, he will say diffidently, 'It went very well. You know Charlie Roach, he's a pretty direct talking fellow. He said to me that it was perfect for the occasion."

"There are so many kindly chairmen who, after a most awful speech, will say to the speaker, 'Well done! Well done indeed'. The speaker therefore goes on believing that he is very good, and goes on boring others for ever and ever.

"Now you know how difficult it is for us to recognize our own weaknesses."

Greg Ryder interrupted: "Nina, you lifted all that from our public-speaking course."

Nina replied, "I know, but I have changed the text, and it is the perfect example of unrecognized weakness."

"I agree, but we don't want those attending both courses to think they are paying twice for a single offering. Think of another example, Nina."

"That's not difficult. I'll give you two. First — now I'm addressing the delegates again — stand up those of you who consider yourself to be mean. No one? Oh, that's good! Next, stand up any of you who consider yourselves to be compulsive talkers — just can't stop talking. No one again. Excellent!

Here's a third. Stand up the bore. You know the bore – he will always insist on telling us about the perfect holiday he's just had, or his most wonderful children and the exams they've passed . . .

"We all like to hear such news from our friends, but during business it is often difficult to find the time to listen to these stories. We're all prepared to listen to short eulogies on family, holidays, etc. but the bore just goes on and on, showing not one picture but fifty. We are expected to produce words of praise and look at each one of them.

"Hands up the guilty person. We're bucking the odds, you know. You can carry out elementary research yourselves right now, and I'm going to give you a matter of a minute or so to think about this research. Consider five or six of your associates or friends. I'm almost sure that you will find at least one of them is a little on the mean side. He or she doesn't stand a round when he/she should, or disappears when the collection for someone's wedding or anniversary comes round; and out of the other five you will find at least one who tells you lengthy stories about his holidays, family, etc., even when he/she can see that you're really busy. There's certainly one who is a compulsive talker, who doesn't let you get a word in edgeways, who just talks and talks, and talks and talks . . . There are fifteen new managers here. Can it be claimed that we are perfect? Do you really think that you're all perfect, that none of you comes under the headings of such people as we meet in business – the mean, bores, compulsive talkers. Please don't look at your neighbour and then consider him to be the guilty person, just look within.

"We don't recognize our weaknesses, as we have said so many times, and we would deny them if they were pointed out to us. Years of experience have taught me that while we so readily recognize the weaknesses of others, we cannot see ourselves as others see us. Furthermore, it is often the weaknesses that we see and deplore in others that are also our own problem areas.

"To find a cure, let us consider a basic principle of

salesmanship. All buyers raise an objection to buying at some stage or another. They may claim that the offer is too expensive, the company's delivery is not up to standard, or they cannot rely on the quality of a product, etc. Once an objection is voiced, it is doubly hard for a salesman to overcome it. Why? Because the salesman then has to prove the buyer's opinion wrong, and no one likes to be put in the wrong. The experienced salesman therefore tries to pre-empt the main objections. The minor ones don't matter, and they may even help the sale along.

"If he feels that an objection may be raised about price, he will talk very early about quality and value against cost, so that the objection can be answered before it is voiced. That way the buyer is not proved wrong. His mind has analysed the salesman's statements and then he, the buyer, decides that his assumptions were wrong and there is no need to raise the objection.

"Simply, when there is no publicity for a viewpoint, there is no argument, but when it is brought into the open, then even if we are in the wrong, we fight to try and prove that we were right after all. We know it is impossible but we bluff our way through time and time again.

"In this session there will be no direct accusations. No one need feel that his or her weaknesses are being brought out into the open. You will be judge and jury, but you will be judging yourself.

"Let me now talk about interpersonnel comparison tests . . ."

Before she could continue, a smiling Ryder said, "Nina, there are five of us here. If you are right, one of us is a bore, one of us is a meany, and all the rest . . ."

Nina quickly interrupted: "Of course it doesn't apply to us, Greg; we are all perfect".

Everyone joined in the laughter, then Nina went on: "If the good manager is to be an outstanding manager, he must understand himself and strive for self-improvement. If he cannot recognize his own weaknesses, how can he hope to eradicate them?

"The director of a direct mail company was brilliant at writing persuasive selling letters, but he could never keep up with the demands of his clients. He had continually to make excuses for not supplying copy on time. He would blame others when in fact the main reason was his own inability to retain secretaries or audio-typists. He lacked an essential executive quality − understanding of human relations − which led him to make unfair demands on his employees, to use sarcasm as indirect criticism, and a loud voice in place of persuasion. He was always saying to his clients that 'the girls are no good these days', while believing he was a patient and considerate boss.

"The only way to see ourselves as others see us, a way that has proved effective over many years, is by interpersonnel comparison testing. This means comparing ourselves with associates with whom we work or have worked, understanding them thoroughly, and knowing their strengths and weaknesses, as they know ours.

"Ask yourself this question, *Am I a good conversationalist?*

"A good conversationalist is a person who can talk sensibly and interestingly about many subjects which are of interest to many people. He will also certainly listen intently . . . when others are putting forward their points of view."

Lewis interjected, "Why he? Why not she?"

"Because," Nina replied sweetly, "all women are good conversationalists, aren't we, Mary?"

Mary readily agreed, and, following some more banter, Nina went on: "Possibly your answer may be that you think you are a good conversationalist by that standard. But how would others rate you? You don't know, and you're never likely to find out. Your friends won't tell you the truth, and you won't believe your enemies if you have any. We are all masters of self-deception anyway. Your next step, then, must be to compare yourself with two other people, one of whom, in your opinion, is a good conversationalist and another who is not so good.

"Consider first the associate, past or present, whom you rate low in ability to sustain an interesting conversation – someone who, in company, never seems to know what to say, or if he does say something, it is usually wrong. You know such a person? Then ask youself the question, *Am I like him?*

"You will find that thought almost incredible. Let us now simulate an in-depth analysis of that person. Is he a poor conversationalist because:

- He lectures others.
- He interrupts continually.
- He becomes annoyed quickly when others disagree with him.
- He veers from one subject to another, losing the trend of what he is saying.
- He never asks a helpful question, but remains quiet until someone asks him a question.
- He speaks abruptly.
- He is never intersted in what anyone else says to him.

"Now ask yourself: *Do I interrupt others? Do I lose my temper?*

"You will find it difficult to mislead yourself. You may shudder at the thought of being like that associate, but you know now that you may perhaps have one or two of his weaknesses, which you must quickly eradicate.

"But on to the associate whom you consider a good conversationalist. The *word* good can mean so little, but *analysis* of the word can mean:

- He always brings everyone into the conversation.
- He has a wide knowledge of many subjects.
- He always listens intently.
- He never pounces when others are talking.
- He is fluent.
- He has a good vocabulary.

"There will, of course, be many other factors arising from the analysis, but having made this analysis, you then have to compare your strengths with those of your associate. You may decide that you compare well, or you may consider that you could improve one or two factors – increasing your vocabulary, for example.

"Now for another example. You believe that Jones is a first-rate designer, but you cannot compare yourself with Jones until you know what is meant by a *first-rate* designer. You must, therefore, analyse the work Jones does:

- Are his ideas original?
- Does he improve on the ideas of others?
- Is he outstandingly good with colour?
- Is he a fine draughtsman?
- How long does he take to research an idea?
- Is he imaginative?
- Why does he always use certain materials?
- Does he continue to study his craft?
- Does he seek the advice of others?

"What you are doing is carrying out an analysis in depth, and it is only when you have done this that you are able to compare your own work with that of Jones.

"Interpersonnel comparison tests can be salutary, but they are most effective in helping us to discover the truth about ourselves. Once these truths are known, we may be able to find the answers to our problems; and also perhaps the reason we are not making the headway in our career that we believe we deserve, why others do not seem to have implicit faith in us, or why our counsel is not often sought.

"Just one more example. We say of someone, *He's a very strong character,* but what do we mean by strong? In what way is he strong? Is he decisive? Is he obstinate? Is he loyal? Sometimes loyalty needs a great deal of strength of character. Does he accept total responsibility? Is he dependable? Is he strong because he never blames others for his own mistakes, or does he pass the buck on occasion? In the latter case, he is perhaps not as strong as we may have thought him to be.

"We must compare ourselves with this person in order to discover our own strengths and weaknesses. We must try to discover whether other people refer to us as *strong* or *weak*, or just as a *nonentity*.

"Interpersonnel comparison tests are successful because they relate to people. Those we choose for the tests are known as targets, and our knowledge of our targets may have been acquired over weeks, months, or even years of close association.

"Sometimes we fantasize about others because our only knowledge of them has been gained from newspapers or magazines, biographies or autobiographies. Sometimes we only learn the truth about our heroes after a biography has been written. For this reason it is of little use to make *targets* of people we presume are brilliant, whom we wish to emulate. If we have no personal knowledge of them, we cannot analyse their strengths and weaknesses, because we only know them by the labels given to them by others. The success of interpersonnel comparison tests therefore depends on the targets we select. It's no use a junior clerk taking his managing director as his *target*, because he doesn't really know his managing director. If you are a general manager, your *target* may be a director or the managing director. If you are an area manager your *target* may be your sales manager. If you are a computer technician, your *target* could be the computer manager. But your *target* must always be someone from whom you can learn more about yourself.

"This is how you carry out your own interpersonnel comparison tests. First choose your *target* or *targets*, then draw up a series of forms, each with five columns:

- The first column is for skill – aptitude, character, intelligence. At the column heading we shall use the word skill as a generic term, measuring all aspects of management.
- In the second column you will analyse the strengths of the

target(s).

- The third column is for self-comparison. You will compare your strengths with those of the *target* and in this column you will place either a plus or a minus sign, to denote your own strengths and the areas for improvement. For example, a *target's* strength could be a retentive memory. If you too have this strength, you will place a plus in column three. If you are the kind of person who easily forgets facts and figures, you must answer with a minus sign, denoting an area for improvement.
- The fourth column is for the *target(s)'* weaknesses.
- The fifth column is, again, for self-comparison. If you have listed your *target(s)'* weaknesses and these are your weaknesses too, you will show a minus sign against them. If your *target(s)'* weaknesses are your strengths, you can put a plus sign.

"As it is just as essential to cover weaknesses as it is to improve strengths, it isn't necessary to concentrate on only one *target*. There may be two or more, because we are always ready to see weaknesses in others that we don't recognize in ourselves until we have carried out these tests. The rule, however, is that if you have two *targets*, you must have two forms, and the analyses must be carried out separately. In this case, however, one *target* will enable you to find your strengths, while the second *target* will help you to discover more of your own weaknesses.

"There can be many other areas of analysis – technical, production, research, salesmanship, teaching, finance. Your form should be as complete as possible, and your analysis can be in greater depth than the examples given, depending on your position and the *target's* qualifications. The deeper the analysis, the easier it will be for you to benefit from it."

Nina again invited questions, but there were none.

Cooper said, "Nina, when you research a session, you cover the ground so well that there are few elucidating questions to be asked".

"Thank you, Philip."

She went on: "I shall hand out interpersonnel comparison forms and invite the delegates to complete them. They will be told that they are for their eyes only, and will not be collected by us nor seen by their associates." Then, turning to Greg, she added: "I haven't drawn up the forms yet, but they will cover seven aspects of management – human relations, innovation, time management, decision-making, administration, communication, and leadership. I'll give examples to help them on their way. For example, under decision-making the strength might be *demanding facts before arriving at a decision,* whereas a weakness could be *becoming emotionally involved in the decision-making,* which clouds thinking; or in the time management section a strength might be *keeping meetings short,* whereas a weakness might be *wasting time at meetings by reminiscing and introducing irrelevant subjects,* and so on."

Nina paused, smiled at her friends, and said, "I think that's about it, except that I'll try to think of a good high note finish".

Ryder said, "I'm going straight to my office to complete an interpersonnel comparison form – no, not for me, but for all of you". He joined in the general laughter.

4   A Break for Lunch

The main building complex held the delegates' restaurant, which could also be used by staff when necessary, and a separate quick service restaurant for the instructors. Instructors had so little time between sessions to sort out queries or run through the following session notes that a lengthy lunch break was rarely possible. Another reason for the separate rooms was Ryder's belief that it enabled the delegates to talk freely amongst themselves without the restrictions of having an instructor at their table. In the evenings instructors were expected to dine with the delegates, but by then the atmosphere was much more relaxed, especially after a drink or two at the bar.

The instructors' dining room was self-service. A long table placed centrally in the room displayed a choice of two hot dishes, cooked vegetables, and also a cold buffet for those who wanted a lighter meal. Intoxicating drinks were not served at lunch time.

After helping himself to a hot dish, George Young made his way to a table occupied by three senior instructors. Philip Cooper heaped his plate with cold roast beef, with a jacket potato on the side, while Mary and Nina, as usual during the lunch break, ate salads only.

The women sat together at one end of the room, and the two men chose the opposite end. Young, on sitting down, was immediately engaged in a controversial subject that surfaced every few weeks. The senior instructors were complaining that, because of the heavy demand for courses, schedules were much too tight. If the instructors were not racing from one lecture room to another, they were hurrying off to catch trains, or breaking speed records on the motorways on the way to running another in-company course.

Young patiently explained, as he had done many times before, that if ever the rush ended, there would be real problems; in addition, MSI instructors were highly paid, and such a pay packet inevitably meant more production per instructor. The alternative was to employ more instructors, with less pay for all. That was the standard response to the critics of Ryder's tough schedules, and it was always accepted, if only temporarily.

Nina and Mary nibbled at their salads, talking of their many commitments and an overseas trip that Nina had to make in the near future. Suddenly Nina switched the subject by saying, "I'll tell you now, Mary, about the idea I'm going to put before the meeting this evening. It is that we should approach Greg pretending that we know nothing of his intended sellout, and tell him that if the opportunity ever arose, we should like to consider a management buy-out. Knowing Greg, he will consider what is best for him, and he may well postpone his decision while he evaluates our offer."

Mary said, "He won't if he has made up his mind, and I'm not at all happy about working for a big international company. There's too much bureaucracy, too many chops and changes, and each change means that someone is thrown out!"

"Mary, listen to me carefully. I believe you and I could go it alone. We don't need Greg. He's a wonderful person, a great entrepreneur, in fact a business genius, but he no longer instructs – not in the sense that we mean anyway – just the odd session now and again. He no longer negotiates the big contracts. Peter's brilliant, but he wants to dominate everyone. Philip is only of value on the financial side, and the world is chock-full of good accountants."

Mary threw back her hair with a sudden movement of her head, a habit she had when the unexpected happened to her. She said, "But only a few minutes ago you were telling me that you were suggesting a management buy-out. It doesn't add up."

"Yes it does. A buy-out would be ideal. Finance would come from a merchant banker, and we'd be in the same position as we are today, but without Greg. Young would of course take over temporarily, and we could all cash in later when we went public. I'm only suggesting an alternative plan in case my first idea is not accepted. I've got a little stacked away, and I'm sure the same applies to you; and, Mary, we can depend on at least six large groups who have relied on us in the past to put business our way. We'll employ more women than men; I think that could be a winner. What do you say? Before you answer, I'm not being disloyal to George or anyone else. Loyalty doesn't mean not making plans for one's own future."

Peter Lewis looked at Philip Cooper's plate, heaped with roast beef, potato salad, and a jacket potato, and said, "I don't know how you do it, Philip! Every day you stuff yourself with more and more food. You have coffee in the morning with biscuits, and tea in the afternoon with more biscuits, yet you don't put on an ounce.

"I only have to look at a potato to put on a pound or so, and today I'm making an exception to my rule and having an extra slice of beef. But it is an exception, you know."

Cooper said, "That's been your theme for years, Peter. You delight in jogging, exercising, playing squash, all to keep faith with the scales. I only have to use my mind. Remember, the mind working full out also uses up calories." He paused, then added, "But let's keep away from diets. There's something I want to talk about with you, and what I'm about to tell you is confidential. Is that OK with you?"

"Of course."

"It's about our future."

"I thought we were going to discuss that at our meeting this evening."

"Yes, we shall. Possibly the right solution will be found for all of us, but we ought to consider alternatives."

"That, I thought, was the objective of our discussion."

"Yes it is, in a general way. But I meant something more personal, which might not apply to any of our colleagues."

"What's on your mind?"

"Us!"

"That I've gathered," said Lewis, and immediately Cooper went on, "Let's assume that Dysons don't want all of us."

"But we've been through all that," said Lewis, "and they may need us more than we need them."

Cooper shook his head. "I'm not so sure. If they do, it will only be temporarily."

"Then we'll get a pay-off."

"Why?"

"They have to, if they make us redundant. It's as simple as that!"

"OK," said Cooper, "but that will be peanuts, not a life pension. Greg might give us something out of his windfall, but his idea of generosity might not be the same as ours. We all admire Greg, and we're a pretty loyal crowd, you know. We understand that we've been well paid for what we've done. We're realists, not left-wingers, dreaming of some Utopia in the future. It's Greg's business, and he was the great motivator, the great builder of the business. We all played our part, fair enough, but without him we shouldn't be where we are today.

"He would never act unfairly, but fairness is a strange word. What one person considers fair, another might consider unfair. I can't see him parting with much hard cash, which means that we'll have to depend for our future on the Dyson crowd."

Lewis said, "Yes, I agree with all that, but what is your

plan?"

"You know Carter Lovell, of course, one of the three largest accountants in the country, with branches worldwide. I have a contact with one of the partners, one of the very high-up partners, too.

"They are concerned that some of their competitors have got in first with marketing consultancy, and it's bringing them extra business. Carter Lovell of course have their own consultancy and training group, but it hasn't been very successful – but then, it's not very well run. They haven't a clue what marketing is about anyway.

"My contact tells me that at a recent meeting of the partners they decided to fight – and that's a word not very often used by accountants – to fight competition by rejuvenating their own consultancy and training division. They are looking for a competent marketing manager. My contact knows my record – he knows the record of everyone in our group, we are pretty famous you know, and also well respected and highly successful. That's worth a lot of money to the right people, and Carter Lovell are after the right people.

"Cutting it short, they would be willing to accept us as joint managers of their marketing consultancy division. They are big enough, and have the finance to give us all the backing that we would ever want.

"I told them I'd make a decision after speaking to you. They want a top-class marketing man and you, Peter, are certainly that. They also want a marketing-oriented accountant to head their consultancy group, and they believe I am just the person.

"What do you say, Peter?"

Once in his office, Greg Ryder hurriedly gulped a coffee and a sandwich, before interviewing a designer with new ideas for the programme brochure to be issued in the autumn. Greg, as usual, was hypocritical, demanding more originality, and sent the man away to return with a different concept.

His next visitor was an instructor who had a personal financial problem. When he had happily left, Greg's secretary rang through with the news that Dr Walker was in the waiting-room. He called regularly to check on the health of all instructors, and to give flu jabs in the autumn and dispense hay-fever palliatives in the summer. When he had been shown in, the doctor, a small plump man with a pinkish complexion and eyes that seemed continually to be looking for symptoms, said, "You wanted to see me, Mr Ryder".

"Yes. It was at your suggestion that I saw Bartlett-Smith, the heart man. I'm seeing him again on Friday. He thinks my condition is due to stress, but Doctor, I do assure you, I have never suffered from stress in my life; neither do I worry unnecessarily, and I do take exercise. I don't smoke, I sleep well, I am not overweight. So might he not be making a mistake?"

Dr Walker answered, "It's possible. New tests will assist his judgement. But if Bartlett-Smith believes that you should now take things easy if you want to live a few more years, then you should do so, stress or no stress. Remember, blood pressure can rise without stress, and you're a wealthy man, so why take unnecessary risks?"

Ryder said, "I suppose you're right. But I can't accept what is possibly the truth. However, Doctor, I am about to take the biggest decision of my life. On Friday, an all clear will help me to make up my mind."

"You won't be given the all clear. You may well show an improvement, even a great improvement, but that doesn't mean that the original diagnosis was at fault. It doesn't mean that you don't have to take care in the future."

Ryder nodded again, saying, "Never in my whole life have I made my health an excuse for slacking at a job, for not doing work that should be done. I've never admitted to any illness, even when I was suffering from an illness. I've always said that I was fine, if anybody asked me. I've never stopped away for a cold, or even flu. Leaders are not supposed to suffer as others do.

"But that's as it was. Things may well have to change. But Doctor, please do me a favour and 'phone Bartlett-Smith. Tell him I'm not a stressful person. I'm sure he is motivated by the idea that all top executives suffer stress, and that might generally influence him. I now have a big decision to make, and I don't want it influenced by someone's wrong opinion of my state of mind."

5   People Analysis

After Dr Walker had left, Greg sat musing for a few moments. He thought of his team in conjunction with Nina's interpersonnel comparison tests.

George Young's weakness was a fear of appearing weak, but that was his — Greg's — weakness as well. That was why, sometimes, he had appeared to be too strong when there was no need. Good old George, everyone thought so highly of George, an excellent administrator and a clear thinker; but he was not a strong leader. Peter Lewis was brilliant as a marketing man but completely self-centred, and always likely to make one enormous mistake; again, not a leader. Philip Cooper had no pretensions to leadership, but he was an exceptional accountant, almost a financial genius. Of the two girls, Nina could run a company, and could run it well, but she would never retain top-ranking associates, for she was too emotional. She was not a good leader. Mary Glynne had all the assets — strength, a good record, ambition, popularity — but had she the stamina for leadership? Had she the toughness which was so badly needed when the chips were down? She could succeed, but only if she had someone like Philip Cooper at her side.

But perhaps he was wrong. When he criticized his team as not being top leadership material, he was not comparing them with others, he was comparing them with his own very high standards. Also, some people when promoted and given extra responsibility showed a different side to their character, and became first-class managers.

Greg sighed, stood up, straightened his tie, and made for the meeting room. Striding into the room with his usual purposeful air, he said, "We want to get two more sessions in today, so on with the show, Mary".

Mary stood up and said, "I shall follow Nina's example, and address you as if you were first-time managers. Nina", she began, "has explained how interpersonnel comparison tests can help you to learn more about yourselves. I want to talk about your relations both with your subordinates and your immediate bosses.

"It is difficult for us to understand ourselves. It's much harder to understand others. But it's what goes on in the other person's mind that really matters. Discover the truth and many problems can be forestalled. What goes on in the mind of the calm friendly man who one day goes berserk and beats up his wife? Why do some people always chase additional work, while others try to avoid any challenge? Why do some boast and brag while their associates are secretive or evasive? Why do so many of us change when we get behind a steering wheel?

"As you all know, it is because we all have a facade. A smiling face may not mean a smile in the mind, and that makes it so difficult to learn the truth about the inner thoughts of others. But when we work with people long enough, they can't hide every one of their hidden qualities − their fears, their dreads, their hates. It is these hidden segments of a person's character that a manager has to discover if he is to pre-empt problems and conduct worthwhile performance appraisals.

"Now picture the scene in your office, factory or shop when the news filters through that you are the new manager. Will you be given the benefit of any doubts? Not likely, even if your company promotes by length of service and not by ability. If the assistant always becomes the manager and the vice-president the president, there will still be some antis amongst subordinates. Why him or her and not me? is a typical reaction, and there are always jealousies. Remember, if they have worked with you for some time, they know your weaknesses as well as your strengths − there is no hiding place in the office. If you expect such reactions, you will be able to handle them, but there will have to be some self-questioning. For example, and this might apply to one of you, you might be thinking, *John and I always argued about research and development. He has disagreed with me more often than not, and he has won his arguments more often than not. How am I going to win him over to take instructions from me whether he agrees with my decision or doesn't agree?*

"Another might be thinking, *It is a fact that Susan and I used to get on so well together until we heard about your promotion. But then, of course, she was always one of your favourites, which didn't matter so much then, but it matters an awful lot now that you're the manager.*

"These are standard reactions. A manager can no longer have favourites. All must be equal. Never mislead yourself into believing that you are loved by everyone. It may happen if you're a real softy, but love is not the same as respect, and as a manager you do not seek love, only respect.

"From now on you must make your judgement of people on their work, and not on their personal behaviour. You cannot let your emotions influence your judgement when you are having to make decisions concerning people for whom you may have a high regard or you dislike intensely."

Greg Ryder held up his hand. "Sorry to interrupt, Mary, but I can't see what you're getting at; you've given some very useful lessons about people, about the way people think − people analysis, as you call it − and that is what you have called the session."

"Sorry, Greg," Mary answered. "Maybe I should have clarified the issue earlier. What I'm heading for is of course the prevention of conflict – one of the most important aspects of management, as we all know."

"You didn't explain that," said Greg.

"No, but I shall. I won't go back to the beginning, however, I'll go on from here. The cause of conflict is people, not machinery; and if a manager learns more about people as well as himself, he will overcome many small and big problems."

Lewis asked, "Are you talking now to us, or are you addressing the class?".

"I'm not sure."

"Anyway", said Lewis, "shouldn't we then call the session handling conflict?"

"No, I don't agree," answered Mary. "I want to drive home the message time and time again that the most important aspect of management is management of people, and if people are managed properly, conflict is reduced."

Greg said, "You've made your point, Mary, and I'll withhold judgement till later. Please carry on."

Mary smiled her thanks, and continued: "I'll begin again. I want you now to think about yourselves more than your subordinates, because the actions that you take will motivate people – perhaps even motivate them to avoid conflict – but the manager as a motivator will be dealt with fully in a later session.

"Now let us think about those working for you, those whom you will have to motivate. On your appointment they will perhaps be anxious about their future. It is up to you, the manager, to take the tension out of their lives, and discover what it is that your subordinates are anxious about.

Here are some of their anxieties:

- One, how will you react to them and their work. How will you respond to their ideas and suggestions?
- Two, whether they still have a safe job. New brooms do sweep clean.
- Three, can they measure up to your demands?

"So you will see that you must let people know where they stand with you, from day one. Yes, a new broom nearly always does sweep clean, but in your case you should only make a sweep when you have carefully evaluated all your subordinates, analysed their behaviour and seen whether they can in fact measure up to your demands. If a new manager doesn't make fresh demands, well, quite frankly, he shouldn't be promoted. There is no division in any organization that runs so well that there is no room for improvement.

"Now returning to you, as managers, are you all confident that you can win through, confident that you will succeed beyond your expectations? The very fact that you have been promoted should give you that confidence, and I'm quite certain that by the end of this course, if you have needed another 5 per cent confidence, you will have obtained it from being here. That confidence will allow you, mostly, to head off trouble without acrimony.

"Every book on management explains that as conflict is a normal part of life, it is therefore a normal part of business life. There's conflict in families, conflict behind the scenes in sport, even conflict between friends. When there is conflict in business, however, quality and production always suffer.

"I'm not referring to conflict between management and unions, when conflict tactics are usually carefully worked out in advance. I'm referring to those conflicts which arise suddenly for valid reasons, or possibly based on rumour. Why is conflict common in some offices and factories but not in others? Why do normal people become so angry as to become almost fanatical?

"I'm not a qualified psychologist, but while I was a personnel manager in a large company employing thousands of people, I learned some lessons and some understanding of why conflicts begin. Often I was asked to solve conflicts which could easily have been prevented by the manager in charge, had he understood more about the way people think and act.

"Why are tempers lost so quickly, and for no apparent reason? Why does Susie continually burst into tears when she doesn't get her way? Why does John always think everyone is wrong except himself?

"Some of the reasons, possibly most of them, are hidden in the past, so that even those who act irrationally are not aware of why they do so. It seems that at an early age we all develop love and hate syndromes, we develop some form of anxiety about parents who are away, we have irrational fears, and all these characteristics are built into our subconscious minds, to affect our behaviour at some later date. When you, as managers, realize this, you will know that there is not some change of character when anyone becomes anti this or that, when previously they have been for this or that. To prove that we are all psychologists in some way or another, you tell me what you consider the main reasons for conflicts beginning.

"Some suggestions, please?"

All the directors knew the answers, but played along with the role Mary was enacting. Cooper called out, "Resentment".

"Thank you, Peter, that's a very good beginning," said Mary. "Now let us consider some deep-seated reasons for resentment.

"Perhaps, way back, preferential treatment was given by parents to a son or a new daughter; then, at school, we found that we were no longer the apple of everyone's eye, we could no longer do as we wished, and we resented our teachers. Later, as teenagers, we resented the questions our parents asked us: *Why were you so late last night?*, *Where did you go?* or *Who did you go with?* In most people such resentments disappear, but in some they become deep-seated, and burst out from the subconscious mind whenever there is a feeling of being unfairly treated or overlooked."

"I can give an example of that," interrupted George Young. "I remember, in one company we were advising, a capable director continually resented every change made, unless he had thought of that change himself. He had had a very troubled early life, and his resentments carried right through to his directorship. As I said, he was very able, but in the end his resentments destroyed him. They caused too many conflicts.

"But even his problem could have been solved if his managing director had had the courage, or the nous, to analyse his performance time and time again, to encourage and praise him while pointing out the problems he was causing by his resentment of colleagues' successes. I agree, resentment is a common cause of conflict."

Philip Cooper said, "May I give an example? I remember that in an office in which I worked some 10 or 12 years ago there was a typing pool, and the manager of that department decided one day to call one of the typists his personal secretary. I believe he was rather fond of her. This really did cause a conflict. The girls took sides, but mostly, they were 'agin' the new personal secretary, who was not all that good at her work either, and often had to be helped out by the other girls.

As the resentment built up, so the output fell and all because the manager was on an ego-building trip so that he could talk about having a personal secretary. When resentment burns, Mary, I agree, logic disappears. The conflict only ended when a director stepped in and moved the girl to another division.

"But he should have stepped in much earlier. He should have read the symptoms aright, and sensed what was going to happen. He should have explained to that manager that it was a typing pool, and no one had secretaries. If stopped early enough, conflict would have been avoided."

Some more examples were given, then Ryder called out, "How about the perfectionists? They can sometimes cause problems."

Mary said, "You are right, Greg, the perfectionist can cause many a conflict, because very few people can live up to his or her high standards." Then she added quickly, "But a perfectionist is not the same as someone who pays strict attention to detail."

Ryder said, "You mean that I'm a perfectionist detail man?"

Everyone laughed, and Mary hurriedly went on, "You may ask how does the perfectionist, solely male this time, cause conflict?

"Usually it is because no one can live up to his standards. He criticizes them or makes demands they cannot meet. Therefore you, as managers, must look out for the perfectionists among your subordinates, and know exactly how they are going to act, and react, to others."

Ryder said, "These days it seems that so many people have either an anxiety neurosis or a guilt complex — and I'm serious, I'm not just spouting psychological claptrap. The neurotic sees problems ahead, difficulties, criticism where none is intended. He seems to discover double meanings in every sentence, in every memo he receives. Even when there are no threats to him, he feels insecure and can start a conflict for no real reason at all. Maybe it's because one of his suggestions has been ignored, or he feels that he should have been asked to undertake a certain task. Whatever the reason, he believes he is being directly insulted, his confidence is undermined, and he goes into the attack.

"These men and women need very careful handling. It's almost useless including them in a performance-appraisal exercise, unless you praise them all the time, for they need continual reassurance that all is well. Strangely, many of them are highly competent. On the other hand, the guilty neurotic always believes that he is at fault, even when he is not. He makes himself ill by his self-doubts or, alternatively, becomes very bad-tempered. If something is wrong with their work and they are criticized, they will not accept the criticism. Their guilt comes to the surface and they fight and they argue — they become very vicious in their arguments. The good manager recognizes the subordinate with this kind of guilt complex, makes allowances for it, and, by skilful counselling, gets the subordinate back in line. Do you agree with that, Mary?"

Mary answered wryly, "Thank you, Greg, yes. But I thought I was giving this session."

"So you are, so you are. I was only helping it along."

"In case you're suffering from a guilt complex," Mary answered with a laugh, "I won't argue with you."

The other directors knew that only Mary could get away with that kind of remark to Greg without starting a conflict.

Without changing her tone of voice, she continued: "I'm not going to ask for any more contributions. I shall begin to feel frustrated." Everyone laughed, and Mary went on again as if addressing delegates: "You will also find amongst your staff the aggressive person, and although aggression, well harnessed, can be useful on some occasions, an aggressive person can quickly change a hard-working team into an argumentative debating society, and work suffers.

"Most people react to the aggressor by becoming aggressive themselves, because, again, the aggressive instinct starts in childhood, and cannot be cured by a manager. The child who finds that his demands are not met and decides to go in for heavy tantrums to win, will continue to play that game over and over again. He or she will never lose that aggressiveness, which can lead to one person making a fortune and another just making a lot of trouble in offices, factories, or shops. It is when the aggressor always wants to dominate others that the trouble begins.

"Again, the answer is always for the manager to be aware of the symptoms and to know that although aggression may be triggered off by someone's act, the real cause of the aggression can go back a long way. To help the aggressor, a manager has to adopt an autocratic stance. He might say, *'This is what you will do, and we can only work together if you accept my decision'.* There is no pussyfooting around with an aggressive person.

"Fortunately with most conflicts the symptoms, if known, show up early, and the perceptive manager knows exactly when to offer counselling, advice, or tough talk.

"Let us now consider some of the standard conflicts which occur in most companies. If any one of you here is a production manager, you will know that demands from sales managers are always ridiculous. If, on the other hand, there's a sales manager here, you will be aware that all production managers are obstructive. Here are two possibly emotional reasons for conflict.

"In some companies conflict quickly arises because those in office, shop or factory extensions will not answer the telephone quickly when it rings, and the poor telephone operator or receptionist is left to deal with irate callers. She, in turn, will become irate herself, and conflict starts.

"A manager must not, in these circumstances, take sides. First comes the investigation and the decision, then a reprimand if there has been neglect, followed by advice, the instigation of new procedures, or further training, upstairs and downstairs.

"When it is a question of production manager versus sales manager, and the chief executive himself is marketing-oriented, he often takes the side of the sales manager; and that can lead to conflict and bad feeling, and frustration on the part of the production manager. If, on the other hand, the managing director is an engineer or production-oriented, he will often come down against the sales manager, to the latter's frustration.

"To repeat, a manager, at whatever level, must not take sides because of personal preferences."

Mary paused for a moment, frowned, then went on, "I think that's enough on that subject. I'll switch now to telling the managers of the need for awareness." She remained with her thoughts for a few moments, then said, "Managers, do you possess the faculty of awareness?

"A manager with great awareness can overcome so many conflicts. His or her awareness encompasses what is happening in the general office, the workshop, the ad. department – an awareness of symptoms." Mary suddenly brightened, her voiced raised, and she went on: "Have you heard of management by not looking? No? I'll explain.

"It is the blinkered manager who never notices an untidy desk, overfilled ashtrays which could even lead to fires, magazines piled high on the cupboard, obviously not to be read, but paid for by the company; who never notices gossipers wasting time, and never picks up a letter from someone's typewriter to read it through, just to make certain that the mail going out lines up with his way of thinking. These are examples of management by not looking.

"It's particularly prevalent in restaurants. So often we see a head waiter bustling from table to table asking the right questions. Are you satisfied? Was the food all right? Did you enjoy it? There's one table where the diner is complaining to a waiter about some aspect of his meal. Does that head waiter go over to help? Not a bit of it! He passes by. He's managing by *not* looking.

"If you are like that head waiter, this session is going to be a complete waste of time, unless of course you change your ways; and, as we said in the first session, we can all change, can't we? If you don't notice conflict symptoms, you won't be able to stop any trouble before it begins. The rule must always be to settle conflict amicably if at all possible. Unfortunately many managers are so preoccupied with their own problems that they are not aware of conflict between others until after it has started.

"Is there one of us asking the question *How are you?* who ever mentally registers the answer? The response might well have been, '*I have a terrible cold, because no one will ever shut the outside door*', but the answer hasn't registered, so there is a possible cause of conflict between Jane, worrying about her cold, and Bill, who won't shut the door.

"A good manager develops awareness, knowing instinctively when something is wrong. His objective is to head off conflict by being aware of changes of moods, appearances, even false laughter.

"The manager who is unaware of what is going on around him, and never notices a change of attitude, is often shocked when a key member of his staff tells him that he is leaving because . . .

"Here are some standard warning signals:

- One, the good mixer who suddenly becomes a loner.
- Two, constant bickering amongst staff.
- Three, the formation of cliques. Whatever the reason,

where there are cliques in the offices or on the shop-floor, they can lead to conflict.
- Four, a high staff turnover.
- Five, a sudden lack of enthusiasm for change.
- Six, an increase in absenteeism.
- Seven, when someone has been given an assignment which is beyond his capabilities to complete successfully, that person will become 'anti' the assignment. He will try to form a faction that agrees with him. Some will, some will not, resulting in conflict.
- Eight, domestic problems. Wife/husband quarrels can spill over into the office, and conflict can arise for no apparent reason. Often counselling in these cases can stop the conflict spreading. Too many of us believe that it is not our business to interfere with someone's home life. It is a manager's concern if it affects production.
- Nine, the risk of conflict between ethnic groups.
- Ten, imagined grievances due to lack of good communication.
- Eleven, failure to keep staff informed. Tell your subordinates your plans for the future, and ask for their views. Secrecy is a constant cause of conflict, because rumours then take over from facts.
- Twelve, look out for such views as, *'Sally's been given a new desk — why? I have to put up with the old one!' 'John has been given an office of his own. Why should he have an office in preference to anyone else?'* Such remarks are symptoms of conflict in the offing".

Mary paused and said, "There will always be conflict, but management's aim is to keep it to a minimum. Again, I emphasize, find the cause, the background, look for the symptoms, and you will find that more and more conflicts can be prevented. Yes, Nina? You look as though you want to say your piece".

"You recognized the symptoms," said Nina, amidst laughter. "I wanted to make the point that being a good listener can prevent conflicts. What people say to you can teach you a great deal if you listen. We don't listen carefully enough. Even idle chatter can give a clue as to how rumours have been spread, and rumours can cause conflict, too. There's a grapevine in every business activity, and a manager should be aware of its value, so that ill-founded rumours can be condemned. That's all, Mary."

Mary thanked her colleague, once more threw back her hair and said, "Now let us turn to one particular reason for conflict."

"Is there more to come?," asked Young.

"George, I can give you a list a mile long if you like."

Young said, "Heaven forbid! Remember, you only have 45 minutes for the session. You've been going for some time now and you haven't yet used visual aids or participation."

Looking at Greg Ryder, Mary said, "As if any of us could ever forget that we have to keep to a time schedule! I promise you the final session will be no longer than 45 minutes."

There had been many occasions when there had been a peremptory call from Greg Ryder to a lecturer overrunning. To run over time was a serious offence in his book.

Mary continued, "The reason I refer to is poor interviewing and selection of staff. All too many managers paint a golden picture at the first, second, and even a third interview.

"It isn't a case of warts and all. It's no warts at all, which leads to subsequent complaints from a new employee: *He didn't tell me that I was expected to work late. She didn't explain that I'd be working in a general office. I'm used to having an office of my own. I was not told that I would have to clock in every morning;* or *My territory wasn't properly defined. I never realized that it would be so small.*" Mary paused, and said, "Finally . . ."

Lewis interrupted, "You mustn't say that, it's against the rules."

Mary answered, "I know Greg's rule, but sometimes it fits in with the natural finish."

Ryder jumped to his feet and said. "Never! Never, never!

The word *finally* always denotes that a session is about to end, and what happens? Delegates' minds switch off. They begin gathering together their notes, and don't hear the rest of the session. There is no *finally* in our sessions. Remember that, and that is an instruction."

Mary laughed aloud. "Sorry, Chief," she said, "I'll start again: Another important factor in forestalling conflict is simply *change*.

"Change almost invariably causes some conflict because usually change results in gains for some and losses for others. For example, the installation of sophisticated machinery will delight the highly skilled technician, but it won't please the unskilled workers, who fear that the installation may cause redundancies. A new central typing pool may please a newcomer who prefers working alongside other typists, but it may not please the resident staff. Moving office or factory may delight those whose homes are nearer the new premises, but those who have to travel further will not approve.

"Changes must obviously be made, but advance explanations and seeking the opinions or advice of others can prevent conflict.

"Please imprint on your mind: *think before you act; think* of the other person's reactions; *think* of the possible conflict which may result. These days, serious conflicts arise between employers and unions, but this subject is not within the scope of our course. Sometimes, however, one has to seek conflict simply because there is no alternative to a showdown. But the rule must surely always be to settle conflict amicably if at all possible."

Mary drank some water before continuing. Everyone clapped.

"Why?" she asked.

"We thought you'd finished," said Lewis.

"Do you want me to start a conflict right now?" asked Mary.

Cooper said with a smile, "Why not? It would make a good exercise, wouldn't it?"

Gruffly, Ryder said, "Mary, ignore them. Please

continue."

"Finally," she began, and Ryder himself had to lead the laughter.

Then, changing her manner, she added, "Every big fire, every burnt-out building, begins with a small flame; and every large or small conflict begins with a small disagreement.

"When you tackle these small disagreements quickly, you have fewer and fewer conflicts. The heart of your job as a manager is people management, and people analysis is a fundamental procedure for handling conflict."

6 Communications

After a short tea break Greg said, "So far it's been ladies' day. George may like to give the next session on Communications."

Everyone readily agreed with Greg, except Cooper. His argument was that the first step should be the training of staff. That, he believed, would get the new manager off to a good start and help to build a team. He was outvoted and Young began his session, as if addressing new managers.

"If any of you are lovers of history and have read some of the instructions despatched by Queen Elizabeth I to her commanders at sea – Drake, for instance – or going back still further, if you have read Caesar's messages to the Senate, or, more recently, perhaps Gladstone's many notes to his cabinet ministers, you will be struck by the length of these instructions, and also how punctilious were the writers. There was no margin for any error or misunderstanding.

"Today all has changed. Brevity is the keynote. Messages sent by satellite or telex can be expensive, and even during cost-cutting exercises one of the first instructions is to keep telephone calls short. Lengthy memoranda, we know, are usually only skimmed through, but these changes have brought about the risk of messages and instructions being misinterpreted. Another factor is that clarity of speech is no longer a part of teaching curricula, either at school or university.

"Men, supposedly, began communicating by grunting at each other. Sometimes when I listen to the youngsters today I think we haven't improved a great deal."

"Too true," said Lewis, "and it isn't only youngsters. You ask my wife. She says all I ever do is grunt."

There was laughter, and Young continued: "This session is about communication, and it has strong links with the previous sessions. Let me remind you, first you must understand why the other person acts as he or she does. Now we can link the two together to consider all forms of communication."

Young glanced around at his colleagues and went on: "That is my opening, but before continuing I want to seek your advice. We have communication sessions in all our management courses. Surely we must change the package a little for our course for new managers.

"What I suggest is that we now have a recorded open discussion. I shall edit it and maybe come up with a new approach. Do you agree?"

"I do, for one," said Ryder, who liked nothing better than discussions which went on and on and in which he could play a big part.

Ryder then took over from Young: "Let's go back to basics, something we do not do for our senior management courses. All communication in business comes into one of four categories – good, indifferent, bad, or none at all when it is needed.

"Bad or indifferent communication, whether written or verbal, is the cause of constant argument and strife, and it is sometimes better not to communicate at all than to do it badly.

"When I was younger, and not so experienced, I would direct memos, write letters, for no good reason other than that they satisfied my ego. Off they went, reprimands, criticisms, urgent directives – most of them unnecessary – and if I wanted to increase my ego even more I would send copies of the directives, etc. to others to show how astute I had been.

"All new managers send out a spate of memos; it's almost the first thing they do. Mostly the memos are of the abrupt kind: 'You will do this', 'You will do that'. They rarely achieve their objectives.

"But going back to myself, I would even send a memo or letter to an associate in the very next office. Surely it would have been much easier for me to walk into that office and explain my mission in a few words. But possibly the reason for some 50 per cent of such messages is sheer cowardice – an avoidance of confrontation or argument.

"This is wrong. It is always better to talk rather than to write. In fact a written communication need only be sent if a record is essential, if the information is lengthy and technical or would have to be carefully evaluated, or if the same message has to reach a great number of people.

"All new managers are advised to make it a rule before sending a memo or directive, or any form of message in writing, they should think three times, then think another twice, and possibly don't send it. Certainly it must never be sent if it has been written while one is feeling irate. Such communications are rarely acceptable, and never bring the right results. Confronting people is a far better method. Furthermore, don't make the same mistake as I used to, and send copies to others unless they really are essential, especially copies to senior management criticizing a subordinate. This is not the way to build a loyal team.

"That", concluded Ryder, "is a beginning for you, George".

But before Young could continue, Philip Cooper said, "I shall be equally brief with my contribution, covering, in the first place, communication faults which I shall number:

● One, communicating with the wrong person.
● Two, bad timing – communicating either too early or too

late. An obvious example of this is a potential strike. Too early, and the negotations may fail. Too late, and maybe the strike is already on.

- Three, not using the right method of communication, e.g. a poster might in some circumstances be better than the distribution of letters.
- Four, the introduction of irrelevant matter – padding the message or report.
- Five, lack of accuracy – not enough information.
- Six, giving opinions and expecting them to be accepted as facts.
- Seven, too much jargon.
- Eight, lack of clarity. As an example of clarity in communication, a message sent by a captain on the bridge to the engineering room is a fine example. There can be no ambiguity, no unnecessary use of words. It must be short. If too lengthy, the initial instruction might be forgotten and that could result in a shipwreck. Too many managers are shipwrecked through not keeping to basic communication rules."

Cooper paused, and then went on, "And now for another factor: There are, in my opinion, three barriers to good communication:

- First, semantics: the use of words and language which can be interpreted differently by different people.
- Second, physical barriers. Noise, for example, can cause misunderstanding, not necessarily corrected by shouting, which often occurs in workshops or in fact in all manufacturing areas. Another barrier may be buzzing on a telephone line.
- Third, psychological barriers. These bear on the likes and dislikes of the communicator. If a manager dislikes a subordinate, he may communicate in a manner which will not only not find favour with the other person but may result in a complete disregard of instructions.

"Finally – oh dear, Greg, that word will keep cropping up!

- One, always choose the most economical but appropriate means of communicating.
- Two, if possible, check to ensure that your message is understood.
- Three, try to imagine that you are the recipient of your own messages. How would you react to those instructions, information sheets, etc.?"

Cooper stopped talking for a moment, and Lewis said, "For an accountant that was very good!"

Cooper answered, "I can think of a few communications I have received from the marketing people which make appropriate case studies of what not to do."

Lewis laughed and said, "I withdraw my remark. All accountants are good communicators."

There was more laughter and Young said, "A good contribution, Philip. Nina, what have you to say?"

Nina Westlake said, "I should like to stress once more the importance of listening."

"Oh no!" said Lewis.

"Why oh no?"

"Because that was going to be my piece."

Young interrupted, "No need to worry, Peter, you can both discuss the art of listening. It can't be emphasized too strongly.

"You continue, Nina, and then Peter can contribute his share."

Lewis said, "Knowing Nina, there won't be too much left for me."

"Oh Peter, there will! I'm only going to try to make two points. The first concerns the big switch-off, when our minds race ahead, when we think we know what the other person is about to say. We are not listening, only working out our responses. There can't be a two-way contribution when one side isn't listening to the other.

"The next point is back to our old friend Freud, and comes under the heading of *neurosis*. There seems to be a legion of neurotic people about who are always looking for hidden meanings in what is being said. Their minds work overtime, trying to penetrate the speaker's underlying meaning, and therefore they often arrive at the wrong conclusions.

"Listening must be part of the two-way communication. It entails checking to see if we have understood what is being said. It also means reflecting, and asking questions based on what we have heard. This applies particularly when someone voices a grievance. If the manager makes up his mind in advance that there is no grievance, he doesn't listen. The result can be that the grievance continues, to the detriment of efficient working.

"Now over to you, Peter, and maybe you'll leave something for me to talk about a little later on."

Lewis said, "You always win, Nina, you know that, but thank you for brevity. Here are some additions to the points you have raised, which I know you would have mentioned if you had continued.

"The art of listening properly is to concentrate and relax. No one listens with complete concentration with pulses racing, fingers drumming, or fists clenched; and you've all met the half-listener who sits forward on the edge of his chair, shoulders hunched, just waiting to disagree violently with everything that's been said.

"To be a good communicator you must recognize these non-listening signals, so that, if necessary, you can emphasize a point, or ask for confirmation that you are being understood. When it is your turn to listen, you must listen quietly, with no sense of urgency to interrupt.

"When we are tense, our mind is no longer retentive, but when we are relaxed, we listen intently.

"How well do you listen? To discover your listening capacity you should carry out an interpersonnel comparison test.

"For example, take John, in your department — a

compulsive talker, isn't he? But how do you rate him as a listener – excellent, good, fair, poor, terrible?

"Now rate yourself on a similar basis as a listener, comparing yourself with John and then (here's the crunch) ask John to rate you. From these assessments you will learn the truth about yourself."

Lewis then said, "Back to you, Nina".

Nina continued as if addressing the delegates: "We know why some people are bad listeners, but even those who try hard to concentrate on the other person's voice sometimes fail because the other person communicates so badly. You therefore have not only to consider whether or not you are a good listener, but also whether you can communicate effectively.

"I'll give you some examples of delinquent communicators:

"There is the mumbler. He swallows his words, rarely raises his voice, and speaks in a monotone. No one can concentrate for long enough on what he is saying to understand it.

"Do you recognize him? Good! Now compare yourself with him.

"Do others have to ask you regularly to repeat your words? If you dictate to your secretary, does she have difficulty in hearing what you say? Do people sometimes have to ask you to speak up?

"Next we have the grasshopper. This is the way he communicates. 'I want to discuss with you, and to settle right away, this question of cutting down staff. It seems ridiculous, doesn't it, to have to consider this when you remember that Julie came here for an interview and we almost had to beg her to join us. But then of course her uncle used to be in Bob's department, and that helped. What was his name? Oh, I remember, Dick Long. He was a first-class designer, but then art ran in his family. I was on holiday with his brother Charlie once – he was a classical musician, didn't play my kind of music at all, I found him rather boring. Now, what were we discussing? Oh yes, Julie. But what about Peggy? She always reminds me of a nurse we once had here in the medical department. Do you remember that first medical department . . .'?

"So he goes on, the conversation now turning to medicine, the original point completely forgotten.

"Think of the grasshoppers you know in your company, and compare yourself with them.

"Another delinquent is the fast talker, whose tongue races to keep up with his thoughts? Much of what he says is unheard, and the concentration of those listening to him soon lapses.

"This makes him a very bad communicator.

"Compare yourself with any fast talker you know, and then ask youself *Am I a gabbler?* If the answer is yes, only a conscious effort on your part to relax and slow down will enhance your ability to communicate effectively. If you want others to understand and be motivated by you, *you must slow down your talking pace.*

"Opposite to the fast talker of course is the slow talker. It is as difficult to concentrate on the jerky sentences of the slow talker as it is on the gabbler. Even the most relaxed person becomes a trifle tense when the slow talker pauses, speaks a few words, pauses again and then, with great deliberation, attempts to make his point. When the listener believes that a most important announcement is about to be made there comes the *ahs*, the *ums*, the frequent use of *you see* and *now let us consider*, and the *I want to be deliberate about this.*

"Compare yourself with the slow talker. It's much harder for the gabbler to slow down than it is for the slow talker to speed up. The effort must be made.

"Then there is the ventriloquist. We don't look to see if the master's mouth is moving, we concentrate on the dummy. But what if there is no voice throwing, no dummy, only a variety of sounds issuing from sealed lips, which we have to strain to hear? It becomes a game of guesswork.

"Too many people try to emulate the ventriloquist, speaking with their mouths almost tightly shut."

Nina concluded with, "Compare yourself. Look in the

mirror while reciting a poem or reading from a book.

"Words provide the material for communication, and the voice is the instrument for shaping that material."

Nina looked at Greg. "I think that will be my total contribution for this session," she said, "I hope it's what you wanted, Greg."

Ryder answered, "Exactly. And now, Mary, it must be your turn."

"Thank you, sir," she said brightly. "I'd like to talk about report writing, because the rules for report writing are almost the same as for all general communication. But first I'd like to raise the issue of poor communication in which management fails to keep staff fully informed.

"Too often, management states facts, gives instructions, without explaining why those facts are so important, or why the instructions are essential to the welfare of the company. For example, rebuilding work in office or factory may cause great inconvenience, and be quite unacceptable to many people, and there will be such general criticisms as, 'Why didn't they do it during holiday time?', 'Why don't they do it in easy stages?', 'How can they spend that much money when they keep telling us to cut costs?' and so on . . .

"Such remarks would not occur if management set out clearly the reasons why the rebuilding work had to be carried out, and why it had to be carried out now; explained why the costs would be justified; and how the work, when finished, would add to the efficiency of the organization or the welfare of the staff.

"Nothing should be written, or spoken, until you have asked yourself this question: *How will they react, how will they discuss the matter with their colleagues, how will they talk about it to their families, if it is something which applies to them personally?*

"The message can then be so worded as to take controversy out of the issue.

"Now to return to report writing.

"Compiling readable, informative, factual, concise reports

is a most difficult, yet essential, form of communication. But do most reports contribute to the welfare of a business?

"The answer is *no*. All too often reports are requested as a delaying tactic — to give someone a job to do, to show one's authority, to make someone else feel important — because it is standard practice, or because a committee doesn't know what other action to take.

"If you are the authorizing person therefore, always be objective and consider these factors; then ask yourself the following questions:

- Is the report necessary?
- Am I likely to read it carefully?
- Shall I take appropriate action after reading it?
- Shall I file it away, to read at some future date?

"If you decide a report is needed, give the go-ahead. If not, think again. Often a brief discussion will supply all the necessary evidence, without wasting time over a report. Managers should be as ruthless in cutting down their requests as in cancelling meetings.

"Here are some guidelines for report writing:

- One, why is the report required? Is it to inform, to persuade, to help in decision-making, or for reference purposes at some future date? The writer must have these objectives clearly in mind before investigating and then reporting, otherwise, although his report may be brilliantly written, it will only provide irrelevant information. The question to be put to the person authorizing the report is: *Please tell me exactly what you require from this report.*

   "Sometimes the person authorizing the report does not think clearly about its objectives, and if it is not clear to him, the report writer cannot succeed in producing a worthwhile result.
- Two, who is going to read the report? If the readership is

to be divided between technical and non-technical people, the writer will have to simplify many of its technical aspects. If, however, the readers are well versed in the technicalities, there will be no need for him to waste time explaining what is already fully understood.

● Three, with research to gather all the relevant information, the following questions should be asked:

Which books, reports, research works, do I need to read?
Whose advice should I seek?
Whom should I interview?
Which areas must be visited?

"Once the answers to these questions have been found, a time limit should be set and adhered to. Without such limits, report researching can continue for so long that the report will no longer be useful by the time it is completed.

"Remember, unsubstantiated claims have no place in a report. Analyse the information. Eventually the report writer will have accumulated dozens, even hundreds of facts, and these will now have to be correlated and checked, so that duplications can be deleted and the remainder evaluated. This is quite a simple matter when a report writer works systematically.

"Having completed the analysis, the report writer will then have to break down the main objectives into subsidiary objectives.

"If these guidelines are adhered to, writing a report becomes relatively simple. The problem most report writers face is a blank page – and a blank mind. Ideas which abound while driving, original thoughts which arise from the dream world at night, or devastating comments which come to mind while viewing television, all seem to disappear when the time for writing the report arrives. In fact you have only to present your research, just as you would if you were making a speech. Quite simple, really!

"Always write reports in the first person. It makes them much more readable than when they are written in the third person.

"The rules of letter writing apply equally to report writing.

"Avoid clichés, jargon, unnecessary technicalities. Too many report writers attempt to build their own ego and, indirectly, their own qualifications, by using technical terms which the reader has to check.

"Use short sentences, avoid emotional language, use plain and simple words if possible, and, remember, there is no poetic licence in report writing. Be positive but not arrogant, and be sure that each paragraph deals with only one point. Remember to be logical at all times.

"Few people enjoy reading reports, and if a report is ill prepared and badly laid out, the chances are that it will only be glanced at. On the other hand, the well laid out, clearly written one can undoubtedly influence minds, and that is what report writing is all about.

"All supporting evidence which does not necessarily have to be included in the substance of the report should be given at the end in an appendix. This may include graphs, charts, drawings, illustrations, and extracts from references quoted.

"Finally, the report writer should summarize his findings and state his conclusions and recommendations."

Mary's contribution was considered so successful, because it was succinct yet covered a lot of ground, that she was applauded when she sat down.

Then Lewis said, "I should like to point out that a regularly issued bulletin for salesmen, or any other personnel for that matter, makes an excellent communication vehicle. We, as you know, send out our *MSI News & Views* weekly. We also teach bulletin writing in our sales courses. Provided the writers of bulletins remember that they are not being written to satisfy their egos, but to motivate others, the bulletins will succeed.

"There is another proviso. Bulletins must keep to the rules, which always are to teach, to inform, and to inspire. Glossy house magazines are, in my opinion, not nearly so effective as regular bulletins from managers telling everyone what is happening and explaining why it is happening.

"Bulletins are also appealing because the successes of various members of the staff can be highlighted in them. They need not be expensive to produce: they can be run off on one of the standard duplicating machines or reproduced on a photocopier. Provided they are well laid out and written with the interests of the recipients in mind and not to show how brilliant the management team is, they will be avidly anticipated by the recipients."

He paused for a moment, then added, "May I continue? Is there time?"

Ryder said, "Why not? You may go on as long as you like."

"Thank you. Then I'd like to make another point. As you know, I was the instigator of making use of noticeboards and posters to communicate with our staff. I also set up many similar schemes for companies where I had been called in as a consultant. I'd like to copy Mary, and lay down some rules for this means of communication.

"Before any notice is pinned on a board, the writer should consider the feelings and views of those who will be reading it. Usually noticeboards are not good vehicles for listing misdemeanours. Avoid the display of blood-pressure-raising phrases such as 'We can no longer tolerate . . .', 'We must insist that . . .', or 'I have asked all managers to report to me if . . .', or notices like 'Absenteeism is now averaging 10 per cent, and is having an adverse effect on productivity and profitability. Mrs Jones of Personnel has been asked to investigate all cases and report to management . . .'

"We know that many newspaper editors and politicians urge management to take a tough stand – whatever that may mean. But toughness does not mean dictatorial or belligerent.

"Also, in the notice referring to absenteeism, which only applies to a minority, why waste the time of all the other workers who will stop and read it? The minority can be dealt with individually, and there is certainly no need for a notice reminding staff that absenteeism is high. It is action that is needed here, not notices.

"Whenever directives are issued or information given, management should ensure that no words or sentences can possibly have a double meaning. If a statement can be misinterpreted in any way, it surely will be; that is how industrial problems arise.

"A careful check should be made for spelling mistakes or typing errors. Such mistakes can result in readers forgetting the message they are reading in their eagerness to belittle management.

"Notices should be kept to one page. Second pages are rarely read.

"Coloured paper should not be used. Black on white makes for easier reading.

"Do not continually use capital letters for emphasis. They serve no purpose, and often antagonize the reader.

"Never write an emotionally worded notice while in a bad temper. It will only cause anger without providing any solution, changing anything, or leading to a better relationship or understanding."

Nina interrupted: "The siting is also very important".

"Indeed, it is! One central board, possibly situated near to the staff entrance in a busy passageway, or next to the staff canteen or entrance lobby, will result in many passers-by passing by, without reading the content of the notices.

"If anyone is late arriving or leaving the premises, if it is lunchtime and everyone is hurrying to queue for food, notices will not be carefully read. Ideally there should be a noticeboard on every floor of an office block or factory, or in every department, and the notices should be duplicated. Main noticeboards should be reserved for social communications.

"Too many notices are left up for too long. Passers-by glance at, but do not study them, on the assumption that there's nothing new to be read. Notices should be taken down as soon as management considers the messages have been read by most employees. I've seen notices on boards 2 or 3 months out of date, which happens when no one has been made responsible for taking down the old notices. Someone must be delegated to inspect the noticeboards every day. It shouldn't be necessary for any notice to remain on the board for more than 7 days unless there is a statutory obligation for it to be displayed at all times. An effective idea is to stick a red arrow to the board, printed with the words *This is new.* Few people will pass by such an appeal.

"Although noticeboards can never take the place of personal messages, they can, when properly used, be good instruments of communication. And that," concluded Lewis, "is my final contribution."

Nina said, "Congratulations, Peter! Excellent!" Then, turning to Ryder, she asked, "Do you think we should cover public relations in this course or in this session?"

Ryder shook his head. "No, nor advertising, nor direct mail, nor outside posters. They are all effective means of communication, but this course is for new managers, and not many will be handling public relations to begin with. We can consider running a new managers' course part two, and can then introduce other forms of communication."

Ryder did not wait for agreement from Nina and went on: "I should like to make another contribution; it covers briefing others. This obviously applies to every manager when delegating. There should be briefing sessions before conferences and exhibitions. Financial directors may have to be briefed before visiting a bank manager to discuss additional finance. Briefing others, although an important part of management, is often treated too casually.

"If an accountant is told, *Get the best possible rate but don't go too high,* what is too high? This accountant may feel he has been most successful in his negotiations, but when he returns, the managing director may disagree, and reprimand him for borrowing at too high a rate.

When briefing, I suggest these are the rules to remember:

- One, write down every factor relating to the briefing.
- Two, explain these factors slowly, and insist on subordinates taking notes, and not relying on memory.

- Three, question subordinates to make sure they have fully understood the notes they have taken.
- Four, never accept, 'Don't worry, I know what to do!' Always reply, 'I shan't worry if you will tell me exactly what you are going to do!'

"I think that is all I want to say. However, I think we should cover some aspects of letter writing, Don't you agree, George, or should the subject be treated separately in another session?"

Young replied, "I think it must come into this session, but it need only be treated briefly." Turning to Nina, he added, "You, Nina, originated our letter-writing and public-speaking courses. I suggest you outline the main features of letter writing."

Nina replied, "I'll gladly do that. Just give me a few minutes, please, so that I can refer to some notes."

Five minutes later she said, "It is worthwhile taking the trouble to ensure that every letter posted − be it seeking business, answering a complaint, or requesting payment of an account − is of high quality in layout, typing, and content. Because of misspelling, poor typing, and bad grammar, many letters are well below standard. Such letters are also usually poorly set out: they are all *I* appeal instead of *you* appeal − *I* believe, *I* think, *I* want, *we* have, *we* produce, instead of *you* will be interested to learn, *you* will be able to . . .

"They are also usually cliché-ridden.

"The average letter is well written, although still cliché-ridden, and lacks warmth. The writer is apt to use six words where two will do.

"Usually, the excuses for bad letter writing are 'Can't get good typists', which sometimes means, 'Can't be bothered to check and correct'; or 'Haven't the time, I have to depend on subordinates', meaning 'We have no training scheme to improve the standards of our letter writing'.

"Strangely, when a manager is visiting a client he will make sure that his appearance is immaculate, yet he will allow another of his company's ambassadors – a letter – to have so little appeal. Bad communications by letter lose business.

"Many departmental managers write bad, dictatorial letters which cause ill-feeling, project a poor company image, and fail in their objective. Surely you will have received at least one letter from a public utility corporation, a car manufacturer, a store, a local authority, which has infuriated you; so don't do unto others as they do unto you. Ensure that *every* letter sent out by you, your department, your company, is well received and enhances your company's reputation.

"Mastering effective letter writing begins with the recognition and observance of three basic principles:

- The need to define the *purpose* of the letter.
- The constant need to consider the *reader* of the letter.
- The need to use *language* appropriate to these two requirements.

"Further letter-writing rules that should be observed are:

- One, *be clear*, which means avoiding ambiguity, making the correct use of punctuation, and placing adjectives and adverbs in the right context.
- Two, *be concise*. Brevity is accomplished by the limitation of padding, caused most often through needless clichés and meaningless phrases. ,
- Three, *be accurate*, not only in facts, figures data, detail, information, etc. but also in letter construction.
- Four, *be complete*, which means providing all the information and answers to satisfy the reader, and fulfil the purpose of the letter.
- Five, *be courteous*. The choice of words creates the tone of the letter. The right one will convey an image to the reader of a warm, helpful, interested human being.
- Six, the layout of the letter must be neat and attractive. Solid chunks of typing must be avoided. *One thought, idea, or subject per paragraph* is a sound guide to follow.

- Seven, sentences should be kept as short as possible: eighteen to twenty words make for easy reading and understanding.

- Eight, information of particular importance to the reader can be given emphasis by creating separate paragraphs indented three or four spaces from the left-hand margin. These may be referenced alphabetically or numerically, or simply given additional prominence by an asterisk or dash.

- Nine, typing must be to the highest standards. These standards should be set, and maintained, by the letter writer, who must not accept soiled stationery, erasure marks, nor any other untidiness in typing.

- Ten, familiar and direct wording should be used rather than commercial jargon. Hackneyed phrases should be eliminated, and replaced by warmer, more expressive language.

- Eleven, the signature on the letter must always be personal – not *per pro* or, even worse, *p.p.* Use of the footnote *dictated by . . . and signed in his absence* should be avoided.

- Twelve, identification of the writer should be clarified by having his name typed below the signature space and, where necessary or appropriate, his title and department.

- Thirteen, make sure that *all* enclosures are enclosed.

- Fourteen, before replying to a letter, make sure that you have clearly understood the points raised or the questions asked. If in doubt while dictating, always play back, or ask for a read back. Don't hesitate to make corrections at that time."

Nina then concluded, "That's all. I should like to close with one of my favourite quotes: *The essential in all communications is to be understood, and to show understanding.*"

7 Making Plans

Almost every tourist arriving at the Cricketers' Inn makes a photographic record of his visit to a typical old English hostelry in a typical rural scene of old England. The Inn, set back on the Hartley Wintney to Reading road, encompasses everything expected by a visiting tourist – thatched roof, rough white stuccoed walls, and a village green adjacent to its own backyard. The cricketers' changing room has been adapted from an old cowshed.

Inside the Inn low oak beams cause regular bumps on visitors' heads, a great pleasure for the USA visitors, who subsequently claim to have been biffed on the head by an old beam, undoubtedly from a tree planted in the Elizabethan era. The fact that only about 5 per cent of the Inn building goes back to that time is immaterial.

The small entrance lobby leads into a large, well appointed lounge, with comfortable chintz-covered chairs.

When the directors arrived at 7 pm, the lounge was almost empty. The waiter explained that Monday was a bad day.

They made for a secluded corner, settled down, ordered appetizers, and talked shop for a while. Then Young said, "We have five evenings together before arriving at a decision, but I must make it clear that there will be no confrontation until Greg has given us his terms of sale and perhaps explained how he has safeguarded our interests."

Lewis said, "George, we all know that you're devoted to the man and will give him all the benefit of the doubt, but as we have said time and time again, loyalty does not mean not safeguarding our own interests, and loyalty is a two-way thing. If a decision is made to put our position to Greg, I'll go along with that."

Young replied quickly, "You all agreed to honour the word I gave that we should not take any step which might lead to my friend's daughter being implicated".

Lewis said, "Yes George, but there may be ways . . ."

Young replied, "There are no ways, and that's final!" He looked at each of his associates in succession.

It was Nina's turn. "Let's go one step at a time. I'd like to put my proposals first. OK?"

There were nods all round and Nina continued: "My suggestion of a management buy-out was put briefly before you at our lasting meeting. Since then I have sought the advice of a friend, a merchant banker. I'll run through what he told me."

Cooper said, "You're wasting your time. I've already told you the problem with that solution."

Nina retorted sharply, "But George, it means that we shall be the bosses. We'll fix our salaries and our share of the profits, and as long as we make high profits, our backers won't complain. We can work out contracts so that if one day we are taken over, we shan't suffer. Obviously we'll have to elect a managing director, or we could rotate as some consultancy organizations do. The first managing director should be the one of us who puts up the most cash, but that person will never, while managing director, be able to kick us around as Greg can, because the rest of us together will hold more shares than the managing director, whoever he or she may be."

Young said, "Greg doesn't kick us around. Sometimes you are irrational in your statements, Nina."

Cooper said quickly, "If we start by quarrelling now, what chance do we stand as a master team?"

"We're not mice; there are bound to be some differences," said Mary.

George Young suddenly realized that in the face of the supreme issue the team were already showing signs of disintegrating. Greg was such a great leader . . .

Nina said, "You're right, Philip, there are problems, and all problems beget feelings — feelings due perhaps to childhood insecurity, feelings that we have to justify ourselves to others, feelings because we don't like admitting our mistakes.

"Look, we can't go wrong. We're all dedicated instructors, determined to do our best for every delegate attending any of our courses. With that philosophy we are bound to succeed, whatever differences we may have."

Young nodded his agreement, but wondered whether the friendship would be likely to break down without a firm, guiding hand. Did he have that hand? He wondered. He wasn't sure.

After further discussion Nina said, "I think it's a winner, and we can put it to Greg now, to force his hand. We need not mention our knowledge of his sell-out plan, just a plan, we can tell him, that we have worked out for ourselves to cover the day when he decides to retire."

Cooper said, "I'll explain to you again why it won't work with Greg. Our net profit after tax, but before dividends, is about £3,200,000, which means taking all assets into account. A fair offer would be about five times earnings — some £16,000,000 or so, it could be £18,000,000. But when a buyer like Dysons are out to get a business and they want it badly, standard values no longer obtain. For example, if we were in a rental business, a competitor who wanted our many rental account customers might offer a very high sum, even if our profits were negligible. With Dysons wanting to buy into a training group, Greg would ask perhaps £30,000,000. No backer would ever finance such a management bid."

Nina protested: "As we don't know what Greg is being

offered, surely it's worth a try, if only to learn what's in his mind."

Cooper nodded. "Maybe", he said, "It could be a good bluff. I suggest we consider it with the other alternatives, later."

Young agreed, adding, "Let's go in to dinner".

Over dinner they all relaxed and did not once discuss their future. As usual, when training instructors get together, they talked and laughed about the problems they had had with difficult delegates – delegates who had walked out, delegates who had ended up in tears, and delegates who had stood up and cheered. They discussed courses that had flopped, and that had been successes in such places as Saudi Arabia and Canada. Then of course came the standard anecdotes about Greg Ryder – how impossible he was sometimes, how unpredictable, how ruthless on some occasions but completely forgiving on others.

Many of the stories were apocryphal and had been passed on through various people over the years.

Lewis who, because he had once won a local competition for wine-tasting, considered himself an authority on the subject, took great care in selecting French wines. Young decided that Lewis only ordered on price. The higher the price, the better the wine – not really a sound policy!

The food was excellent, and they returned in good spirits to headquarters soon after 11 pm, to be greeted in the entrance lobby by a flashing blue light. This denoted that Greg Ryder wanted to see his main board directors urgently.

"Now that," said Nina, "is going to be the end of a perfect evening!"

Young rang through to Ryder, who told him to bring the team to his office right away. On their arrival Ryder greeted them with, "How can you spend so much time over dinner?"

Mary said demurely, "But how did you know we were dining out, Greg? We could have been running round the fields, exercising, like you always tell us to."

Ryder grinned broadly, "You went to the Cricketers' Inn.

Remember, I have spies everywhere. However, the reason I asked you here is that I want us to have a creative conference now. We're not generating enough new ideas."

Young said, "Be fair, Greg; it's 11.15 now. Do you want us to work all night?"

Ryder shrugged his shoulders. "Time has nothing to do with it. We didn't succeed by clock-watching."

Cooper sighed. They all knew that Ryder was in one of his impossible moods.

The meeting ended at 3 am.

8 Motivational Forces

The team made a big effort not to appear tired next morning. There were the usual smiles, quips, and alert movements.

"No complaints?" asked Ryder.

"Of course not," said Lewis, "we enjoyed the meeting".

Greg said, "That is exactly why we are so successful, and that is why you are successful – because you are all prepared to pay a price to succeed". Then as an afterthought he added, "Anyway, we all sleep too much!

"Our first session is Motivation, isn't it?"

Young said, "We did agree that, earlier. The subject is vitally important in our opinion. It may well takes us all day today to cover.

"The sessions will follow the findings of our research into motivation, carried out by our research division some 6 months ago. The results gave twenty areas, or main areas, of motivation. We shall try to cover all these motivation forces in the widest possible way; by that I mean discussing the implications of motivation both in business and outside business."

Young paused, then went on, "We're pretty good ourselves at using all the motivation forces".

Ryder smiled broadly. "You're not pretty good, you're the best – no, the greatest!"

The whole team beamed its delight at the praise.

Young said, "Thank you," paused, then continued: "I'll open the session by asking delegates to tell me what they consider to be the greatest of all motivators. The response will be incentives, bonuses, profit-sharing, because most people believe they are motivated to try harder if they are well rewarded, or even over-rewarded, for their efforts."

Looking towards his chief, he said, "Greg, you have spoken many times to managers on the subject of pay as a motivator. May I ask you to open the session? You don't need any rehearsal time or thinking time, because you have expressed your views so often – and they're strong views. Summed up they mean that pay is not a motivator, but *can* be a demotivator."

Greg thought for a moment, then, with furrowed forehead, said, "This is a course for new managers, and new managers are hardly likely to be in a position to suggest pay increases or pay incentives; or is your objective the new manager himself, and how pay affects him? Is he or she motivated by some form of reward for effort?"

Young replied, "Yes, a manager has to be motivated – yes, you will indirectly be clarifying the position for the managers themselves, so far as rewards are concerned. In addition, a manager still has to motivate, even if his staff consider themselves underpaid. This is particularly so when there is a set scale for pay increases, years of service counting more than ability. But if rewards depend, as they should, on ability, then usually a manager will be consulted about the pay of the staff, and what special pay increases should be offered. If he isn't, the board of directors are to blame if they do not control a well-motivated company."

Greg nodded and said, "As you wish, I'll open the session. Give me a few moments to collect my thoughts."

This he did in some 30 seconds flat. "Even those most highly paid executives," he said, "believe they are not unduly rewarded for their efforts. This applies to the chairmen of some of our greatest companies. Recently, I was speaking to Charles Armitage, chairman and chief executive of Dysons."

The facial and stomach muscles of the directors tightened, and they all hoped that they showed a lack of concern at the mention of the name Dysons. But if proof were needed of Ryder's connection with Dysons, a connection which might lead to a sell-out, surely, the fact that Ryder had mentioned the name was proof enough.

Ryder continued: "Armitage is a very highly paid executive, yet he told me quite seriously that in view of his company's success, he believed he deserved more".

Young interrupted: "May we use that as an example in the course?"

"Why not? It's true!"

"But perhaps told in confidence . . ."

"No, he told me that he had mentioned his views to a journalist, and the article is soon to appear in one of the management publications."

"Good!" said Young.

Ryder went on: "The point I want to make is that if Armitage were given another £100,000 a year or more, he couldn't work harder, or more diligently. The fact is that whether someone is the chief executive of one of our largest companies or a manager just starting out, no form of pay increase or bonus or incentive motivates such people to make a greater effort over a long period."

Lewis said, "But surely you don't believe that the opportunity to receive a good chunk of the profits of a company doesn't motivate people, especially executives, to increase profitability?"

Ryder answered, "You're wrong. All outstanding chief executives are self-motivating, and can never give anything but their best to the job. But we must keep to our objective. We are concerned now with departmental and divisional managers rather than chief executives. I brought up the subject of Armitage of Dysons to show that whether someone is the manager of a small branch or chief executive of a large company, they both usually consider themselves underpaid.

"But if a manager is a good manager, then, as I said, he is self-motivated and will always give of his best. The only way that profit-sharing does sometimes motivate is in cost-cutting exercises. Most managers spend too much money, or want to spend too much, but for a time anyway, if they are offered a share of the profits, they do tend to agree more readily to cost-cutting exercises. But even that doesn't last long.

"However, back to our new manager. He or she always gives 100 per cent effort to the job on arrival, whatever the reward, but that 100 per cent quickly drops to about 80 per cent, which is about average, and it applies however he or she is rewarded. Remember, managers need motivating just as much as do the managers' subordinates. Subordinates react in the same way as managers. On arrival at a new job they are usually prepared to give 100 per cent effort, but this drops to 70 per cent or even slightly lower after a while, whatever they are paid. Of course there are always really ambitious managers whose efforts will not drop much below 90 per cent. They want to forge ahead. They are motivated to succeed because they want promotion. It is these managers who will be determined to motivate their subordinates to a greater effort than 70 per cent.

"But let me digress for a moment. In the marketing field, employees of distributors can be motivated by special promotions – holidays abroad, free gifts, various prizes. In selling, salesmen are motivated by commission, because there is a direct link between effort and reward. This, however, doesn't apply to the majority of a country's work-force."

Lewis asked, "How about the production bonuses?"

Ryder replied, "Yes, they work well, but only when management has been weak, and production therefore is at a low level. In such cases more efficient management could quickly increase production; but the old management can only try what will turn out to be an expensive incentive scheme. For example, if we accept the coal industry's figures, many mines were unprofitable, owing to poor production, and that was due in turn to poor management. The work effort was down to 50 or 60 per cent of potential. When incentives were introduced, production shot up, and even non-profitable mines were made profitable. But even so, in comparison to mining elsewhere, profits are still not high. Good management would have brought about a higher figure, higher returns, without all the hassle; and this in turn could have led to higher wage settlements for the miners. If a company is run efficiently, it has never been proved that various profit-sharing schemes motivate the work-force to greater effort. Yearly bonuses are equally ineffective.

"Don't misunderstand me. I agree with profit-sharing schemes. I agree with giving employees a slice of the action, as long as it is borne in mind that these are not motivators but are a fair method of reward – that's all."

Before Ryder could go on, Young asked, "Don't you think it's dangerous to tell delegates that the average employee only works 70 per cent of his or her capacity, while managers may begin at 90 per cent or more and then drop to about 80 per cent?"

"No, its not dangerous at all."

"But everyone believes he or she works to capacity."

"But that's not true! If it were true, why are time-management courses so much in demand, and that applies to self-organization only. There's also personal effectiveness, which comes under the 60 per cent heading: for example, letters badly typed through sheer negligence, mistakes made through incompetence or lack of training, packaging that breaks down because of slackness in a despatch department, telephones answered badly. The list is almost endless.

"Maybe I was exaggerating; probably 70 per cent or less would be nearer the truth, but that 70 per cent can be increased to nearly 80 per cent by good management, good training, and, most of all, good motivation. Additional awards, however, will not make the bad worker good or the good worker more effective. Most employees have to be motivated by some other means."

Ryder paused, ran his hand through his hair — a habit of his — then continued: "Take a newsagent, for example. He or she will put in 7 days a week's work, taking hardly any break. The same effort in an office or factory would almost inevitably lead to promotion, provided the employers were themselves motivated by the need to be successful.

"That newsagent is not usually at all well rewarded, certainly not commensurate to his efforts. So what motivates him? Security? Personal pride? Doing his own thing? It is certainly not money.

"Ask any salesman his first thought on closing a big order. His mind won't immediately switch to the commission he has earned. He will, firstly, be feeling proud of himself — proud of his achievement, proud of winning a challenge."

Ryder took a deep breath, relaxed his shoulders, smiled at his colleagues and said, "Well, that's about all. The point I have really tried to make is one that is not understood by the majority of managers, let alone new managers. So many of them feel that if only the directors would pay more, there would be no trouble with the work-force — no slacking, everyone would be happy. But that is a fallacy.

"The manager has to look for other ways to motivate, but unfortunately he usually looks within, and, looking within, he decides that he, himself, should be receiving a higher reward. Then he allows his thoughts also to become the thoughts of his subordinates.

"Although pay must be adequate and fair, even good employees will still consider themselves underpaid. But as most of them know their market value, they will not be as demotivated as they would be if they really were underpaid."

Young interrupted saying, "Sorry to stop your flow of words, Greg, but referring to your newsagent example, how about the many would-be entrepreneurs — those in computers, electronics, travel, property — who will leave a good job to start their own companies? Advertising agencies is another example. Surely they're money-motivated?"

Ryder shook his head. "I don't believe so. Later, they

become profit-motivated, as we all have to be in business, because success is measured by profitability, and we cannot stay in business unless we are profitable. But in the first place it is usually a longing to get away from restrictions – away from being bossed around, away from someone who won't accept one's ideas, a feeling that one is not being appreciated. When someone contemplates starting up on his or her own, their words to their wives, husbands, or friends are not *Think of the money I'll make* but *I want to be on my own, I want to make an investment for our future, to put my own ideas into practice. I don't want to work for someone else all my life.* Is that OK, George?"

Young said "Yes, that's fair enough, But I still believe that some are motivated by a chance to become rich."

"Of course that plays a part. But mainly it's to get away from frustration.

"Now I'll move on to my second point. Bonuses, pay increases, incentives, should be given not because they are long-term motivators, they are not, but because they are sound management policies which inevitably lead to a happy environment, and that in turn leads to higher productivity, whether it is in the office, shop, or factory. But such incentives, employers and managers should remember, can only be based on increased profitability, and there is always a problem if profits fall.

"Thirdly, no form of motivation will ever succeed, however loyal a work-force, if that work-force is not paid a fair reward for its efforts.

"And that," concluded Ryder, "completes my views on pay as a motivator – or rather, as a demotivator."

"It won't be easy to put across," said Mary.

Greg answered, "We shouldn't consider whether it is easy or difficult, but only whether it is right. There is too much nonsense talked about pay as a motivator. As if X, the brilliant boss of Giant Y, would only work at full capacity if paid another million a year! Nonsense, the X's are not built that way. They are more likely to be motivated by the headlines in the papers – *X, the highest earner* or *X gets a million* – that's one up for them against fellow X's."

Then, hearing a knock on the door he changed his tone and added, "Ah, here's the coffee. I'm motivated to have a break."

9 Long-Term Motivation

After the coffee break George Young said, "As you all know, I believe that the answer to many motivational problems is the understanding and application of human relations. For this session I intend to treat the subject in a more general way. I shall be grateful if you will hear me out without interruption. We can have a question time and a time for discussion later."

Ryder interrupted to say, "How long will it take?"

Young replied, "About 45 minutes."

Ryder said, "You are suggesting a 45-minute talk without delegate participation, without visual aids?"

"Yes. I believe the session content is such that there will be no problem in holding the delegates' attention throughout the session. It is the one session which lends itself to a straightforward talk."

"Very well, George," said Ryder. "But I'll interrupt if I feel that a delegate might lose interest."

"That's fair enough!"

Young stood up as if addressing a number of newly appointed managers and began: "You, as managers, are looking for motivational forces which will raise the efforts of your subordinates from perhaps 60 per cent, as it may be at present, to 65 per cent; then on to 70 per cent and 80 per cent, and to holding that, with temporary surges up to almost 100 per cent. Being only human, we cannot maintain 100 per cent efficiency or effectiveness all the time, but an understanding of the application of the principles of human relations will help that optimum to be reached time and time again. These principles are so obviously the right motivational forces that they have to be emphasized over and over again. Why? Those engaged in problem-solving know that we seek hidden causes, use computers to provide us with more and more facts, when the solution to the problem is both simple and obvious. This seems to apply particularly to psychologists and professors studying human resources. They are for ever carrying out research, then stating the obvious in a very complicated form. There is nothing complicated about human relations.

"Let me begin by talking about possibly the greatest motivator of all – *praise.* It applies to all of us in all walks of life. Prime ministers revel in it, judges preen themselves when praised by a higher court, hard-nosed trade union leaders mellow when appreciation is shown for their efforts by fellow trade unionists, and the housewife whose home sparkles with reflected light gives an extra polish after being complimented by a neighbour. Wives generally are starved of it, husbands yearn for it – yes, I'm still talking about praise – and schoolboys try that little bit harder when Dad says, 'Well done!' Everyone in business, from the most junior clerk to the top executive, reacts with extra endeavour when someone has praised them for work well done. Very few executives praise their staff for the good work they do. Is it that they fear they may subsequently be asked for a raise in salary?

"Giving praise does not mean being a weak, friendship-seeking manager, but the reverse. The weak may flatter; the strong give praise when praise is due.

"Why is it so hard for people to say anything complimentary? They love being complimented themselves. Showing appreciation can work miracles, if the appreciation is honest. It makes people want to give of their best, to help you and do things for you.

"We all suffer from this lack of appreciation. Let's look outside the business sphere for a moment. I was talking the other day to the head waiter in charge of room service in one of the most famous London hotels. He had been with the company some 30 years, was well paid, and he worked very hard indeed — far harder than he needed to. He said, 'At one time I would not even leave the hotel if it was my time off, but now I do sometimes go out for a breath of fresh air'.

"'You must be very happy in your work to work like that,' I said.

"He shook his head. 'Not really,' he said. 'In fact, I don't know whether I've really ever been happy.'

"That puzzled me, as I am sure it is puzzling you, so I sat back and waited for him to continue. 'You see,' he said, 'the management here has never given me one word of appreciation for anything I've done. I stayed in all day when staff was short, but nobody thanked me for doing that. Nobody appreciated the fact that I was doing work which should have been carried out by waiters,'

"When he paused, I said, 'If they had appreciated you and praised you for what you had done, would you have felt better?' The answer came quickly, 'Very much better. I wouldn't have minded what I did, and everything would have been worthwhile.'

"His managers never understood the value of honest appreciation. In fact they would probably have scoffed at the very idea. Possibly they'd have said, 'We pay him well, don't we? Isn't that enough?'

"No. It is not enough! Here was a man who had spent his life looking after visiting tycoons and film stars, yet he was so starved of appreciation that he didn't think his life's work had been worthwhile.

"Why is it so difficult for so many people to appreciate and show appreciation for work done by others? The majority of managers, it seems to me, would far rather make a sarcastic remark or reprimand someone than give praise for work well done. Even the minimum of praise can work miracles — that's an absurd word to use but you know what I mean."

Young was now in full flight and continued: "You can prove I am right if you wish. Make one day a praise day, and judge the effect.

"You have so often heard the expression *If only I were appreciated, I'd feel different.* Shop assistants, telephonists, those on the factory floor, all have made that remark at some time or another. It's no good using understatements when you're praising people. A curt *You'll make it* or *You're not too bad* isn't good enough. People want to hear the actual words of praise when they do well, and in spite of what they may say, in spite of their manner when they are being praised, the fact is that inside them they do want to hear those magic words.

"Answer this question honestly: *Do you enjoy being praised?*

"Think carefully. You do? Then remember that so do other people, and you as newly appointed managers can motivate your subordinates as much by praise as by anything else — certainly more than by a bonus or an increase in pay.

"Iacocca, the man who turned the failing Chrysler car into the great company it is today, never fails to tell everyone that some of his success was due to the fact that he knew how to encourage other people by showing appreciation of what they had done.

"*Give praise lavishly* is one of his sayings.

"I have often given talks on this subject — probably with little effect, I don't know. But on one occasion I was approached by the sales director of a company manufacturing kitchen furniture on a large scale. He told me subsequently that what I had said was all very well in theory but not in practice; it certainly didn't apply to the men working in his factory. They didn't seem to react to anything except money, and they didn't react very much to that!

"He couldn't see eye to eye with me. I said to him, 'Have you ever addressed your workers, have you ever talked to them? Have you ever told them that they had done things well? He answered that that was not his function, that was the job of the works manager.

"'You're wrong,' I replied, 'it's your job as well. Talk to the men one day — have a meeting with them, tell them about the future of the company, tell how much you appreciate the way they have turned out the equipment. Make sure you pick a day when the equipment has been well turned out.'

"Some time afterwards I received a letter from him telling me that he had given his talk, and subsequently production had increased and a deputation had gone to the works manager to tell him that they felt much better now they understood some of the difficulties of the company. They were now helping to overcome those difficulties.

"You will remember I mentioned earlier the fact that praise, when given, should be given lavishly. You may ask, *Can it be overdone? Can it seem like flattery?*

"It's never flattery if it is the truth; it is only flattery when it is a lie. Remember, I said it must be honest praise, honest appreciation. Most people, then, will always give their best when they are praised, but they will rarely show any improvement under criticism.

"But of course there has to be criticism some time. We'll deal with that a little later. Usually the 'I'll tell'em straight' fellow — the man who wants to be blunt and who wants to call every spade not only a spade but a bloody shovel — will rarely get the best out of people."

Smiling at Ryder, he went on: "The managing director of our company, Greg Ryder, does practise human relations. He wouldn't thank me for telling you that, but he does. He does criticize as well but he does it in a fair manner.

"He tells the story of one of our typists who was not very accurate. She would present letters which were not 100 per cent right; they weren't even 70 per cent right! Her erasures were not neat and tidy, and there could be words misspelt. One day he walked into the office. He stopped at her desk and picked up a letter. It was perfect, there wasn't an error in it. Although in the past he had complained to the manager for whom she worked about the letters that were being sent out, he hadn't mentioned a word of his complaint to the young lady. Instead he said, 'Now this *is* a good letter! I'd like to show this around', which he did. He showed it to one or two of the others, and congratulated her again. 'That's excellent work, isn't it? Copybook stuff. Well done!' and he patted her on the shoulder.

"From that day onwards that typist rarely made a mistake. Every letter she sent in was as good as it could be.

"Remember, you can always find something to praise if you look for it, and when you find it, it can change the ways of people more than anything else will ever do. *It motivates.*

"I've heard Peter Lewis tell the story of when he was a salesman, calling on factories. Walking through a factory one day, he noticed many of the workers were smiling and laughing, so when he saw the manager later, he said, 'It's so good to see them all so happy out there, they seem to be enjoying their work. That's a lot more than I can say about those working in many of the factories I visit.'

"'That's because we look after them well,' said the factory manager proudly. That manager, who in the past had proved very difficult, changed his attitude towards Peter, who left with a big order. His objective in giving praise had not been to win favour, but because of his belief in giving justifiable, honest praise when it was due."

He was about to continue when Ryder interrupted, holding up his hand. "Hold it for a second. I don't want to interrupt you, George, but there is a point I must raise. I appreciate your kind remarks about my knowledge of human relationships, and I'm sure Peter will appreciate the fact that you've told his story, which I've heard on so many occasions myself. Is that human relations, or isn't it?"

They all laughed, and Ryder continued: "It sounds good to me, George, and you are a master at explaining every facet of human relations. But these days, do you think it might be considered a little bit corny? It's all tough talk now, isn't it? Get tough, be tough, act tough, cut costs, make 'em redundant . . . Not quite in line with human relations as you have been explaining."

Young answered, "I see your point of view, Greg, and some may hold a similar viewpoint, but that doesn't mean that we should not teach the truth. We all use platitudes on occasion, and you are the first to reprimand us when we use them too often; but platitudes are only the truths of yesterday spoken today. It doesn't make them any less true, does it? The fact that some people don't want to live up to these truths, or even recognize them, doesn't alter the fact that they are truths. The same applies to human relations. The fact that this subject has been taught for so many years, the fact that it was practically all included in Lord Chesterfield's letters to his son, do not change its values. Praising others, giving justifiable praise, may sound corny but it's a great motivator, and as such, we should teach it."

Ryder said, "Carry on, George. If there were more people like you in the world it would be a better place."

"Thank you," said Young. "I won't disagree with that!"

More laughter.

Young went on: "Well, if a proven motivator comprising justifiable praise and honest appreciation is on the corny side because of present-day conditions, you'll think my next motivator even cornier.

"When I say it's a motivator, it's really a demotivator. But both aspects have to be considered.

"A motivator is essential in business. On the other hand, when we demote we stop motivation, and one of the greatest of all demotivators is criticism.

"Nobody wants criticism, and even when folk ask for criticism, they still don't want it. The strange part is that when you strongly criticize a man's work, you rarely improve it, whereas when you praise his work, it invariably gets better. Even when someone demands criticism of you, tells you he respects those who criticize him fairly, tells you that criticism will help him, he doesn't mean it.

"An author might well say to his agent or friend, 'Just give me fair criticism'. He doesn't want fair criticism at all, he wants fair praise. Even indirect criticism is a demotivator. Again, I must tell you another Peter Lewis story:

"A salesman said to a restaurant proprietor while selling deodorizing units, 'We can take all the smells right out of your restaurant'.

"Now what does that imply? That the proprietor had a restaurant which smelt. He could have said the same thing in a variety of different ways, none of which would have been offensive. He didn't get the order!

"Criticism rarely gets anyone anywhere, yet people are so ready to criticize. Dramatic critics and literary critics work at criticism, they have to do it; but you and I need only criticize as the very last resort.

"Try criticizing a waiter and see if you get any better service or any better food. I've lunched with many a man who has tried to show his importance by shouting at the waiter, demanding this, demanding that. I'm always scared to have lunch with these people really. I wonder what the waiter may have done to his food!

"Tell the taxi driver that as you're in a hurry to catch a train why the hell is he going the longest way round? Why doesn't he go this way or that way? Do you know what he will do nine times out of ten? He'll make certain that you do miss your train. Put your trust in him, however – it sounds foolish but there it is, it's a fact of life – tell him that you are relying on his driving ability to get you there on time, and he'll get you there if it is at all possible.

"When anyone criticizes factory workers, they should always walk on a few paces and then turn around and look at the faces of those operators.

"Recently, we did a consultancy job at a shoe factory where the managing director's son had not been in the business very long. He was showing me around and it was obvious that he did not know the shoe trade at all well – certainly not as well as his workers – but to try and impress me he was making the most absurd statements.

"'Pull that a bit tighter, Harry', he said. 'I think you'd do better on the bend with that, Bern', and so on. If he'd turned around and seen the expression on the faces of Harry and Bern, he would have gained some idea of what they were thinking. He hadn't even made his point, because none of the men made any attempt to carry out his instructions.

"Another strange thing about those who criticize is that they dislike receiving criticism. They will lay it on thick and fast, but if someone turns around and criticizes them, their face becomes red, their lips tighten, and you wait for the explosion. They can dish it out all right, but they can't take it.

"This morning I was looking through the *Daily Mail* and I read an article by that well known journalist, Lynda Lee Potter. She was writing about a broadcaster who has been many, many years in broadcasting, during which time he had, she said, broken the hearts of authors, poked fun at interviewers, was an arch exponent of the wittily wounding word, vicious insult, and contemptuous denigration.

"When he finally got his marching orders, he said, 'I'm not going, I'm not going, this is the focus of my life', and then burst into tears.

"The one lesson that broadcaster had never learned was that if you hand it out, you've got to be prepared to take it. Over the years any mild criticism of him, any slight innuendo suggesting that he was not a Shakespeare nor had he knowledge of the Divine, had had his hackles rising and his nervous system affronted – a simple example of the fact that those who criticize most can take it least.

"Consider the John Blunts of this world. They are outspoken about other people; they delight in their bluntness, and they believe it is appreciated. Well usually it is not. Others may say to them, 'I respect you for what you have said', but they don't really respect them at all; and I've never yet met a John Blunt who could accept criticism of his own way of life.

"If you want to demotivate anyone in your organization, the easy way to do it is to keep criticizing them. Tell the telephone operator she's too slow and she must do something about it or else! Tell the typist that her work is ridiculously bad and she won't last long if she carries on like that! Tell the production manager that his systems are cockeyed! Tell the salesman that he'd better learn to work his territory properly or . . .! You can demotivate them all.

Young ducked below the table, to the surprise of his audience. Straightening himself, he grinned and said, "Remember, I'm addressing delegates, not the managing director and his colleagues, so I'll tell them why I ducked just then. I did it because I knew that mentally you would all be throwing bricks at me. Many of you were thinking that I was being very wishy-washy – I think 'wet' is the right word, isn't it? I was acting like one of the 'wets'. You, or some of you, will believe that if the telephonist is slow, she should be ticked off. If the typist's letters are badly set out and you don't tell her, how will she ever put them right? If the production is dropping, why shouldn't you slate the production manager?

"Of course, you're right! You may criticize, provided you do it in the right way.

"Many years ago when I was a young and, businesswise, rather an innocent man, I used to study hard, with a view to improving my future prospects. I read books on management, books on salesmanship, books on finance, but most of all books on how to succeed in life.

"At that time advice came freely in newspapers, magazines, and in books, on how to be successful. There was a magazine published then called the *Efficiency Magazine*, owned and edited by a Mr Carson. I revelled in that magazine. Every month as soon as it was issued, I studied it avidly. Everything taught in that magazine was right, but one aspect of his teaching was consistent, it was one that I have just tackled.

"*Don't criticize*, he would write, *never criticize. Nobody wants criticism.*

"If a friend asks you to tell him if you like his garden, he isn't asking for any criticism – he doesn't want you to tell him there are too many weeds in it. If someone proudly shows you a picture hanging on his dining room, he doesn't want to hear from you that the apples don't look at all like apples and that you don't like modern paintings anyway, you think they're ghastly. He wants you to praise his painting.

"I felt I could help that man. I felt that I could contribute to his magazine, and I disagreed with his policy of writing the complete *Efficiency Magazine* himself. He had no outside contributors so I suggested that I could contribute to add some zest to his monthly publication. I telephoned him, asked for an appointment, arrived at the appointed time, received a big handshake and a hearty welcome, and then, 'Well, how can I help you, what can I do for you?' A very good approach.

"Because I didn't know how to criticize, I told him straight away what was wrong with his magazine. I explained, at least, I began to explain, how I could help him by contributing monthly articles.

"Then came the explosion! He called me a variety of names; he told me that he had studied business writing for over 20 years and what did I know about it anyway? He didn't actually throw me out of the office, but he came very near to that. I had rarely seen such anger. That visit to the magazine proprietor taught me a lesson I've always remembered.

"If I had begun with that magazine proprietor by telling him how wonderful the magazine was, how much I enjoyed reading it, how it was top priority on my reading list, how avidly I read every article and appreciated everything he wrote, he might not have liked my criticism but I think he would have been a little more receptive to it."

Young threw up his arms as if guarding against some missile. "Well," he said, "you know what I was doing then. Someone was throwing the book at me again. Someone was saying to himself, 'I don't like this round the corner stuff. Be direct is my belief. If you have to hurt people, hurt them quickly. Do you mean to tell me that if you give a man the sack it makes him feel better afterwards if you've said a few kind words first? He's still got the sack, hasn't he?'

"Quite right. Those few kind words won't save him from being out of a job for a little while, but a helpful remark and some praise for some of the work he has done may well help him to retain his pride and, most of all, to retain confidence in his ability to seek another position.

"Therefore the rule should be: *If you must criticize, try to temper your criticism with a little praise first.*

"There is another way in which criticism is partly acceptable, and that is to blame yourself for acting in a similar way to the person you are criticizing. For example, when perhaps blaming a salesman for time-wasting, you could say, 'I remember when I was a salesman, I used to spend probably 20 minutes to half an hour a day at coffee, meeting some of my friends in a regular meeting place where we would criticize our bosses and moan about conditions generally'. A completely wrong attitude! It took me some time to learn that I was wasting my time, but I did learn one day, and my experience can help you."

Young smiled, looked at his colleagues and said, "Well, I'm back to you now, not the delegates. I think that's all about criticism. I said no interruptions, but you're all looking as though you want to say something."

Peter Lewis said, "George, I've never heard anyone explain human relations as a motivator as you do. I've heard it from you on several occasions and you've always held my attention and I've always known you are right. But can any of us copy you? Can any of our instructors give it the same verve, the same enthusiasm, have that look in the eye which states *This is the truth, you must learn?*"

Young sat down, drank some water and said, "If we believed in that philosophy, we couldn't carry on training. I don't think there's any instructor in our organization who can teach salesmanship as well as you do, Peter. I don't think there's any instructor who can live up to your eloquence when teaching finance and accountancy, Philip. As for the girls, they're in a class on their own."

"Girls?" said Nina.

"Sorry, young ladies."

"Young ladies?" said Mary.

"Well, ladies."

"We're only teasing," said Mary.

"I know," said Young, "but the fact is that there will always be outstanding instructors, and instructors who are not quite so good. Ours, even if they are not quite so good, are still far, far better than anyone working for our competitors; and these men and women can learn the sessions, they can be trained, as we know . . ."

"Hold it," said Peter. "I appreciate that they can learn accountancy or salesmanship, but to explain human relations does need firm convictions."

"Don't you believe our instructors are convinced that human relations is a great motivator?"

Ryder interrupted, "Let's stop this conversation. I'm sure they are convinced, I'm sure they have belief in it − they've listened to you enough times, George, and I'm quite certain that under your guidance they can put over extremely good sessions. They may not follow your explanations word for word George; but they will make quite clear the points that you have made so far, and will continue to make, that praise is a great motivator, honest appreciation is a great motivator, and criticism is a demotivator. But if you criticize at the same time as you praise, or take the blame yourself, then it can still motivate. OK? Carry on, George."

Young stood up again and said, "My next motivator is just two words − I'm sorry.

"To prise a few words of praise out of some people is difficult, but to get them to apologize is even harder; and I mean apologies not only to your own bosses but also to your subordinates, if you are wrong. I know that you feel that you are never wrong, but that, as we know from the early sessions, is why you must look within yourself, compare yourself with others, and then determine whether you are being pig-headed, and not being truthful with yourself.

"There are other people who do say they're sorry, but in such a manner as to make you feel that you are in the wrong and they are only apologizing to show you their fine qualities. Yet there is no more certain way of making someone who is all set for a quarrel ease off and become ready to shake hands than by saying those simple words, *I'm sorry.*

"This apologizing business comes naturally to some people, but others have to learn it. It can be learned, it can be so developed that it comes naturally to you. It doesn't mean grovelling or whining – get that right out of your mind. *If I'm right, I'm right, and I won't admit that I'm wrong* may be OK for the man who's on top and can stay on top, but it isn't good enough for anyone else."

Young paused, then said, "I'm talking to you, now. Just to prove my point, the boss over there, Greg Ryder, is the first to say *I'm sorry* – and don't we appreciate it! However, from time to time he criticizes us, and I believe he does it in the nicest possible way, although sometimes he can be very, very tough. That is acceptable from him, because he does give praise, also. But sometimes," he looked at Greg, "you know you are wrong; and when you know you are in the wrong, what happens? The intercom flashes and a voice says, 'I'm sorry for what I said. I've been thinking about it – I'm wrong'. We all so much appreciate those few words from you, Greg."

Ryder said, "Thank you, George. I always appreciate the truth. You'll never find another me!"

When the laughter subsided, Young continued, "Now to the next factor in human relations".

Nina interrupted, "George, I'm sorry to interrupt you again, but there's something on my mind. To be the kind of manager who will carry out your teachings you have to be a very nice person, and it's an axiom that nice people always seem to finish last."

Young smiled. "I'm glad you brought that up, Nina. *Business* – that's the excellent glossy magazine sponsored by *The Financial Times* – had an article in this month's issue called *The Life of O'Reilly.*

"Tony O'Reilly oversees the Heinz empire, whose turnover is about $4 billion a year, and his is a fantastic success story, well imprinted on my mind. Hold on a minute, I have the magazine here."

Young delved into his briefcase, extracted the magazine, flipped through the pages and said, "Oh yes, here it is: *In London, New York, and Pittsburgh, O'Reilly has a reputation for charm, dynamism, frankness, generosity, and for putting into practice his beliefs on human relations. It is tempting to think of him as a chief executive who gives the lie to the axiom that nice guys finish last.*"

Mary Gwynne called out, "Fix, fix, fix! You arranged with Nina to ask the question, didn't you?"

"How did you guess, Mary? What a brilliant girl you are!

"Now on to my next point before there are any more interruptions. I'm now going to ask all of you a question. When you enter a restaurant with guests – no, not this time one where you are unknown, but where you are well known – do you or do you not like being greeted effusively and by name?"

There were nods of agreement all round.

Young continued: "Why? Because you are being made to feel important. The late J.B. Priestley, when writing one of his books on the things which delighted him, mentioned the fact that he liked to be recognized by head waiters and doormen, etc. He was big enough to admit that such recognition made him feel important. Unfortunately too many managers are apt to make their subordinates feel unimportant, especially when suggestions for improvements are made. Possibly the reason for this is that the manager feels that he has been made to feel unimportant by not thinking of the idea himself. But we've covered that ground before.

"Another point. Why are so many people name-droppers? We all know them. We do it ourselves sometimes. It's because they want to feel important.

"Why do tycoons delight in seeing their photograph in the newspapers? They'd like to see it daily if it could be managed by the PRO. They will claim that its all good for the company. Rubbish! They want to be made to feel important.

"I was recently at a party where I was introduced to a doctor. I thought he was a GP and told him the story about one of my relatives who was a GP in the south of England, and all about his trials and tribulations. I asked him where he practised. That doctor went to endless trouble to let me know in a roundabout way that he was not a GP at all but a consultant physician – and one of the most eminent at that! Why? He could just have accepted my story and said nothing more. He didn't, because he thought I didn't recognize how important he was.

"Dr Johnson wrote: *No man is much pleased with a companion who does not increase in some respect his fondness of himself.*

"That, I think, sums it up pretty well. When, for the right reasons, a manager makes a subordinate feel important and that he is doing an important job, he is motivating him to greater effort. Whether you employ in your department garage attendants, truck drivers, draughtsmen, or shop assistants is immaterial. Whoever you employ, whatever job they do, is important; part of the jigsaw puzzle which, when complete, represents the company.

"Now there are two sentences which I would like to have indelibly printed on your mind. When they are used they will invariably make the other person feel more important.

"The first is *I want your advice.* We always feel so important when anyone asks our advice. The second is *Can you help me?* We really do like helping other people, and we feel important when we are able to give them some help.

"That's all. Remember, then, making that other person feel important is a great motivator."

Mary Glynne said, "You are, of course, absolutely right, George, but you must also remember another fact. The manager himself must not feel too self-important, and too many managers, bustling around, do win that name for themselves."

Young nodded. "You're right, Mary, but why do they put on that act? Why do they have to try to impress others with their importance? There's usually one reason: their own bosses do not make them – the managers – feel important and neither perhaps do their subordinates. That's why they have to impress other people. They are almost begging others to tell them that they have an important job to do, and they are important people. You'll usually find that the bustling, hustling, self-important type of manager has over him a chief executive who is cold, quite unimpressed by human relations, and doesn't believe in building anyone up. Most problems stem from the top, and then work their way downwards, in exactly the same way as do so many brilliant concepts.

"But on to other factors in human relations. There are, of course, several motivators which we shall present after lunch, but my talk on human relations ends with two points, often considered unimportant. One is a demotivator, while the other is a gentle, but acceptable, motivator.

"The first relates to our tempers. We all lose our temper at times — outbursts come quite naturally to most of us — but my plea is to try to restrict them to hollering, bullying, menacing, shouting matches with our bosses. That's fair enough, isn't it? He can answer back. He can also lose his temper with us."

Young smiled at Ryder and added, "And, of course, our fellow associates — our fellow directors or managers. But even with the latter, there should be as few outbursts as possible.

"With our subordinates we should be more circumspect. In fact we should attempt to cut out the shouting altogether. Except at times of high unemployment, when there is a fear of losing a job, losing your temper with subordinates doesn't work. It always demotivates, whether it is from fear of losing a job or not."

Nina interrupted, saying demurely, "But George, losing our temper is supposed to be good for us. We're told by psychologists and psychiatrists in newspaper articles and on TV that neuroses disappear, anxiety vanishes with our spots, the air is cleared and we all feel mentally refreshed when we have an outburst. That's the claim, anyway; and so often we read about husbands and wives, especially in the film world, who enjoy throwing things at each other and then, immediately afterwards, happily make love. What do you say about that?"

Young answered, "That is a claim that is made, but is it valid? It's all a question of whether or not we have a conscience, whether or not we are more concerned over our feelings than those of other people. We all have arguments, and they're good for us, but I'm talking about the violent tempers so often used by managers in an attempt to get their own way. My wife and I have arguments, of course we do, but we don't throw plates, and we don't go into tantrums, for one very good reason. In a tantrum we nearly always say things we don't mean, but which can hurt for ever.

"But we're not here to discuss the quality of marriage, or irate wives and difficult husbands, only motivating our employees to try harder. The truth is that when we unburden ourselves – you know the sort of thing: 'I soon told her where to get off!', 'I slapped him down so hard he won't make that mistake again' – we may well be unburdening ourselves by moving the burden on to someone else's shoulders. We don't win over the other person. We may think we do, but after the outburst you may be sure the person who is on the receiving end of that verbal violence will tell his friends, associates, his workmates, and his family, that he was altogether right, and the boss, for all his shouting, was wrong.

"Reprimand, by all means – that, as has been mentioned earlier, must be done on many occasions – but without losing one's temper.

"There are some people who can get away with it. They are usually very, very nice people whose bark is known to be far worse than their bite. They may shout a lot, but they don't shout viciously, and they don't undermine another person's confidence. Subordinates will say of such a person, 'Oh, he's gone off the deep end a bit you know; the old man does that on occasion', and then perhaps laugh it away. But those people are few and far between. Don't try to emulate them.

"So my advice to managers is, if you can, when you boil over, shout in your own office, or go into a field. Then, when you have made up your mind on the clarity of your argument, the base of your discussion, the facts that you wish to explain to a subordinate, have that subordinate in and lay down for him what he should do in the future — but never in a violent manner.

"Now for the small but important motivator: it's keeping promises. Most people keep the big promises but, unfortunately for many, break the little ones. You know the kind of thing: 'Yes, of course I'll tell Mr Jones what you've said', 'Don't worry, I'll find a new supplier for you', 'I'll get that door fixed, leave it to me', or 'Of course I'll send flowers'. These promises are so often broken and forgotten.

"Keep those little promises and you, as new managers, will find that they are little, but most acceptable motivators."

Young paused again, then continued, "There's one point about human relations I must mention: Because we are supposedly normal human beings, we cannot live up to the tenets of human relations 100 per cent all the time, or even part of the time. We can't even reach 90 per cent, but maybe with a little extra effort we can reach nearly 70 per cent, and if we aim for 100 per cent and finish up with 60, we shall still become powerful motivators of people."

10   Time for Reflection

They had agreed on a 30-minute lunch break. Greg Ryder ordered chicken sandwiches and coffee to be served in his office. Rapidly he annotated memos and reports, used his tape recorder for three urgent letters, agreed with the general manager on building expenditure and then spoke to Mr Gross, managing director of Grossley Industries. Mr Gross boasted that he only dealt with managing directors – no salesmen for him. The result was the booking of a series of in-company courses. That left Greg just a few minutes to finish his coffee and sandwiches and to spend some time thinking.

His first thoughts were of his wife, doctor, and consultant, who had, each in their own way, tried to impress upon him the necessity for him to have a complete lunch break. "Lunch," they all said, "should take at least 45 minutes, followed by a half-hour sleep".

Ryder smiled. *Why sleep,* he thought to himself. *I don't even feel tired.*

His mind switched once more to the future. Had he made the right decision? Involuntarily, he nodded. Yes, he was sure he had.

During a war-scare crisis, a friend, the managing director of a multinational group had said to him, 'I'm expanding. I don't run my business on newspaper headlines'.

He, Greg Ryder, had decided that he wasn't going to run his business on health reports. What risk was there, other than the standard risk that happened to everyone? He could be knocked down by a bus, he could be killed in a car accident, or he could pick up a germ which could destroy him.

Ryder eased himself out of his chair and left the office for the afternoon session.

Mary Glynne hurried to her bedroom, having noticed when she crossed her legs for the last time before lunch that a ladder had begun wending its way down her ten denier stockings. She much preferred stockings to tights, believing they were more feminine and, equally important, less costly. Provided they were bought in pairs, there was always another to take the place of one that laddered.

In her room she drank a glass of orange juice, sat on the bed, and gracefully rolled down the offending stocking, replacing it with the new. Then she moved to the stool in front of her dressing table mirror and briefly inspected her appearance. She had another matter on her mind – Nina's proposition.

Had she the courage to invest in her own future? She had seen so many of her old associates branching out on their own, but she could hardly remember any of them succeeding. It was easy enough to advise clients to buy new computers, take on additional staff or increase advertising expenditure, when one did not have to find the cash oneself. But when you were on your own, every penny had to be accounted for, and if the cash flow were not right, there would soon be problems. Yet it was a great opportunity. A group of women management consultants, plus training of course, would have tremendous PR appeal.

But could she and Nina work happily over a long period? Could there be close co-operation between them? They worked well together without really liking, although respecting, each other, but would that continue if, for example, one of them were to fail in an assignment or wanted to borrow from the partnership cash reserve?

She didn't get very far with her deliberations, and decided to leave the matter in abeyance, to be reconsidered later. What she really wanted to do was to stay with Greg. She so greatly admired the man.

She sighed. If only he weren't so happily married!

Feeling a little more relaxed she left her room, to be greeted by Ted Noble, an instructor with an ambition to take every lady instructor to his bed. He said, "May I see your bedroom?"

"Of course," Mary answered, "why not? I'm going away next week, you'll have ample opportunity to look at it then. So long!"

Peter Lewis decided that an apple was sufficient for his midday needs. He required exercise, but then he always required exercise. A holiday mountain climbing was his ideal.

Returning to his room, he undressed, eased on swimming trunks, and with a towelling robe as cover, made his way to the pool, where he swam some twenty lengths. Back in his room, he took a shower and considered Cooper's proposal.

A very tempting offer. Unlike the other directors, he felt no personal loyalty to Greg Ryder, and thought Greg was getting a bit past it anyway.

Lewis knew his own worth, both as an instructor and a marketing consultant, but did not want to spend the rest of his life teaching or advising. He wanted to be the boss. He wanted to press buttons and make others jump. He was only concerned with what was best for him, but he was honest enough, and while he was working for Greg he gave 100 per cent effort.

Another thought entered his mind. Working for a group of senior partners in an accountancy organization, and a very large one at that, might mean he would have to stay put for most of the year. Like Ryder, he enjoyed visiting many parts of the world. Travelling was another of his hobbies.

Also, as with Ryder, decisions were given on the spot. It was yes or no; there might be an argument, but it was still yes or no. Would that happen with the senior accountants?

He dressed again without arriving at a decision. He did not know of Ryder's evaluation of him − that he was too selfish to hold a top job.

11 More Motivational Forces

Ryder said, "It seems that Motivation is taking up all the second day. I assume you are including performance appraisal?"

Before anyone could answer, he continued: "Incidentally, I agree with your criterion that if a manager cannot motivate his subordinates, he can only remain for ever a below-average manager."

Nina said, "Performance appraisal will be a complete session after tea; but another point, Greg, that we have to consider, is the manager who works in an environment which is anti any form of motivation.

"For example, the newspaper industry. A journalist told me the other day that if he asks for a message to be delivered, the response may well be, 'that's not my job!' A telephone operator refused to pass on a message he had wanted dealt with urgently by another editor. When tackled with the problem subsequently, her excuse was that it was against union policy, the union policy being that if a telephonist was supposed to be a carrier of messages that was a different kind of job, and she should be rewarded accordingly. How do you motivate such people?"

Young answered, "You are referring to the 'them and us' syndrome so prevalent a few years back, Nina, although it isn't so widespread these days. It still causes problems in the car industry, shipbuilding, the dockyards, and certainly in the press.

"We know this from experience, because we have carried out consultative work for the *Daily Gazette*, and of course one only has to read any of the spate of autobiographies written by ex-editors or ex-trade unionists, to be appalled by the intransigence of some trade-union officials, and the awful weakness of management. I believe that no such 'them and us' conflicts would have arisen if management had been of a higher calibre in the earlier days. For all that, there are difficult people whom it is almost impossible to motivate, although a good leader with an understanding of human relations can change them, over a period of time, especially if he sets the right example. Fairness is always respected, weakness is not. Truth is respected, lying is not. Commonsense is respected, foolish decisions are not.

"So let me turn to you, the new manager. You will have to handle difficult people as well as those who are more amenable to reason, but your task is to motivate all your subordinates, not just the nice ones.

"There is one proviso: most difficult people can, as I have said, after a time be won over; but you can never win over or motivate the fanatic. Don't try. Either put up with the fanatic if he is worth putting up with, or part company from him as soon as you can.

"Now I want to refer you back to yesterday's session on interpersonnel comparison tests. But as there is no one here whom you know well enough to compare yourself with, I want to ask you to look within.

"Why? Because so much about motivation is not acceptable to some managers, although such managers would find those same motivational forces quite acceptable to them if applied by their superiors. Your attitude now should be: *I'll accept your teachings until they are proved wrong in action, over a period of time.*

"I must ask you the question I posed before, and which you must think about for yourself. Are you a Mr, Mrs, or Miss 'S'no use', or 'Tain't possible' – words spoken by two well-known cartoon characters?

"As you know, most of us are consultants as well as instructors. Our clients pay quite heavily for our advice, but when we give it to them, so often we are met with a negative reaction, summed up by 'S'no use' or 'Tain't possible': then employees are always *different,* their manufacturing process is always *different,* their chief executives are always *different,* their region is *different,* their marketing problems are *different.* In fact they're living in a *different* business world altogether.

"What it all adds up to is the response of those cartoon characters to all suggestions – 'S'no use because . . .', 'Tain't possible because . . .'

"So far as you managers are concerned, it may be hard for you, but you must not allow these thoughts to obtrude. You have come here to profit from our research and our experience, which, summed up, means: *if you want to motivate others, you've got to keep to motivational rules,* whether you like them or not.

"Some of you, I know, will already be thinking to yourself, 'I can't do that, I'm not made that way'; but you have been born with one great right. You always have a choice. You can choose whichever way you want to act: you can choose between being a successful manager or a 'nearly' manager, and always remember that the largest club in the world in business is called the *Nearly Club.* It comprises those who have *nearly* made it in business, as well as those who have nearly made it in sport, the theatre, television, politics . . .

"To those in the *Nearly Club,* everything and everyone else are to blame for their lack of success. They were so *nearly* there so often, they *nearly* got that job, they very *nearly* got that promotion, but . . .

"Those who succeed generally understand that they cannot learn just from their own experiences. They could do, if they lived to be 1000 years old, and they could then drop ideas, motivational forces, what you will, after trying for a year or two – or even 3 years. They would still have 900 years or so to carry out their tests. But we don't live that long, so if we are to succeed, we must learn from other people.

"The reason I am labouring this point is because when you leave this room, when you have lunch together – when you walk together, you will criticize, as you have a right to do, and you will be very nearly using those words *Tain't possible* and *S'no use*. But before doing so, think – and think hard. Then make up your mind to put our lessons into action, come what may. I can assure you that if you have never before practised human relations, you will find that the changes that happen are so rapid that they will surprise you.

"But to change the subject now, we have moved away a little from direct human relations to setting an example, and I want to emphasize that this either is a great motivator or a great demotivator.

"If a manager is known for taking an extra long lunch hour and always returning looking well dined and well wined, that will have an effect on his subordinates. Why shouldn't *they* take a little extra time? Then, if that same manager one day reprimands them, this reprimand will not be so acceptable because they feel that he, himself – or she, for that matter – breaks the rules too often. It's the same with the manager who sets a bad example by his inability either to dictate or record, or even to write, a decent letter; or his inability to keep to a timetable. If he is late in the office most days, how can he reprimand others who also arrive late?

"But let us move on again. There are other factors in motivation and I shall explain them by relating experiences among our consultants and training team. First, I'm going to call on our marketing director, Peter Lewis."

Young paused, then said, "OK, Peter, don't worry. You're not going to have to attend every new management course to give one anecdote and then disappear. Your story will be related by others, or we may record it, or put it on video. We all know that delegates respond extremely well to what we call our visual or verbal proof stories.

"However, on this occasion, Peter, I am handing over to you, and, as we discussed the matter last evening, you know very well what it's all about. So tell us your true story, Peter, of someone proving that status is important to all of us, no matter what level we are in an organization.

Lewis said, "I can't understand you people. You sit here all day and then, as soon as we have a break, you sit down some more. Why don't you jog, swim, or walk?"

"Why should we?" asked Greg Ryder, and regretted the question when Lewis came back immediately with, "To protect your health. We all work under pressure. The antidote is not rest, but exercise."

Ryder smiled. "You win, Peter. We'll start a course on how to be physically fit, and you will run it 100 per cent. If we all go bankrupt through exercising instead of thinking, it will be your fault!"

Everyone laughed dutifully, except Lewis, who attempted to start an argument. His first words, however, were brushed aside by Ryder who said, "Let's get on with the session".

Lewis nodded and went on: "I want to explain the importance of status as a motivator, and how I learned that lesson. It happened some years back, when I was the field sales manager of a company selling air deodorizing and purifying units.

"The units we were selling at that time produced ozone. One of my top salesmen, Albert Green, was certain that he was about to obtain the biggest order of his career from Lever's, the giant margarine and detergent organization. They then had their London headquarters near Blackfriars Bridge – a massive building housing a large restaurant and canteen for the employees and visitors, besides the offices, etc. Green explained that he had won over the manager of the catering area and the order was almost in the bag. He wanted me to accompany him, to make sure that if there was a last-minute problem, I could make decisions. Three of our large units had already been installed in the restaurant area and he had been told by the manager that the tests were going well.

"Although I told him that he was quite capable of closing the order himself without any help, I naturally agreed to accompany him when he insisted. We met outside the Lever building on the following Monday at 9 am. On entering the lobby, Green was greeted by the commissionaire as an old friend. Good selling, I remember thinking, because at the training school which we ran for our air-conditioning division we always stressed that two people should be won over in any organization – the commissionaire who helps to get you in and the secretary who can arrange an appointment for you with her boss.

"We were waved through with the words, 'You know the way, Mr Green', and soon we were in the basement catering area. On arriving, I noticed several women preparing vegetables. Some were even peeling potatoes, although a potato-peeling machine was standing idly by.

"Green said, 'If you wouldn't mind waiting here for a few minutes, Mr Lewis, I'll see if Gerald Mann the manager is ready to see us.' With that, he was off, and one of the ladies turned to me and said, 'Are you wiv 'im?'

"'Yes', I said.

"She sniffed, and that sniff did not denote a warm friendship. A plumpish, red-faced lady, who had hardly looked at me, made off, also in the direction of the manager's office. I said to one of the younger girls who did not seem to mind breaking off from her sniffing and cleaning in order to chat, 'I'm sure you like our air-purifying units that have been installed. They really are good for you, you know. They will keep the air fresh and clean. You have a caring management, willing to consider spending money mostly for the benefit of those who work here.'

"The girl answered, 'We're not 'aving 'em'.

"That shocked me, and I'm not easily shockable. 'Why?' I asked.

"One of the plump women replied, 'Your bloke upset

Maggie'.

"'And who's Maggie?' I asked.

"'She's just gone out, the one with the red dress.'

"'Oh yes, what upset her?'

"'Well Maggie has been made supervisor. She's in control of us, and your bloke couldn't spare the time even to say good morning to us, or tell us what he was up to. He made silly jokes to all of us. He likes the young girls, doesn't 'e. but Maggie's the boss you know, and what she says goes.'

"'And what does she say?' I asked.

"'That your things give us headaches, runny eyes, and sore throats.'

"'And do they?'

"The girls giggled. One answered, 'Anyway, Maggie's told Mr Mann that we don't want 'em'.

"'But your Mr Mann said they were doing a splendid job.'

"'Well, we still don't want 'em.'

"I tried to win them over. When Maggie returned, I attempted to make my peace with her, but it was no use. Later, a disconsolate Green arrived to tell me the bad news. I didn't have to ask him what happened.

"'He wants them taken away', he said. 'We've lost the order. Someone didn't like them. I don't think you could have helped, Mr Lewis. It would only have embarrassed you if I'd asked you to join us. He was so adamant. I don't know what went wrong.'

"'Maybe' I said, 'you failed to remember the importance of the chief potato peeler'.

"'What?'

"'Never mind. Let's make some more calls and try to make up for not getting this order.'

"'Yes, let's do that. But what did you mean about the potato peeler? I don't understand . . .'

"'Well', I said, 'you lost the sale because you didn't show enough respect to the lady who was in charge. She wanted to be consulted, she wanted her opinion sought. You ignored her. You won over the commissionaire because you respected his uniform, his appearance, his manner, the fact that he was obviously the boss of all he surveyed in that lobby: but some of the most important people who could influence the sales for you were those actually working under the conditions you were trying to alleviate. Maggie was very concerned with her status, and you didn't recognize that status. Come on, let's go and do some work.'

Nina said, "An excellent story, Peter. Surely the moral behind that story was covered earlier on in the need for us to feel important."

"Yes", said Lewis, "but there is a difference. Maggie wasn't trying to prove how important she was, she was simply status-conscious. Her status in the eyes of her colleagues was all-important to her. They were expected to take a lead from her, and that status was undermined when someone failed to consult her, especially as the others had expected that to happen."

"Did you retrieve the order"? asked Cooper.

"No, we didn't. It was lost forever. I think the management decided to put in a full-scale ventilation plant."

"What you are stressing," said Young, "is that status depends on recognition by others."

"That's right," said Lewis. "but it taught me another lesson: people, whether of low rank or high, like to have titles.

"Within a few days of returning to the office after that call on Lever's, I reorganized our sales team. Wishing to motivate the status-seekers, I made new appointments. A salesman could become a senior salesman; if he then achieved success he could become an inspector, and then a supervisor.

"Now, quite frankly, the work of the senior salesman, the inspector, and the supervisor, was exactly the same − to help other salesmen. But each step meant that someone had achieved greater status. I went on to make district managers, area managers, followed by regional managers. It was Maggie's views that made me realize just how much status meant to some people, and one should create positions within an organization to cater for that need.

"Once that need has been filled, most people are motivated to achieve a new status and will be continually motivated to retain that status.

"That completes my contribution for the moment," said Peter.

Mary said, with a laugh, "I'll use that case study, for sure, only I'll change the venue."

"You dare!" said Lewis.

Ryder interrupted: "Please continue with the session. Does anyone want to add to our claim that status is a strong motivator?"

"Yes", said Nina, "only to emphasize that desire for status motivates nearly everyone. After all, why does anyone want to be chairman of a committee, for example? There'll be no thanks before retirement, only endless criticism of everything that's gone wrong. But what makes up for it is the respect, almost reverence, of the members who, when they introduce friends, say, 'This is the chairman' or 'This is the captain'.

"Why do managers, as Peter said earlier, like their name printed in gold letters on their door? Surely not because someone might never find them! No, they want us all to be constantly reminded of their status; and as happened in the case of Maggie, once ignore the status and you've probably made an enemy for life.

"Why does the person who was once quite happy to be known as the ratcatcher now have to be called a chief rodent exterminator? The reason probably is that the job couldn't be filled if people still called them ratcatchers. There is no motivation in becoming a catcher of rats, but a rodent exterminator – that's a different proposition."

Ryder said, "I think the point has been made now. Status is a motivator. Next please?"

Cooper said, "I'd like to tell a story relating to a problem raised earlier, the problem of motivating those employees who are in a rut. Probably they have been with the company many, many years, and they are not willing to accept innovation or change. They are in fact quite happy living in their rut. But that is not acceptable to an efficient and well run company. We all dislike using fear as a motivator, but sometimes there is no alternative. Here is my story.

"There were three frogs jumping their way down a muddy highway. From the sheer enjoyment of living they pranced and leapt in and out of a rut made by a tractor. After one particularly long jump a little frog named Harry landed badly, and became stuck in the mud. At first this didn't worry him, and his two friends passed him by. Then he found he couldn't move. His two friends returned to help him. They began tugging, pulling, they pushed and heaved – all without success.

"Suddenly from out of the mist there loomed another tractor. It was making use of the rut in the road, and as it came nearer, the two frogs made one last desperate effort.

"They tugged at Harry but it was no use, they couldn't budge him. At the last moment the two frogs jumped aside, leaving their companion to meet his end.

"They stood sadly by the roadside as the tractor passed, bemoaning the fate of poor Harry. Suddenly, to their surprise, there was a slight plop and Harry had rejoined them.

"Harry," they cried simultaneously, "This is marvellous! How did you get out of that rut?"

"Well," answered Harry, "I had to get out, so I got out!"

"That kind of thing happens in life. Often we are forced out of ruts through changed circumstances."

Cooper paused, then continued: "You all remember Roper. I couldn't motivate him even to begin to appreciate how much computers could help productivity so far as his division was concerned. His response was always, 'I'm too old to change now'.

"I told him the story of the three frogs. I remember him looking quizzically at me as I concluded, but his expression changed when I added: 'The time has come, John, for you to copy Harry the frog. You're stuck in your old rut, and no one can shift you except yourself. If you don't get out now, maybe you won't be with us long enough to reach your retiring age'."

Again, Cooper paused, then added rather diffidently: "That's an example of using fear as a motivator. It must only be used when there is no alternative, and there was no alternative in Roper's case. But it worked. He became a changed man and you, Greg, gave him a very nice golden handshake when he retired last year."

There was some discussion about the advisability of using fear as a motivator, but eventually they all agreed that it had its place, and should be left in the course with the story of the little frogs.

Young then turned to Nina to invite her contribution.

She said, "We mustn't forget that we are instructing newly appointed managers. This, then, is how I would talk to them.

"We are asking you to change your point of view, possibly even to act against your previous ideas of motivating forces, but you have to be motivated before you can motivate others; and you are faced with so many demotivators. The most prevalent is the 'Why should you?' syndrome.

"This sentence is used by possessive mothers, fathers who believe that whatever their family does is correct, business associates, workers in factories, and employees in offices. There's little Johnny who always plays on the wing and has been transferred to a mid-field position – or perhaps he has been asked to play for the reserves. 'Why should you?' asks his father. 'Why should you do it?'

"How much wiser if he were to explain to young Johnny that it's quite likely he isn't the best footballer in the team, and possibly it would do him a great deal of good to play for the reserves.

"Young Mary Smith works later at the office. 'Why should you?' asks her mother, and repeats, 'Why should you? You aren't paid overtime; they take advantage of you . . .'

"In the selling field, the enterprising salesman may want to work on a Saturday morning. 'Why should you?' askes his wife. Well-meaning friends and relatives can do so much to demotivate, by undermining our confidence in those who employ us.

"A manager, aware of the *Why should you?* syndrome, always establishes the reason for, and the importance of, changes or special requests."

Nina finished, and Ryder said, "Excellent, Nina. May I now make another contribution?"

They all echoed politely: "Of course".

Ryder said, "There are other specific motivators. Should they be highlighted? They cover working conditions, enjoyment of work, activity targets, employee benefits, quality circles . . ."

Mary interrupted: "If you want to detail every aspect of motivation, we must also add promotions, general amenities and of course medical welfare. But I believe that we shall be overdoing it if we stress every motivator. It's enough perhaps to mention them. "I think we've covered the ground well as far as the new manager is concerned."

Ryder said quickly, "Very well, I agree".

Nina said, "I think we must emphasize the management objective of seeking excellent working conditions, enjoyment of work, and get-togethers in the shape of quality circles to solve problems . . ."

"Agreed", said Mary icily, "but you rightly used the word management. Top management should instigate such disciplines."

"Nonsense!" said Nina. "Every manager, new or old, can improve conditions, etc; it's almost a priority for the new manager."

Ryder stopped the discussion getting out of hand by saying, "You are both right. Let's leave it at that."

Young said, "But I would like to elaborate on two motivators that Greg touched upon, and they are consultation and explanation. Both of them have such high motivating potential. You'll remember Bisset, in the order department.

"He would never tell anyone what he was doing, or why he was doing it. He wouldn't put his staff in the picture, and that resulted in rather a disconsolate staff, in spite of the fact that Bisset was always adored by everyone who worked with him.

He was so kind, so helpful, so generous, yet they were 'agin' him because he caused such problems. Work was handed out without explanations, followed by reprimands if it was not carried out quickly or efficiently.

"He neither consulted nor explained, and was always criticizing modern youth for not being willing to give that little bit extra, to take more interest in work. Yet he wouldn't give the incentive of explanation or consultation to get the best out of the younger members of his staff.

"He was the type who was always right, and everyone else was always wrong."

Cooper said, "Now we're getting into the realms of delegating, a strong motivator we have also only barely touched upon."

"I agree," said Young, "but you'll remember that our decision was to give delegating a full session to itself".

Cooper smiled and said, "You're right, I had forgotten. Sorry, George. But surely it should be mentioned now, as you are raising the subject of Bisset."

"Right, it will be." Then, turning to Nina, George said, "Do you think it would be a good idea if we acted out a few sketches for videoing, depicting the rights and wrongs of consultation and explanation? They could be based on Bisset's story. You're the expert in that field, Nina. Would you like to take on the job of working something out? You're far better at it than I am."

"Praise," murmured Nina, "but justifiable praise! I agree, I'll do all I can. It's a good idea anyway. Just a few simple shots showing the right way to bring in subordinates and the wrong way, without actually delving deep into the realms of delegating."

Cooper, looking at his watch, said, "We're nearing the end of the session, and after tea we shall be covering performance appraisal. But one point still concerns me. The complete session is based on caring for the individual, something we hear so much about. But those who sometimes stress their caring attitudes are mostly uncaring people — at least, I've found them that way. I remember when Greg engaged me he told me of the four principles of his company: one, respect for the individual; two, to win respect of the individual for management; three, that marketing was everyone's concern; and four, that quality was not just important to production, but to every aspect of business, whether it be writing a letter or answering a telephone call.

"I believe that we, in this organization, do mainly keep to such rules, but any of our management consultants will tell you that the majority of companies not only don't have these rules but they don't believe in such ideas anyway. How can we impress upon managers that they must adhere to the first two principles, which means putting into practice George's belief in the effect of good human relations in industry?"

Ryder stepped in quickly. "That's a non-starter, Philip," he said. "If we, as instructors, cannot by our eloquence, enthusiasm, dedication and sincerity win over the delegates to our way of thinking, then we're not doing our job properly, and no one can say that we ever don't give of our best. If we can't persuade those who attend our courses immediately to put our teachings into action, then we shouldn't be in the training business. It's the academics who fall by the wayside in that respect, Philip, not practical people like us. Do you accept that?"

Cooper said, "I'd better, or there might be some criticism in public, and that's against George's beliefs."

There was general laughter, in which Ryder joined. Then he continued: "We are all so motivated because we are high quality instructors first and foremost, and therefore we shall be able to persuade the majority of those managers attending this course to carry out the principles we outline.

"Let's leave it at that. But I would like to clarify what respect for the individual means. It means never putting him or her in a position where they will feel a loss of dignity, or degraded in any way. A simple example is one we have already met, reprimanding someone in front of a colleague. As you said, Philip, sometimes those who pretend to care most care least; but that doesn't affect our teaching or our principles. The main principle is putting people first, because it's people who build a company, in the same way as it's people who can drag a company down.

"But can you give uncaring people a caring attitude? That, I don't know; although, as I said much earlier, people can change, people do change, and people can make themselves change.

"Putting caring into action means that every chief executive, for example, should want to know if serious problems face any of his employees. If the organization is too large for that to happen, then the chief executive should make his wishes known to his managers, so that they can be responsible for showing a caring attitude to those in need.

"Ill health can cause serious problems: say a husband is away, or a wife is ill, and there are children to be cared for. Flowers sent to someone in hospital is an act which is highly thought of. Congratulations when a baby is born is also much appreciated. This caring attitude may have to be adopted by those who don't really care in the first place, but if they adopt it, they will find as the months go by and the years unroll, that the effort has become a worthwhile habit.

"Of course those in industry should not have to be philanthropists, because a business is not a philanthropic institution, but most companies contribute to charities. They should remember that the first and foremost important charity is their own employees. In the larger companies there should be a specific procedure for helping those in need, and every chief executive should be very happy indeed if he ever hears the words 'They're a wonderful company to work for'.

"That means they are a caring company, but it does not mean that they are a company without discipline, without strength when strength is needed, or without the ability to correct when there are faults. Caring means paying adequate salaries – possibly, just a little above the normal. But it does not mean giving way to trade-union demands if those demands could result in redundancies in or uncompetitiveness by the company. Caring, in fact, means doing everything to satisfy customer needs, because only by satisfying those needs do jobs become safe.

"Some people claim that caring means that everyone should share the same restaurant facilities – the directors should eat with the engineers, the maintenance men, the cleaners . . . That's fair enough. There's nothing wrong with it, but it need not be a good dictum either. Often men and women in factory, shop, and office do not want to have their bosses around them when they are eating. What it does mean is that basically the directors and managers, should be provided with the same type of food as the rest of the employees, except if a client has to be entertained.

"Employees should know that every firm lives by satisfying its customers and so winning their goodwill. If that goodwill is going to be strengthened by entertainment, no employee should ever complain.

"Ultimately, it all comes down to quality. There should be high quality caring just as there should be high quality products, quality in communication, quality in service. A company imbued with quality is also, almost inevitably, a caring company. As I said earlier, caring can so often result in security, because employees always give of their best to a caring company. It is such a strong motivating force.

"I must reiterate that caring does not mean being weak or vacillating. Why do I have to emphasize that? Because you, as managers, will often believe that you can be too kind to people, too nice to people; but, as someone said earlier, nice people do often come first.

"Philip told the story about the frogs in a rut and how the frog jumped out because he had to, and how that story motivated an employee to pull his weight. That was not uncaring. In fact it was caring, because the alternative could, at some time, have been dismissal. To motivate people for their own good, by any fair means can also mean caring for them.

"Finally – yes, I'm the boss so I may say finally." There

was the usual laughter, and he repeated: "finally, it is usually only the strong leader who can carry out all the principles of human relations and caring."

Greg Ryder stopped talking, looked around the room, drummed on the table with his fingers — a sign that he was off on another track — then said, "One point concerns me about the session so far: there is not enough participation, too much talking. George said earlier that human relations is a subject which doesn't lend itself to a great deal of participation, but for all that we must work out how we can form syndicates and discussion groups, and perhaps someone will be brilliant enough to plan a motivating game which can also be played by delegates in syndicates. Mary, you're good at that sort of thing. Think about it, will you?"

"Of course, Boss," said Mary with a smile; then added: "but may I just have a final word?"

"No," said Ryder adamantly, "you may not. I want to show you all that I'm a very caring boss, and I know this is tea time, and George really can't do without his cuppa."

12 Performance Appraisal

After the tea break Mary said, "Greg, you have such strong views on performance appraisal, I suggest you begin by explaining what you believe to be wrong with it. Your thoughts might also be in the minds of many of the delegates attending the courses."

Young interrupted. "I must defend Greg, he's not at all anti, but . . ."

It was Ryder's turn to break in. "Don't bother, George, I don't need defending. I'm only anti because performance appraisal is often incorrectly used, and in my view it is better not to appraise at all than to make a hash of the job. Mary, I appreciate your reading my mind. I do want to open the session and now I don't have to pull rank to do so.

"The greatest weakness of performance appraisal is its attempt to appraise personality defects and character weaknesses; and from my researches this usually takes up some 60 per cent of any setpiece appraisal. I'm not suggesting that we should not appraise people to ascertain their personality and character defects, but this aspect should be aired when the defects show up, not some months later.

"In any event, whatever the time lag, no one agrees with an

accusation of being weak, churlish, irritable, short-tempered, argumentative . . . If we are churlish, for example, it is due to our determination to be efficient, unlike those with a couldn't-care-less attitude.

"We know that we must strive to discover defects for ourselves, through interpersonnel comparison tests, because we rarely believe the criticisms that come from others. Such appraisals by management therefore can only be set against standards agreed by the person being appraised – all very simple, when applied to a salesman – and nearly every writer on performance appraisal insists, as I have done, that standards must be set, and gives as an example standards set for salesmen. Why? Because it is so difficult to set standards for those in other activities. A sales manager will also have targets for advertising, training, costs, etc.

"The problem lies in extending these standards to office managers, computer operators, typists, receptionists, waiters, service engineers, film photographers, post office staff . . . The list is practically endless.

"When management by objectives was the vogue, managers did try, but mostly failed, to quantify their objectives. Imagine trying to quantify the daily tasks of a secretary. The standard of a letter – yes, that is a standard which can be set – no erasing, no alterations, no misspelling . . . But how do you set a standard for how much typing there should be in a day, how many telephone calls should be made and answered, how much personal work for the boss should be carried out, and in what detail the boss's diary should be updated . . .?

"Pretty tough, that! Is a manager to be judged against the number of estimates or proposals sent out each day, irate customers converted to satisfied customers, or telephone calls made to suppliers?

"Such standards can be set up if there is enough expenditure of time and money, if forms are completed and computers used extensively – but for what? Do we want performance appraisal to cause a massive increase in paper work?

"Management by objectives is no longer fashionable, yet if

performance appraisal is to be successful, some kind of standard has to be set.

"A simple example of negative standards is someone falling behind with their work. No standards have been set, and yet, if a secretary is days behind with her mail, obviously standards have not been achieved, and the reasons for this have to be examined. Does this secretary work for too many bosses? Is her time being misused? Is she given lengthy dictation, instead of her boss using a recorder? Is the environment wrong? If steps are taken to rectify such bad management errors, the onus is simply on the secretary, assisted by the appraiser, to explain why she is still unable to keep up with her work.

"What is the objective of performance appraisal? Surely it is to motivate employees to correct mistakes, eradicate weaknesses, strengthen their strengths, and so increase production in whatever field they operate.

"When men or women in any division of an organization look forward to being appraised, they do so generally in the belief that they will be told how good they are — that they are in line for promotion, and possibly, will be offered an above-average salary increase. Sometimes kindly appraisers will dangle a host of carrots, and those appraised will leave the meetings extremely happy. But this can only be done once, twice, or possibly three times. After that, unless the promises have been turned into realities, those appraised will be put off these meetings for ever.

"As I mentioned earlier, rarely will anyone agree that, even when standards are set, they are responsible for a fall in standards. That is another problem. If you are appraising me right now, you will tell me that all I am telling you you have heard before, several times before. I am being repetitive, and therefore falling from the high standards that a managing director should set for himself. Right?

"Right!" came the low key, half-hearted response.

Ryder continued. "When you have been punished, or reprimanded long after the event, you see no justification in the punishment or reprimand. For example, if, when at school, you indulged in a spot of cribbing, you will remember that if the punishment came late, it was not acceptable to you. Why? Because you had already cleared your mind of the incident, and had thought it forgotten. Punishment at the time may not be willingly accepted, but a realization that you have deserved it will make it much more acceptable than if the criticism comes some 6 months later. You cribbed, you deserved your punishment. But a month or two later your perspective has changed: you weren't cribbing at all, only helping a fellow student. Again, true or false doesn't matter.

"But if you're corrected on the spot, then no excuses come readily to your mind. You take your punishment, however reluctantly, and you bear no grudge. The same punishment handed out later can rankle for months. The analogy with performance appraisal is surely now clear to you. Throughout life we accept a reprimand if it is given at the time of the misdemeanour – sloppiness in the office, a salesman neglecting a customer, poor workmanship . . . All can be corrected at the time with no lasting hard feelings.

"How to criticize has already been covered, and if the rules are kept, then appraisal criticisms will be adjudged fair; but this will not be the case 6 months later. Then, the feelings of the person being assessed are always *Why bring that up now?*

"My views are that a 6-monthly or yearly assessment has its place in personnel management, provided the personnel manager is a highly qualified assessor. However, most managers are not too good at setpiece appraisals, but can assess adequately on a daily, weekly, or even monthly basis. They are not then bound to the formalities of the setpiece interview.

"Let us consider those about to be appraised. Nothing can alter the fact that whatever misgivings they may have, those about to be appraised look forward to being told how good they are – as you do, as managers, when being appraised by your superiors. A typical remark by those about to be appraised is 'I like to know where I stand', which means *Please tell me I'm perfect, and detail my future career developments.*

"Never, never, never believe anyone who tells you at the

beginning of an appraisal, 'I like it straight from the shoulder'. They don't mean anything of the kind!"

Young said, "May I ask a question?"

"Sure."

"Isn't the reason for a 6-monthly or yearly performance appraisal to enable an assessment to be made over a period of time – you have partly mentioned this yourself – rather than to make instant decisions about how someone is doing? Secondly, surely criticism should be made on a daily or weekly basis if necessary, so that when we go to the yearly performance appraisal there can be not only praise but suggestions as to how a career can be developed, because past mistakes are no longer occurring?"

Ryder said, "Putting it that way, yes. Obviously I didn't make myself clear. What we have to do on the course, as George said earlier, is to re-emphasize that people are motivated by praise and by being made to feel important.

"Human relations is an ongoing process, and praise and criticism must be given, as I mentioned earlier, at the time when they are earned. Again, as mentioned earlier, if these actions are taken, the setpieces will also become more acceptable. Does that answer you, George?"

"It certainly does!" It was the answer everyone expected from George.

Cooper said, "In my department I carry out Greg's directive, which he drummed into me when I was appointed. When you appraise people, look upon it as a discussion, and forget the word appraisal. I sometimes think," he said, "the only thing wrong with performance appraisal is the expression performance appraisal. How much more acceptable to say to someone, 'Come and see me at 3 o'clock so that we can have a chat about your job and how it relates to the objectives of the company'. That, in itself, makes people feel far more important than telling them that you are going to appraise their performance. So, in my department I have carried out this dictum. We do have a yearly setpiece appraisal, which I call a discussion on how both subordinates and manager can profit by past mistakes and can add to their strengths, so that we can all look forward to a good future.

Looking at Ryder, Cooper smiled and said, "I well remember your words of advice: deal with people's problems quickly and fairly. Only then will yearly appraisal be worthwhile, because there will not be a series of recriminations."

Ryder said, "Thank you, Philip. Now for some rules for standard appraisals."

"Another interruption, please?" asked Young.

None too happily, Greg agreed.

Young said, "Set appraisals are, surely, necessary, if only for the purpose of keeping records of staff development. Managers change, and newcomers should be aware from records of the strengths and weaknesses of their staff. A managing director may well demand such a record when considering promotions.

"That is right not only for the giant organizations or the armed forces but also for small or medium-sized companies, although directors may know most of their employees' strengths and weaknesses.

"Obviously, if a personnel manager is employed, he or she will want to keep records. Please don't misunderstand me, I'm not in favour of reams of company print-outs, but believe that records are needed. But more of that later."

Ryder said, "Yes, we'll cover keeping records in detail later." Then, turning to Mary, he said, "You are the most experienced of all of us in performance appraisal. Please take over and tell us what should, and what should not, be done to build up a good performance appraisal exercise."

"You won't like what I'm going to say!"

"But I'll respect your views, as you respect mine."

Mary smiled, brushed back an odd strand of hair which was a millimetre out of position − a gesture well known to all of them, especially Ryder. They all felt that there was a special relationship between Ryder and Mary, and they were not far wrong.

Mary said, "I agree, emphatically, that there must be regular appraisals; but I don't agree with your conclusion that the setpiece yearly appraisal is often a waste of time. If those weren't your exact words on this occasion, Greg, you have used them to me in the past, although at the moment you are bending over backwards to be fair to those for and those against. But you have said, and I must repeat, *if a performance appraisal fails, it is due solely to the ineptness of the appraiser, be he manager, personnel officer, or managing director.*

"When a meeting is well conducted, there is no ill feeling, no antipathy, and the person appraised, much as you may think otherwise, does look forward to being appraised again. But you don't want me to speak at length on my beliefs.

"This is a course for new managers, and new managers must be taught how to conduct performance appraisal exercises. Delegates will want a set of rules."

Ryder nodded.

Mary continued: "A problem can be the dreams, and even fantasies, of those to be appraised. They want to hear of career development, but since cost-cutting exercises are now almost mandatory, resulting in much leaner organizations, there are fewer opportunities for advancement. This has to be explained to those being appraised. They must be told that management is only concerned with profitability allied to the care of its employees, and each employee is a profit centre. The way that profit centre is developed can result in some of the dreams coming true.

"At all appraisal meetings, what we, as appraisers, should do is to explain that opportunities can be self-made. Too many employees look to management to create opportunities, when it is within the scope of many of them to create their own, by being better at their job, and this must be set against standards achieved or not.

"What the appraiser must not do is to fall back on the clichés – pull up your socks, put your shoulder to the wheel – or make such valueless suggestions as 'Do that and I'll put in a good word for you when John X retires, or when he is moved to another department'. Such carrot-dangling is not only foolish, but unethical."

Ryder said, "I'm not disagreeing with you, Mary, but I thought you were about to give us a set of rules".

"Sorry, you're right, Greg – so here they are:

- One, be careful about arriving at conclusions during the daily, weekly, or short-term appraisals. People change when circumstances change. For example, a family bereavement, illness, debt problems, wife or husband problems, can affect a subordinate on a temporary basis. Make a note of these occurrences, and save up your immediate decisions so that at the yearly or setpiece appraisal you have enough evidence to enable you to give the right advice, help, or criticism.

- Two, make certain that you are not criticizing a subordinate's work when the problem lies with a management directive or change of policy which could affect, perhaps only temporarily, the smooth running of a department.

- "Three, can an appraisal be truly objective? It is very difficult, but it can be done with training. We all have prejudices, but most of us are able to keep them under control, or at least, to hide them. But unfortunately some have prejudices about which they are almost fanatical. The opposite is the person who is very calm and easy-going, yet has a deep prejudice against people with red hair, spots, short haircuts, long hair styles, slovenly dress, no eye-to-eye contact. Others have the standard prejudices, concerning religion, district or area, country or colour. Appraisals must fail if prejudices are allowed to dominate the thoughts of the assessor to the detriment of the subordinate."

George interrupted, "May I add something to that?"
"Of course."
"Sometimes we have irrational prejudices: for example, we

may resent a different scholastic background, or a university graduate, when we have been deprived of the privilege of such an education, or we can even be prejudiced against someone with more sex appeal than ourselves. Most of us are prejudiced against those who boast, those who consistently depress others with their views, or those who will tell funny stories badly. When the appraisal takes place, I agree, we must fight hard to put these prejudices aside. That's all."

Mary thought, a typical contribution from dear George Young. She continued:

- "Four, has management set a job specification? Does each employee know exactly what is expected of him or her? Does management regularly update that specification after discussion with a subordinate?
- Five, at the regular discussion meetings the manager should pinpoint the areas of success, and also show how areas of poor performance can be improved. Management should seek the views of subordinates as far as their particular tasks are concerned.
- Six, appraisal is a vehicle for improving performance, improving interpersonal relationships, and motivating subordinates to greater success. An assessor should constantly remind himself of these priorities so that he can maintain his own enthusiasm.
- Seven, in life generally – for example, sport, acting, or farming – most people want to know how their accomplishments are measured. In sport there are clearly defined objectives: a batting average, a bowling average, aces at tennis . . ."

She smiled and went on: "My father always wanted a boy. He didn't get one, so he insisted that I should attend every village football match, cricket match, tennis match, and he usually performed in all three."

Lewis said, "I always thought you ought to have been a footballer or a rugby player".

"That," said Mary, "would have been a good idea, then I could have put an armlock on you, or thrown you around when you annoy me, as you do occasionally".

"Sorry," said Lewis, "I only meant to be funny".

Mary continued:

> "On the stage, actors are expected to give excellent performances, not once but night after night. They are measured by standards – perhaps against actors or actresses of the past who played similar parts. Critics also make sure that standards are recognized. These factors can be pointed out to subordinates, so that they will fully understand that they are not alone in trying to achieve and maintain standards; otherwise they may be wary, or even suspicious, of the exercise.

- Eight, a certain failure in performance appraisal is when the subordinate believes that the standards set are impossible to achieve. Standards set must be by joint agreement.
- Nine, a great many benefits are derived from performance appraisal besides improving performance. There is the identification of training needs, areas of delegation, and a better understanding between management and the subordinate. If the latter is not the outcome of a meeting, the exercise has been a waste of time. Subordinates must know that during appraisal time they will be allowed to talk about themselves and their problems. They will not have to listen to someone prating on about successes in the past and how others have done so well and 'Why can't you do the same?' They want to express their views, make suggestions for improvements – in fact at times they almost want to appraise the appraiser, particularly in areas of conflict, which means that the standards in that department have not been maintained. Whether managers' or subordinates' objectives are achieved depends solely on the abilities of the appraiser and the standards set. So let us now move

on to the setting of standards."

Ryder laughingly interrupted, "Remember that, when next you have to appraise me!"

"That's a risk I wouldn't take."

"You would, you know, and you'd enjoy it," chuckled Ryder, then added, 'I won't interrupt again".

"Thank you. We all judge, and are judged, against standards. You mentioned sales, Greg. Yes, it's very easy to set standards for a sales department, and so it is for a credit control division. The standards set can apply to cash collected, the length of time debts are outstanding, how many dissatisfied customers complain about wrongful demands or an 'unless' letter that has annoyed them . . . You, Philip, know that management accounts must be on time and accurate, if they are to be a guide for the future. If your department doesn't measure up to that standard and accounts arrive late, so that decisions are delayed, that fall in standards can affect the smooth running of the business. But of course in your department, Philip, there is tight control, and standards are maintained. There is also a set standard for our computer operations; there is the standard checking of invoices against orders. You have standards related to time, the time it takes to do a job.

"Let me give you some more examples:

- A. Standards can be based on the way a competent person should do a job. There can be a time factor or an accuracy factor, and they can be based on past performances. If Jones is a competent person who sets the standards, and Smith does not reach those standards over a period of time, then we must look for the reasons why Smith has fallen below the standard set by Jones.
- B. Standards may be based on the present, future, or past statistics.
- C. Is efficient training given, to enable the standards to be achieved?

- D. Is experience essential if a standard is to be maintained? It is no use asking a newcomer to achieve a standard set by someone very experienced in that task.
- E. In manufacturing, quality standards should be set, and if a works manager does not aim for zero rejects or zero breakdown on the production line, that works manager should be asked at his appraisal interview for reasons why the quality has not been maintained. If no adequate reason can be given, he or she should be shown how to achieve the objectives, or replaced, always provided that management is not at fault by agreeing to lower standards, or insisting on unrealistic cost-cutting. Sometimes management can be blamed for what seems to be a works management failure.
- F. In a post department letters have to be sorted so that they are on the desks of executives or those concerned with the mail by, say, 9 am each day. That is a standard. If the standard is not achieved, it has to be noted by somebody. There is a standard time when mailings must be taken to the post office or the letter box, say 5 pm, and if letters are not available from the executives to be posted at the time, then, again, those standards are falling. Is that the fault of the executive or the fault of his secretary? This must be discovered and highlighted, if necessary. There are standard allowances for packing materials, envelopes, etc., which must also be adhered to. These types of examples would allow an appraiser either to praise for efficiency or point out the cost to the company when standards are not maintained.

"So you will see, Greg, it is possible to set standards for perhaps 75 per cent of all employees, without keeping to the strict rules laid down by the now often discarded management-by-objective technique, which merely cause ulcers for those managers determined to set standards for operations which could not be standardized."

Before Greg could answer, Mary hurried on: "Another

example is the transport or distribution sector. It is easy to discover by research the average number of packages, goods, units, despatched each day, and thus a standard can be set for the manager of that department. He in turn can set standards for those who handle the packages.

"When these subordinates know what they have to achieve, they will be motivated to try for even better results. Why? Because in business, as in life generally, most people like a challenge. If they are told that 100 units should be despatched every day, and they only despatch 90, the result is unhappiness. But when records are broken and 110 despatched, pleasure results; and even more pleasure when they are congratulated by the appraisers at a later date.

"It isn't difficult, Greg, to fix a standard for brochures or advertising matter, by laying down dates when copy must be in the hands of the advertising agents or newspapers. Those who use the telephone to contact customers can be judged by the number of calls that need to be made each day to ensure customer satisfaction. Standards can surely be set for those who indulge in absenteeism against those who attend regularly. There can be standards set for staff turnover. If it is too high, who is to blame — the staff or the manager? This can be discovered at an appraisal meeting."

Greg interrupted. "I'm not disagreeing with you, Mary, but how do you form a standard for, say, enthusiasm or innovative thinking?"

Mary replied, "To use one of your favourite expressions, Greg, there is nothing more contagious than enthusiasm — except the lack of it. Commonsense is necessary in all forms of appraisal." She hesitated, then added, "As it is in most other aspects of life. When a manager notices a fall in standards, he should check for the reason. It could be that there has been a drop in enthusiasm, which is easily spotted. Then he has to discover the cause, which he can surely do at the weekly or monthly appraisal meetings. Enthusiasm can be increased when a subordinate is fairly appraised, knows what is expected of him or her, and knows what has to be done to achieve objectives, i.e. the standards set.

"Let me sum up. I'm in a bit of a muddle about the numbering and lettering, so I'll start again:

- One, set standards person by person, area by area.
- Two, identify in each area the tasks for which standards can be laid down.
- Three, set the standards against each of these tasks.
- Four, agree these standards with the staff concerned."

Mary took a breath, then continued: "We can argue for ever about the pros and cons of performance appraisal and standards, and there will always be many, as we said before, who will shout, 'S'no use' and 'Tain't possible'. But my experience in personnel has taught me that most of those who carry out performance appraisal exercises discover that it is a great motivator of people. If it fails, it is because the rules have not been adhered to. It is being carried out in a haphazard way, instead of being carefully researched.

"Most important of all, managers are not taught how to appraise. The managing director sends a memo introducing performance appraisal interviews throughout the group, and stating, 'You will be one of the appraisers'. That is the way to fail.

"If a manager is lacking in confidence or cannot win the confidence of his subordinates, then the performance appraisal exercise should be scrapped until it can be properly conducted. That is what I shall tell the new managers attending our course. That will please you, Greg, won't it?"

Greg replied, "You've forgotten, Mary, that I already told them that in my opening address. What next?"

Mary answered, "Here are some of the pre-interview initiatives which must be taken into account. I think I'll return to lettering now:

- A. The manager makes up his mind what action he will take at the interview after seeking advice from others and his own records, and following reference to previous performance appraisal meetings.

- B. If the person being assessed has not met standards, all the facts must be considered and generalizations forgotten. An employee will always have excuses for not meeting targets. Someone or something else will always be to blame. Only facts can negate such excuses. If the employee can prove you wrong, the word will spread, and forever afterwards your judgement will be questioned.

- C. The assessor must leave prejudice behind. Forget labels people have won for themselves, such as, 'She's catty', 'He's a bore', 'He's sly', 'She's uncooperative', 'He's workshy', and so on. You only require facts which can be proved. You must also forget the halo effect, i.e. identifying yourself with the employees' similar interests, past or present.

"Most problems amongst subordinates arise through skill deficiencies. The simplest example would be a telephone-receptionist, who may not service incoming calls or operate the switchboard effectively. All that is needed to improve her skills is training. Nearly every skill problem can be solved through training, and the assessor must know exactly what training can be offered. If there is no organized training in a company, then of course the assessor has a difficult task. In point of fact it doesn't seem worth while, in those circumstances, to have performance appraisal at all.

"It is management weakness in this area which makes so many setpiece interviews a waste of time. Subordinates must be encouraged in self-development – to study textbooks, undertake postal courses, attend seminars – but in the main training has to be organized by management, and continually updated, to line up with performance appraisal decisions."

Young interrupted, "I agree most strongly", he said, "with the need for training; but we must emphasize that it is management itself which is often in most need of the training . . ."

Nina stopped the flow of words, saying, "George, I was about to continue on that subject".

The ever-polite Young immediately apologized, and Nina went on: "All of us have been frustrated time and time again by rudeness or, at best, lack of interest on the part of staff in shops. We have had to stand and wait while assistants have had a private chat and have become more and more irritable at the lack of attention.

"Under an appraisal system the standard for shop assistants can be well defined. Assistants are told that they must put the customer first.

"The good and observant manager will bring about customer care, not by shouting or remonstrating, but by training. Assistants must be shown that even if they are serving one customer, there is no need to ignore another completely. The good manager will set standards, and look for the differences between those standards and what is actually happening.

"For example, if a bus doesn't run on time, there has been a loss of standard. It is necessary therefore to concentrate on the time difference, to discover why the bus is late. There must be no sidetracking – keep to the differences, and the solutions will very quickly be found. It is only when the assessor finds that the differences are not caused by lack of attention or skills that he must begin looking in other directions, rather than remonstrating with the person being assessed.

"But back to our bus. If no reason can be found for the bus being late, if there are no hold-ups due to roadworks, no problems with parked cars, no difficulties with travellers taking a long time to board the bus, the assessor will have to concentrate on the skill of the driver. Are his skills up to standard? Can they be improved? Most drivers think they are expert: there isn't a driver living who doesn't think the other man is wrong – that we know. But, again, driving skills can be improved by training."

"An assessor in a retail store should have his mind on one thought only: the customer must come first, and anything that

occurs which doesn't put the customer first is an action that is
below standard."

Cooper said, "Nina, I'm enjoying this session. I didn't think
I would, because, like Greg, I am not wholly convinced of the
value of setpiece appraisal following many mini-appraisals.
I've changed my mind, and I feel sure that new managers will
form their own judgement, based on facts which we provide,
and will inevitably come to the same conclusion as I have.

"You are right to emphasize again and again that
subordinates must not be wrongly assessed or blamed when
the apparent fall in standards is caused by management
weakness – no, hold it! I know you are going to interrupt and
say that I am only repeating what I have already said, but it
happens so often." Cooper then took a slip of newsprint from
his pocket and said, "This item of news bears out the case. The
caption reads *Secretaries aim to cut pay link with bosses* and the
article refers to a bank – I won't name the bank because they
don't have an opportunity to respond. Otherwise, I'll read the
article in its entirety:

> Secretaries employed by X Bank were reported yesterday
> to be 'fed up' with being graded and paid according to the
> status of their bosses.
>
> Being paid on these terms was unfair because a junior
> manager might use his secretary far more than his seniors
> use theirs, they said, calling for pay in line with
> responsibility and quality of work.
>
> Dissent among the group's 8000 secretaries and typists
> was pinpointed in the results of a survey by the X Group
> staff union, which is preparing to negotiate a change in the
> system."

Nina said, "Philip, I'm very upset with you."

Cooper's face blanched. He didn't want to upset Nina. He
greatly admired her, and preferred her to Mary.

Nina laughed. "Don't worry, Philip," she said, "I cut that
snippet out and I was going to use it as an example."

"I'm sorry," said Cooper.

"You needn't apologize; its all in the same cause, isn't it? Now I'll continue, if I may. All right, Philip?"

"Of course."

Nina continued, "Back to our cutting. If the X Bank manager was assessing his staff and criticizing lack of enthusiasm or drive, or that standards were not being met, not knowing the truth could lead him to the wrong conclusions.

"The assessor must discover the real cause of falling enthusiasm, which is, of course, that the staff secretaries are fed up with being punished for working for the wrong boss. But that won't come out initially. Only after continual probing will the truth emerge."

Nina paused for reflection, then said, "I don't want to keep harping on the same subject, but so often problems arise through bad directives from top management. When a managing director sends a directive, he rarely uses the 'What if . . .' technique – so old but so valid. 'What if the staff don't react in the way we expect of them?' 'What if the strategy doesn't work?' 'What if the staff are not skilled enough to carry out the directive efficiently?' 'What if staff shortages make the directive impossible to complete?' 'What if it leads to a strike?'"

Cooper said, "It seems as though managing directors and chief executives need to be assessed, but I suppose they are assessed all the time, by their shareholders, by merchant bankers, by the City pundits. If profits increase every year as anticipated, if the customers are satisfied and if there are few complaints, if the staff go about their work with enthusiasm and pride, then that chief executive can say that he has been assessed and his performance is right up to standard. But if that doesn't happen, there should be some board set up to assess chief executives, especially those of public companies. They should be assessed to discover why they have not achieved the standards expected of them."

"I agree with that, wholeheartedly," said Nina.

Greg said, "Are you suggesting that I should be assessed by some independent assessors?"

"Not at all," said Nina. "Your profits are increasing every year, your staff are happy, there are few complaints — no, you assess yourself, and you'll come out on top all right, Greg."

Ryder said, "I'll go along with that — we'll call it a mini-assessment. Now who is going to continue?"

Mary said, "May I point out the need for constant revision of the job specification? If there's a change in the duties to be carried out, that should be noted, and the subordinate should be made fully aware of that change, otherwise the assessor will be assessing against wrong values.

"Another factor is the belief by some managers that experiences alone will result in greatly improved standards; but that is not necessarily so. Experience can mean the repetition of mistakes, and if there are not many mini-assessments, the mistakes will continue until the setpiece appraisal. The aim of improving standards is, as we know, increased production, and we must remember to drive home to the managers that production does not mean goods being manufactured on a production line. It means any work they are doing or controlling — maybe it is innovative thinking, operating a computer, designing a brochure, answering telephone calls or confirming quotations. The standards must be high for all activities; the assessments merely check on these standards. Now, to repeat the objectives at an appraisal, they are to discuss all problems appertaining to the person being appraised, to find the true cause of problems which could affect productivity, and to consider all actions that person could take to overcome problems and increase productivity.

"At the interview, as we know, these factors can only be brought to light by an interchange of ideas, so that on completion the person appraised will believe that he or she had thought of most of the solutions and will feel most pleased with themselves.

"Remember, the objectives are to motivate subordinates to do better and enjoy their work, and to encourage them in self-development. It is therefore easy to understand the importance of the opening remarks at an appraisal, whether that is a mini-appraisal or a setpiece. A badly thought out sentence can jeopardize the interview; even the tone of voice matters. The appraiser should not be overwhelmingly friendly, neither should he sound as if he wishes for forgiveness in advance for his temerity in questioning the ability of the subordinate. Avoid this kind of greeting: 'You know I don't like this job at all, but those above have laid it down so we have to do our best, haven't we? You know why you're here, so let's get on with it.'

"In public speaking we teach the value of key sentences to be memorized, to enable the speaker to discard his notes. The same applies to appraisal exercises. Well thought out key sentences should be prepared in advance. After the interview, try to imagine the thoughts of the person assessed.

"That seemingly friendly smile, that warm handshake as he or she leaves the room, matter very little. What do they say to their friends and associates, or their family? Do they complain of the time wasted? Do they say, 'He never considers our viewpoint at all; all he wants to do is talk, talk, talk about himself, and how great he was in the past'?

"Difficult to imagine? Right! Then there is always the grapevine. It's only by learning the truth, by whatever means, that the assessor can be certain of an improved session for the next assessment.

"Unfortunately too many managers are only concerned with how clever they were at the interview, and will tell others, 'I caught him out!', 'She knows she can't mislead me', 'She learned a thing or two from being with me!', 'He knows he can't pull the wool over my eyes', and so on. But managers must remember that the grapevine also works in reverse, and what they have said will also filter down, and possibly, be filtered down in a twisted form.

"There is another problem – dare I say it? It is assessing pretty girls, especially young girls who have a great appeal to middle-aged managers."

Lewis called out, "I take great exception to your exposing the truth about me, Nina!"

There followed a hilarious discussion, until Nina went on: "Well, I've made my point. Finally, don't rely on your memory of past assessments and your general knowledge of the subordinate. Always make notes – but we'll talk about documentation later. Make notes after the assessment, not during it. If an assessor cannot remember the few salient features of an interview until the session is over, he should not be an assessor.

"Here is the pre-appraisal checklist:

- One, check the job specification before the interview.
- Two, check if the specification has been changed in any way.
- Three, check all directives issued by management which could affect or influence a subordinate's work.
- Four, has there been any marked difference between the actual performance and the standards set?
- Five, check if standards should have been changed, perhaps owing to influences beyond the control of the subordinate.
- Six, analyse differences between performances and standards. That will highlight problems.
- Seven, consider problems which have arisen and which have reduced performance.
- Eight, consider how to solve these problems.
- Nine, ensure that during the interview there are no interruptions by callers or by telephones ringing.
- Ten, reread all notes from previous performance appraisal sessions.
- Eleven, remind yourself that you must not let personal feelings or prejudices result either in antagonism towards the subordinate or friendship which could influence the assessment.

"That's all," said Nina. "I'm handing back to Mary now for the interview. I'm not as good as she is; she had so much experience of performance appraisal when she was in personnel. She has probably carried out more appraisals than all of us put together."

Mary almost blushed. There was a slight pinkish tinge in her cheeks as she said, "Thank you, Nina".

Before she could start, Greg Ryder said, "Let's do it differently, Mary. I'm sure you will produce a video of an assessment, so let's act out the scene now. You assess me, Mary. You've been assessing me indirectly during this session, haven't you, with your digs at management. Well let's bring it all out, step by step, and then highlight the important factors in the assessment."

Mary's eyes widened and her lips set. "Oh no!" she said, and repeated, "Oh no!"

Greg said strongly, "I'm not afraid of the truth, you know".

"I know that. Of course you're not. But I'm afraid of even hinting that you are anything less than perfect when in fact you are the perfect managing director."

"Come off it, Mary! I know my weaknesses, and you know them as well, so why not highlight them? Just check me against standards."

"We've already brought that up, Greg. You were checked against profit standards, and you came out on top."

"That doesn't matter – that doesn't matter! It can be repeated," he said hurriedly. "Now, off you go."

"Sorry," said Mary, "I always obey your commands, but not this time. I haven't got the nerve."

"How about you, Nina?" asked Ryder.

"Never!" came the succinct reply.

Cooper said, "No subordinate in any company can ever publicly appraise his boss. You know that, Greg. The only persons who can appraise the boss are his wife and the shareholders, if there are enough of them, who can vote against the boss and give him the thumbs down. But of course if he owns all the shares, there isn't anyone who can appraise him at all. He has to appraise himself. He has to discover for himself if, in any way, he falls below standards. You're good, Greg, and you know it, but I sometimes think that 30, 40, or 50

per cent of the managing directors in this country really do
need someone to assess them."

Ryder shrugged his shoulders. "I thought it was a good
idea," he said, "but I can see now it probably wouldn't work.
I'd get upset and start shouting, as I usually do."

That broke the tension, and everyone joined in the laughter.
Ryder said, "Do it your way, Mary."

"Thank you," said Mary. She then changed the tone of her
voice and in a more authoritative manner said, "I am now
addressing the new managers."

Only pausing to stand up, she continued: "We can discount
those few managers, and I hope there are none amongst you,
who delight in the power it gives them when carrying out an
appraisal. They know the person being appraised is suffering
from some stress and they make that stress worse by
themselves becoming domineering and demanding. It's so
cruel, so unfair! In case there are any of you who could take on
this mantle when appraising subordinates, I ask each of you
again to use interpersonnel comparison tests: to think of
someone you know who is domineering and power-struck, to
accept that that is a weakness, and it's a weakness which you do
not wish to emulate.

"On the other hand, there are managers who themselves
suffer from stress at the thought of carrying out the
performance appraisal interview. The only cure for both the
domineering manager and the one under stress is training. If
that is not on offer by their companies, they should form their
own training groups. You who are here can so easily help your
colleagues by setting up such groups, using our training as a
basis. Practice, and more practice, will make a manager into an
appraiser who is helpful and intent on building a
subordinate's career.

"So think about that. Write a performance appraisal manual
if you wish – that is also learning while doing.

"Remember, you are setting out to help subordinates solve
their problems. That, in itself, is a worthwhile effort.

"Ask the subordinate at the beginning of the interview how

he or she thinks they have fared since the last meeting. Allow the subordinate to talk first and so become more relaxed; then adopt the 'open question' technique, which invites a full response.

"Closed questions are an invitation for the subordinate simply to reply 'yes' or 'no'. The closed question should only be used occasionally, and for specific reasons.

"A closed question might be: 'Do you obtain a quotation before ordering typewriter ribbons?' The open question would be, 'How do you go about replacing used typewriter ribbons?' That open question gives a subordinate an opportunity to express views.

"The response might be: 'I look around the office to see if other typists have spares' – a good answer. 'I suggest that we change our supplier; I heard that X ribbons are excellent. A friend of mine uses them and is very pleased with their quality.''

"These answers allow the assessor to form judgements based on the opinions of the person being assessed. A 'yes' or 'no', although perhaps the right answer on occasion, would not be so helpful in this case.

"Sentences used for open questions can begin:

- How do you feel about . . .?
- What do you think of the change in office routine . . .?
- Tell me why you are 5 per cent above (or below) target.
- Will you explain your reasons, and I am sure you have them, for being late so often.
- How important to you is . . .?

"The assessor now has the opportunity to listen and consider, but whatever the response, the assessor still has the opportunity to extract more views from the subordinate.

"For example, to the unpunctual person the assessor might say, 'I know you believe that the traffic problem is your main difficulty and that you cannot leave earlier because of getting the children to school, but the standard we agreed was that you shouldn't be late more than five times in 3 months, which we both thought reasonable. Even this is not usually acceptable in an office such as ours, but we made it acceptable to help you. But you will agree, Mrs Jones, that you haven't met that standard.

"'Now we could increase the standard to ten times in 3 months, but is that fair to your colleagues in the office? Why shouldn't they be late ten times in 3 months? You'll agree that this is a problem which has to be solved in fairness to you and your colleagues; so let us try to find a solution together, so that in 3 months' time you will be happy coming to this assessment meeting, knowing that you have met your standard.'

"And that, new managers, is what we call the 'think and talk through' policy, which inevitably follows a subordinate answering an open question.

"Try to avoid tricky questions: for example, 'Are you in favour of a new quick-service counter?' Such questions are sometimes unfair because a subordinate has not had the opportunity perhaps to think around the subject. He or she may have views but not wish to express them. Far better to use an open question: 'What do you think of our new quick-service system?'

"The assessor should try to avoid alternative choices if that is possible. For example, 'Would you prefer that we buy a new desk and redecorate the office, or would you rather move to another office elsewhere?' It is unfair to ask for an answer to the alternative because the subordinate has had no time to evaluate whether he wants to stay where he is or move to another office. A hasty answer may be given, which may well be held against him at some time in the future.

"During question time it has been stressed so often – but it cannot be too often – that the assessor must listen carefully. Why do I continually repeat this? Because we also like to talk, and most of us dislike listening. A real effort has to be made if we want to evaluate our response to a subordinate's answer to our questions.

"Now for a few quick rules, since I can see Greg getting his bored look . . ."

Ryder shook his head. "Not at all. I was only thinking how well you are conducting your session to make us all appraisal-minded. Enthusiasm is the one characteristic of all successful people, and you, Mary, are a great enthusiast. Please continue, at length if you wish, or with brief rules – it's for you to decide."

Lewis said, "Which, translated, means that you'd better keep to short rules or we'll all be late for dinner".

"What a lack of enthusiasm!" said Cooper.

Lewis answered, "Not at all, it's just that I'm an enthusiastic eater."

"Please," said Ryder emphatically, "let us continue with our work."

Mary said, "I am an enthusiast, so I'll abide by the rules; and as an enthusiast I shall teach by the rules. So let's have the rules for interviewing:

- One, don't help the subordinate if he or she begins to hesitate. Let them search their minds for the truth as they see it.
- Two, don't jump to quick conclusions. Make a full appraisal only at the end of the interview.
- Three, be sure you have understood the subordinate's remarks, statements, objections, by using questioning techniques based on such sentences as 'Am I right in assuming . . .?', 'Tell me if I'm wrong, but . . .', 'As I see it, you believe . . .', 'Do I assume from that remark that you don't believe . . .?'
- Four, is the subordinate not reaching standards and therefore making excuses? Has he been promoted beyond his plateau, beyond his capacity to succeed?
- Five, the assessor should keep to a standard sequence, thought out in advance; and check during the interview that he is not being sidetracked away from that sequence. Let us go through the sequence briefly:
  A. Ask the subordinate how he feels he has performed

against a set target.

B. Ask his reasons for not reaching the target, or his reasons for exceeding it by so much.

C. Let him highlight his successes.

D. Ask if he believes that further training could help him reach even higher standards.

E. Ask him or her how they see their career developing. The assessor must know in advance what rewards can be offered to the subordinate at some time in the future, as that is a question most subordinates may well raise. The same applies to promotions. Always remember that the assessor must also be performing to high standards, and must consider how someone else could appraise him carrying out performance appraisal exercises.

"At the conclusion of the interview, find some aspect of the subordinate's contribution for which honest appreciation can be given, or at least commend him or her for co-operation during the meeting.

"After the subordinate has left, the assessor must check back on himself to discover how he has fared during the interview. He should ask himself the following questions. Did I put the subordinate at ease from the beginning, and throughout the interview? Would he or she consider that I had acted in a pompous, dictatorial, or argumentative manner? Did I listen carefully? Did I avoid interrupting while he was making a contribution? Did I blatantly reject opinions? Did I aim for, and mostly obtain, agreement on vital issues? Did I tackle all problem areas or only the easy ones? Did I avoid the sensitive areas? Did I become emotional when the subordinate insisted on disagreeing with my viewpoint? Did I blame myself for some past mistakes? Did I give praise where praise was due? Did I try to score points to show how clever I was? Did I try to help the subordinate to a better future? Did I reset standards, if that was necessary? Did the interview enhance our relationship? What must I now do to ensure that action is taken both by the subordinate and myself to improve standards?"

Mary paused, then continued, "So it's a case of appraiser, appraise thyself. Now let us consider the notes to be written up, or the form to be completed, so that at some future meeting the appraiser will be able to check the past interviews. But first an apology. I have mostly been implying that the subordinate is male. That's not because I believe that men need more help than women, it's only that I couldn't keep repeating he or she.

"Now here are the headings for note-takers:

- One. How did the subordinate's results over the past 6 months compare with the standards set?
- Two. How did output compare with the standards? If below standard, what were the reasons given? What actions have been taken to improve standards or skills?
- Three. If the quality standards have been maintained, what was learned from this discussion of the strength of the subordinate which could assist others to reach similar standards?
- Four. Responsibility to others. If it is a manager being appraised, many factors have to be considered. Communication, was it good or bad? If bad, what were the reasons? Did the manager show that he believed he had responsibility for his subordinates, and was ready to do everything possible to help them? Did he give helpful, factual, impersonal views of his subordinates, and how they all got on together? Was a good team built?
- Five. Judgement. Did the subordinate seem lacking in judgement and commonsense? The subordinate would never admit these weaknesses, so it is up to the assessor to try and work out a plan of action to help him overcome them before they inevitably lead to problems.
- Six. Acceptability by others. Were the standards low in general appearance, manners or language? If he or she seemed to be disliked by colleagues, were the reasons discovered? If not, they would have to be discovered by the next meeting. Were ideas to enable a subordinate to

change outlook floated?

- Seven. Timekeeping. Good or bad, or fair? Note reasons and set standards for following months.
- Eight. Wastefulness of company property – envelopes, stationery, stamps, packaging materials, private telephone calls, placing orders without authority and before obtaining other quotations to make sure the prices were right.
- Nine. General information. How does the subordinate seem to view the assessment, company policy, remuneration, expenses, etc?
- Ten. What requests were made by the subordinate for knowledge relating to his future career? Did he seem to believe that he was entitled to a position which you, as a manager, knew he could not achieve? What actions must be taken before the next meeting to enable the subordinate to be more objective about himself and his future?
- Eleven. General impression of the subordinate – the type of person he appears to be, garrulous, too quiet, bombastic, etc. All these factors might affect his reaching standards so far as production is concerned. Is he innovative? Is he a reasonable person? Did he complain about the way he had been treated? Did he complain at the previous interview about the way he was being treated, and is there a possibility that he will be making the same complaint at the next interview? What action would be necessary to help this man over his problems? All these points must be checked carefully before the next appraisal meeting.
- Twelve. Was the date fixed for the next appraisal? What specific improvements have been suggested for achievement by that date? What action was suggested so that these improvements could take place?
- Thirteen. Give a rating for the subordinate. This rating could be against subordinates who have achieved better standards. He could be rated against his own accomplishments, previous standards, or his general

behaviour. All previous data must be taken into account in this summary. It must highlight the subordinate's strengths and weaknesses. Again, the usual standard methods of marking can be used."

Mary paused. "That's about all," she said. "At the course we shall naturally provide printed forms to show the managers how to document the interviews. Different forms should be used for different jobs. For example, the transport manager may have to use different words on his form from the service manager. But in the main the points are the same for all employees.

"On the form there may well have to be a section devoted to standards which must be achieved within the next 6 months or so. For example, it could be that the manager has been told he must reduce the costs of his department by 5 per cent. A filing clerk might have a section devoted to the number of files which have to be handled, and the number of filing cabinets to be serviced.

"Finally, to be an assessor is a great opportunity to be, as Donne said, 'involved in mankind': to help people, to tell how they can reach greater heights, and show them their achievements will be recognized. The manager himself may be judged at some time in the future on his ability to pick out potential winners. It only remains," concluded Mary, "to remind everyone here that we shall need many visual aids, possibly a film of an assessment – forms I have already touched on – and a workshop, organized to allow managers to carry out video assessments; but this, our first rehearsal, has, I think you will all agree, covered most of the relevant ground in the time available, not only now but at the course. At a later date, arising out of the course for new managers, we should instigate a 3-day course for performance appraisal alone. I'm sure it would be highly successful, especially on an in-company basis. Let's be honest now, we didn't have one before because you, Greg, were not a believer in performance appraisal. It's as simple as that. I hope we have helped you to change your mind,"

Ryder said, "You certainly have. I can see now that it can be a most helpful exercise in human relations, in communication, building a team spirit and of course motivation.

"But success will depend on the quality of the assessor. I am still against personal appraisal, unless the appraiser is someone who has been trained or has had extensive past experience of the job, or unless he has been tested by examination and is respected by the staff.

"If the appraiser is 75 per cent objective, that isn't good enough. It's got to be in the 90 per cent range. Yes, Mary and Nina, you have convinced me that performance appraisal is a great contribution to improvement in productivity and personal relationships. To prove my new-found belief, I shall be sending out a memorandum next week to all members of our staff telling them that performance appraisal is from now on a must — a setpiece once or twice a year, with mini-appraisals of course weekly, monthly, or every day. I shall lead the way by appraising some of you. Then we'll see if that works.

"Now I want to change the subject and make a comment regarding our first session tomorrow. Earlier we talked about the need for all managers to have at least some basic knowledge of finance to cover some of the following subjects, taken at random: profitability, cash flow, fixed asset finance, rations, application of funds, added value, budgeting, investment appraisal, discounting, financial information as offered in management accounts, rates of return on capital, on sales — or per employee. Not only must the balance sheet be understood, but its implications must be recognized as well. What is meant by share capital, loan capital, working capital, credit control ratios . . ." He paused, looked at Cooper, then said, "But we have a course — Financial Training for the Non-Accountant — and that lasts 3 days. Can we compress this information into a matter of one or two sessions? I don't believe this is possible, except in restricted areas. For example, as you know, we teach

Finance for the Salesman, to help the salesmen overcome the objections of customers who are not quite clear whether they can afford the price, whether they can afford to buy at all, or whether they can meet the instalments. We also have Finance for Sales Managers and Finance for Service Managers, because they are specific example which can be covered in a session, relating to specific tasks. But I don't think it can be covered in a general way.

"As far as new managers are concerned, I believe they should wait a while and, perhaps after 6 months or so, attend a 3- to 5-day financial course for non-accountants. But what they should know from the beginning is one vital aspect of finance, accountancy, call it what you will, and that is . . ."

He paused, and there was a chorus from his colleagues, "Cost control!"

Ryder laughed heartily. "How did you guess?" he said.

Lewis answered, "Well, you send me memos on the subject once every 4 or 5 weeks – at least that's what it seems like!"

"I must have been sending very bad memos, because you still waste too much money."

Again there was laughter as he spoke in a non-controversial manner.

"I hope you will all agree, however, that the first priority of a new manager is to understand what it means to keep costs down. The new appointment to management gives someone the opportunity to show he is manager, and one of the ways so many of them start to express their authority is by permitting expenditure which, if they understood what cost-cutting meant, they would not find necessary.

"For example, there is a request for a new typewriter, when there may be other typewriters available for use in the office. If an investigation into other sources available is made, if the answer is 'No, but I'll look into it', fair enough. But more usually a manager asked by a typist for a new machine will agree to it immediately. The manager wants to show his power and authority.

"There is always a demand for extra staff: 'We need an extra maintenance engineer', 'We must have another filing clerk'. Requests will pour in, many of them not worth consideration.

"But if I'm not careful I shall be giving you a whole session on cost control. Philip, I'm sorry! I know you have worked out a full session, but I'm sure you will use it later. For now, a session on cost control is sufficient for the new managers."

Cooper smiled. "Don't worry, Greg. I'm not looking for any more sessions. As your financial director, I have quite enough to do."

"We're still friends, then?"

"Of course. I'll be only too pleased to give a short talk on cost control."

Ryder shook his head. "You don't even have to do that, because I'll do it."

13   More Discussions

Lewis said, "Let's celebrate."

"What?" Young asked.

"We must celebrate having been successful in the past, and being determined to be even more so in the future."

"I'll drink to that," Young said, "and let it be champagne."

"Yes, and pay for it ourselves," Cooper said, moodily.

Nina said, "Surely that could be put on the expense account?"

"You know very well it can't," Cooper answered sternly, then added, "you all get away with little bits and pieces which escape my eye now and again, but certainly champagne would never get a counter signature."

Young said stiffly, "I have never attempted to get away with anything."

"OK," Cooper replied, "don't let's argue. Who'll choose the champagne?"

Nina replied, "As we're paying for it ourselves, let it be house champagne. I've never known anyone who could tell the difference between a fairly good and a very good champagne anyway. Bad and good, yes; good and outstandingly good, yes; but not fairly good and good."

"A brilliant analysis!" Cooper said. "I'm always amused at those who pretend to know so much about wines. I watch them in restaurants, swirling the liquid around the glass, sniffing, tasting, sniffing again, rolling it around their tongue and then, looking thoughtful, saying to the wine waiter, 'Yes' — and they do that with the house wine."

They all laughed, Lewis rather diffidently, because he had been one of those who had so often carried out this swirling, sniffing act.

Two bottles were polished off before dinner, and a third with the meal. Everyone became extremely merry. Over coffee Young said, "Whose turn is it now to state a case for our future?"

Quickly Cooper replied, "As you know, I dislike any form of evasion, therefore I shall tell you of a suggestion I have put to Peter, which he thinks is a reasonable solution to our particular problem. Naturally our views are not final until we know how the present problem is being solved by Greg, but if it is not solved, I'm certain that Peter and I will go ahead with my plan." He then went on to explain the offer made to him to take control of the consultancy division of Carter Lovell.

Young said, "Surprise, surprise! In spite of what we said at our first meeting about the difficulties of getting an executive post similar to our own, there are obviously such opportunities around."

"Yes," said Lewis, "but in all fairness I must explain that the total package offered to us is not as good as we are now getting, although they have promised us incentives in the future; but I never rely on promises. So far as we are concerned, we would both far rather stay where we are. We have been set targets, and I'm fully aware of what happens in business if targets are not reached."

"You wouldn't fail," said Nina.

"Maybe not," Lewis answered, "but I'm not too happy at being controlled by accountants. They lack breadth of vision, they dislike innovation, and in the main they only pay lip service to long-term planning so far as marketing is concerned."

"Thank you!" said Philip Cooper, severely.

"Not you, Philip, you've been brought up by Greg."

Cooper said, "I must partly agree with your summary so far as the large general accountants are concerned. But you did tell me that you were 90 per cent sure that you would go ahead with my plan."

Lewis patted Cooper's shoulder, as a friendly gesture, and said, "Right! I only wanted to put things in perspective. With accountants, I'm just above being a nothing. Here I am part of the Royal Family. It makes a difference, you know. But still, though wrongly, I'll go ahead."

Mary said, "But you may not be a part of the Royal Family for long," then added quickly, "and as we are in a confessional mood, I too have to tell you our plans. Nina and I have decided to go it alone in management consultancy and training, with an all-women team. We know at least two clients who will move over to us, and the novelty will, I am sure, receive a great deal of press publicity. We'll have to face problems, that's for sure, but I believe we can be successful."

Young asked, "But how about costs? We've been through all this, haven't we? There'll be precious little income for 6 months, and then only a dribble for the next 6 months."

"We've thought of that. We have some capital, and we're prepared to take out mortgages. Our banks will back us; we can do it."

Young smiled a little grimly and said, "It seems I'm the only one left now. I haven't made any plans."

Lewis, intending to be humorous, said, "You can always become a transvestite and join Nina and Mary."

"That," said Young, "is not very funny."

"Sorry!"

Nina said, "You have no worries, George, you are the one person on the board whom Greg will look after, I'm sure of that!"

Young shook his head and muttered, "I'm not so certain"; then, on a more cheerful note, added, "well, the decisions have been made. You have solved your problems, but are there provisos? Do they depend on Greg selling out? Do they go by the board if he doesn't sell out?"

Cooper said, "Speaking for Peter and myself, we would rather stay here."

"That goes for us too," said Mary.

Young said, "Good! Then I've changed my mind. I'll speak to Greg on Friday evening. Somehow I shall explain our fears for the future."

"You couldn't do it" said Mary. "You almost worship the man. You couldn't even tell white lies to urge him to tell us the truth. But I can do it."

Mary's eyes sparkled. "I don't mind very much if I don't quite tell the truth, so long as I can learn the truth from him. I'll probably say that there's a mole at Dyson's and that was how we got to hear what was going on."

Young said, "That's most unethical and most unfair. You will cause doubts in the minds of the Dyson directors if Greg tells them of your conversation. No, Mary, I must do the job. No one else!"

Lewis said, "Surely it's much more unethical to negotiate the sale of a business without consulting fellow directors, even if they do only own a share apiece? I'm sure that's a breach of some company rule."

They agreed that Mary should speak to Greg. The only adverse vote was from George Young.

"Carried!" said Lewis. "We need not meet again until Friday, when we can have a dinner which will be unbelievably miserable, or unbelievably joyful."

14 Don't Spend – Spend – Spend

There was a tenseness in the air when the directors met in the conference room at 8.45 on the Wednesday morning.

"The problem we have," said Young, "is one of working for lesser men. Greg can be so overbearing, so dictatorial, and ride roughshod over everyone if he wants his way, but he's still a leader of great quality, always leading from the front. He produces more ideas in a week than most of us can think of in months. He can oversee every marketing strategy – he knows immediately when a design is right, when an advertisement is good or bad, whether a brochure has customer appeal – and he's a great motivator. How can we then work for someone more run-of-the-mill? Somehow, I can't see Philip and Peter being motivated by an executive team of accountants, and Nina and Mary will most surely miss the guidance they receive from Greg.

"I've made up my mind that I couldn't work for anyone else. I've talked it over with my wife and we have agreed that if the worst comes to the worst, I shall retire early; we'll tighten our belts and manage on what we have. Yes," he repeated, "I'll retire."

At that moment Greg Ryder entered the room and, on

hearing the word 'retire', said, "Who's retiring?"

"I feel I'm ready for it," said Young.

"Nonsense! You must never retire; that's for the non-achievers, or those with an inbred fear of the future; or those who worry too much about horrific press reports on the state of the economy. No, George, you won't retire until I do, and that," he added slowly, "may be this week."

Every muscle in the room became knotted, every heartbeat ticked over that bit faster.

Mary said, "Why do you say this week, Greg?"

"I'll tell you now. I've been keeping it secret." He paused, and they all thought they were about to hear about the Dyson affair.

They were wrong!

Ryder went on, "Recently I have been paying regular visits to one of those Harley Street witch doctors. He believes my heart needs changing – I shall get the final verdict on Friday. If it's really bad, and I don't believe for one moment that it is, maybe I shall say goodbye."

Noticing the expression on the faces of his directors, he laughed aloud. "Don't worry, you know I have a plan for everything, and that, at the moment, does not include my retirement, whatever my wife or the witch doctor say. I think it's something temporary, and even the doctor has admitted that it could be so, although tests show a clogging of the arteries. I'm awaiting the results of a new series of tests. Anyway, if the worst comes to the worst, I can always have a bypass operation. I'm not concerned, and neither need you be, although obviously I have contingency plans for every eventuality."

Nina said, "Surely, then, we are entitled to hear your plans."

"You'll have to wait until Friday. Now let's forget all this talk of retirement and doctors, and continue with our work."

Ryder, who had been feeling tense himself, due to his dislike of discussing his health problems, relaxed. He was glad he had told his colleagues the news from Harley Street, but not at all concerned that he had avoided mentioning the Dyson affair. He knew from long experience that a negotiation is only completed when an agreement has been signed. The signing was due to take place at the offices of their solicitors, also on the Friday. *It's going to be a busy day,* he thought to himself.

Remaining standing, he beckoned to his co-directors to be seated and said, "Off we go. You are the new managers and I am the instructor. Good morning, managers."

"Good morning."

"There's no time to cover financial management fully, as we do in our standard 3-day course. The subjects included in that course, which you should attend, or study in textbooks, are:

- Why business needs finance.
- How it is used and obtained.
- How to read profit statements and balance sheets.
- Capital employed, profit and return on investment – what they mean and what affects them.
- Financial ratios for assessing profitability, solvency, and use of assets.
- How to read an annual report.
- Different costing methods and their advantages and disadvantages.
- How to prepare and use budgets; the practice of budgetary control.
- How to use management information to help run the company.
- The relation of cash flow to profitability.
- Pricing systems.
- Micro computers in relation to handling financial information.
- Capital investment appraisal techniques — the advantages and disadvantages of the various systems."

Ryder put on his sternest expression and continued: "Now for an important sector so rarely dealt with by those teaching financial matters: to control and, if possible, reduce costs.

"Think of the past when your ideas for spending on this or that seemed to be turned down so regularly by the directors. Why couldn't you have that new desk? Why couldn't you have a computer to take home to help you with your work? Why did they always seem to object to your using taxis when you were in a hurry? Why was your request for a dress allowance for the receptionist turned down?

"But now things have changed. You are yourself part arbiter of expenditure. Now you can show the importance of your position by dispensing rewards. A 'yes' will always win appreciation, sometimes even affection. 'No' will result in condemnation and criticism of you as a manager. What a challenge! One under which many managers wilt.

"When Jane the typist complains that her chair is uncomfortable and puts in a request for a new, expensive resting place, there is no debate. 'Certainly', comes the immediate response. The cash is not going to come out of the manager's pocket but from the company's overflowing coffers.

"Maybe the manager will say, 'Let me know the cost', but that won't make any difference. He'll still agree, later.

"When that salesman, who works mostly on foot anyway, tells his newly appointed sales manager that his car is too small and he needs a larger model, the wish is granted, although the reason for the request is probably known to the sales manager. The salesman has a growing family or wants to tow a caravan.

"There are many areas in which costs can be reduced without affecting production, enthusiasm, or loyalty. If there has to be a refusal, don't blame your own bosses as most managers do. Don't use the excuse, 'Sorry, they won't spend the money'. Explain why it is so important to keep costs down, that every demand for expenditure must be judged on its merits, and that a free-for-all could jeopardize jobs.

"Your experience, if you are on the marketing side, will be to discover that that person who never has any time to devote to any task and is always overloaded with work will readily find the time to fly to Italy, France or the Middle East, because perhaps of some technical query. He may be away for 3 weeks, and the journey need not have been necessary in the first place, but that person enjoys travelling. The problem could have been solved by telephone, telex, or letter. Of course there are occasions when such journeys are necessary; I am only suggesting that you question every item of expenditure carefully, whether for an inexpensive book or diary, an extra telephone, or a new local office. Judge on facts, not generalizations, likes or dislikes, or in order to win affection.

"You will remember that in the past, when you were refused requests to buy this or that, you were upset for a while; others will be upset with you when you put up the bar. But don't worry. If you are respected by your subordinates, you will be forgiven if they know that you have made a careful assessment, not an on-the-spot decision on what is, to them, a burning issue.

"For example, remember Jane – she wanted a new chair. You will personally examine the chair. Is it damaged, can it be repaired? Is it uncomfortable because she happens to be overweight; or believed to be uncomfortable because she has taken a dislike to it? Will a new chair be any more comfortable? How long has the chair been in use? Has someone else in the office recently been given a new chair? That is a powerful motivation for others to plead for more comfort.

"It has been taught at courses, and in many books, that to keep costs down a manager should think of the firm's money as if it were his own. Would he, then, still allow the expenditure?

"If you win for yourself the reputation of caring for the company's money, watching every penny spent, you will be considered a highly qualified manager on the way to promotion. Why? Because you will be the odd one out in twenty or even more managers who so enjoy authorizing purchases by subordinates.

"Let me give you another example: unnecessary increases in stocks. Most works managers hold more stocks than they need, just in case they should run short. To have thousands of pounds tied up in extra stocks can be most expensive, and dangerous if cash is running short and the cash flow is not positive.

"Here are some more examples. You will undoubtedly have some control over printed matter. Cost-cutting does not mean that you must buy cheap print, but neither does it mean sanctioning expensive artwork which may not be necessary to meet required quality standards. Print must satisfy a customer but not necessarily artistic designers.

"Never, never sanction a purchase without first checking on price. I have known many a manager shocked when requested to countersign an invoice for payment.

"The manager had no idea that the cost would be so high, but at the invoice stage it is too late to take action. No orders should be placed without quotations being checked, particularly as regards to direct mail campaigns, advertising, and sales literature.

"Always demand alternative quotations, and even if a high quality expensive brochure is needed, careful thought may enable you to pare it down, cut out a colour, reduce the size, use slightly less expensive paper, without losing any of the quality demanded.

"No subordinate should be allowed to place orders without your authority, unless you have earlier agreed that regular orders may be placed for repeat stationery, etc.

"But let me digress. Almost daily we read of companies in financial difficulties, companies eager to sell out, because they fear the future, companies having to call in consultants or company doctors who try to put things right. There may be manufacturing problems, production development problems, marketing problems, all of which could have been solved by the management. But a company doctor employed by a very well known group of accountants told me that the main cause of most companies' difficulties was lack of financial control – inability to get costs down.

"Sometimes the worst offender may be the managing director, who delights in investing the company's money in expensive cars, yachts, an apartment in the South of France, and so on. Such actions have ruined many a small to average-sized company.

"Company doctors are well aware of, and have little sympathy for, the bosses who want to increase their status and their ego by buying status symbols at the company's expense. Most outstanding chief executives, certainly those I have known, seem to live quite modestly. They do treat the company's money as their own."

Ryder paused, took a deep breath, and felt his heart palpitating a little as he went on: "When a company doctor is called in, his first task is always to cut costs or to sell off unused assets. Only then does it come home to management how wasteful its members have been in the past.

"I know budgets are set, but too many managers believe that they are good managers if they spend all their budget, regardless of decreased turnover, for example, They are wrong!

"Another management mistake is to place large orders so as to obtain increased discounts. Nearly always this results in discarding stock owing to changes. Stationery is a prime example.

"Don't be mesmerized by discounts for large orders. Know your requirements, and meet only those requirements. In addition, do not increase staff unless there is a very good reason to do so.

"You will have constant demands from those who are looking for an easier life – 'We must have an extra person . . .', 'We need two extra in the stores . . .', 'We can't do without an additional receptionist . . .', 'We want one more tea lady . . .' Maybe the requests are justified, but your immediate response must be 'Why?' Then listen carefully to the reasons given. On average you will find that about 60 per cent of demands are not valid.

"It is better for a manager to be respected as a good leader, a fair-minded person, a good communicator, or a good example to others, than to try to win over the hearts of others by unnecessary spending of company money.

"Now back to where I was before I digressed. You will form syndicates, and each syndicate will be provided with suggested cost-cutting exercises as guidelines. It will be up to each of you to discover the areas in your own department which will enable costs to be cut. Each member of the syndicate will in turn explain his problems, and listen to the problems of others. The syndicate is for the purpose of seeking all-round advice, to enable each of you to benefit. Later, syndicate leaders will return, and report on the decisions of their members."

15   Managing Time

All the directors agreed that Ryder's opening that morning had been successful, although there was some feeling that the message would be a little too near the knuckle for some of the delegates. Many managers were themselves wasteful of their company's money, and eased their consciences by agreeing the righteousness of their causes.

Ryder had left the room during the coffee break. Now he was back, and looking at some notes.

He said, "Next on the list we have Time Management until lunch time, and Delegation this afternoon. Let me summarize: Time Management followed by Delegating, and after tea, Problem-solving and Decision-making. Agreed?"

Nobody disagreed.

Ryder continued, "Thursday will be devoted mostly to staff training . . ."

Lewis interrupted: "Which should include Selling Principles, as allied to Customer Care."

"I agree," said Ryder.

Young said, "Too many managers quickly become rutbound, don't want to change anything. It was agreed that we include Creative Thinking, and Innovation."

173

That being rubber-stamped by everyone, Ryder went on. "Well, there shouldn't be disagreement, we've been discussing the programme for weeks past, although we agreed not to finalize anything until now. We are progressive people, even yesterday's ideas might be out-dated by today. However, we have all been in management training for a long time, and I'm sure that by Thursday we shall have covered all the main sessions.

"On Friday, in my absence, I want you to consider films, syndicates, workshops, etc."

Nina said, "But we haven't completed Thursday yet, have we?"

Ryder answered, "You're right, Nina, but we haven't got our timing right either. No allowance has been made for question times, syndicates, etc. When we work out the exact programme, you'll find that we have just enough time with the sessions we already have to take us on to Friday evening. It will be a full 5-day course. The final session on the Friday, which we, however, shall give tomorrow, Thursday, will be Situation Adaptable Leadership. Agreed?"

Once more they all agreed.

"Very well," said Ryder, "now for the session on Time Management. Would you make a start, Nina? Like Performance Appraisal, you have always been closely concerned with Time Management systems."

"No sir!" Nina replied, quickly. "As with Performance Appraisal you, Greg, have never been really happy with Time Management. Therefore, you should voice your views in the first place, and then we can decide on the pattern of the session. Subsequently, I'll willingly give the main features of Time Management."

Ryder shrugged his shoulders. "You're making me out to be an old reactionary," he said. "You're wrong, as I have said so many times. It is only that I've seen so many bandwagons jumped on by managers and just as quickly jumped off, and forgotten. They usually originate either in Chicago or in New York. Why is it that we don't originate many here? Why aren't they originated in Germany, Italy, France . . .? I don't know the answer, but it's all beside the point."

Nina said, "It is not beside the point, Greg. It doesn't really matter where the new developments come from."

Ryder replied, "I'm not referring to new developments, I'm referring to so-called new concepts which, for a short period anyway prove highly profitable to their innovators. They play on people's weaknesses for shortcuts to success: the new BX scheme for improving human resources, the D Plan for futurism, the 1-2-3 system for closing sales, or the Z plan for all to benefit by returning to childhood practices.

"But that's enough. I've ridden that hobbyhorse too long. Let us now get on with Time Management."

Young said, "One more interruption, please?"

"For you, and only for you, yes."

Young went on: "Look at it from the delegates' point of view. You have long taught us that we must not sit on a fence; we must dictate policies, be positive, there must be no *ifs* or *buts*. Now we have two sessions which can cause conflict in their minds."

"A good point, George, but with 90 per cent of our teachings the delegates have no reservations. They can't dispute, for example, our planned selling formula. They can't disagree with the facts presented in self-analysis training. There is no resistance to our Effective Leadership sessions; but all managers, both here and in the USA, have had reservations about two subjects – Performance Appraisal, and Time Management. In these two, and only these two subjects, do I think we should clear the minds of the doubters in our audience by giving both sides of the picture, which means showing the right way to tackle the subjects by not going to extremes. This, I now believe, is our objective with Performance Appraisal, and it should also be our objective for Time Management. May I proceed?"

"Please do," said Young, politely.

"Very well, I am now addressing new managers." In the adopted role he continued: "This session will save you from being overworked and over-worried, that is of course if anyone here is overworked or over-worried. But if you aren't now, you will be frequently in the future.

"The subject is the management of time. There are two ways to achieve the objective of an 8-hour day becoming an 8-hour working day. One is by hard labour; the other a simple but just as effective way.

"First, the hard way: this depends on a special kind of diary-cum-filing-cabinet, in which a manager completes many entries on various cards each day. Every minute has to be accounted for: time for priority tasks, thinking time, arguing time, being friendly time and, if you have a pretty secretary, possibly a lovely time – no, perhaps we'd better miss that one out!"

He didn't get the hearty laugh he expected, so went on: "Data will be vital to the future workload – times for meetings, for meals, etc., and more et ceteras. The idea for this massive prepared record has caught on. We have to ask ourselves the reason.

"I think possibly because it seems so impressive to others to have a personal filing system, a specially designed diary, to save time. It makes a manager seem such a busy, well organized person. For me this system does not achieve its objective. It is enjoyed by few, except those who like ego-building and some who delight in filling up forms. The person who claims that such a giant system helps him to save many hours of time, which can be devoted to important matters, is usually an ineffective manager anyway.

"Consider for a moment the activities of top executives who work their way to the top by sheer ability and determination. Almost without exception, when they become managing directors, there is not enough work to keep them busy. Because they are brilliant, they will have to build around themselves an equally brilliant management team. Once they ruled over production or marketing, research or finance; but now others take the burden of such work from them. Now they only receive their management reports and attend meetings of their own calling.

"They make the big decisions. They decide on future strategy, but still they have time to spare, although they will rarely admit it. As I mentioned earlier, if they don't have the time to spare, it is because they spend too much of it on outside commitments and committees.

"Such people don't need super personal filing systems. Never believe the top executive who bemoans the fact that he has little time to spare for the things he enjoys – his garden, his family, his golf. Almost certainly, he gets more enjoyment from being chairman of activities quite unrelated to his business, often necessitating monthly dinners or luncheons. Incidentally, I do not know one top executive of a large and successful company who keeps a mammoth personal filing system.

"Something similar happens with middle managers. There are many working for badly managed or uncaring companies who are distraught because they never seem to have enough time to get their work completed each day. But even such managers seem to find the time to do what they want to do, such as entertaining their staff and associates, believing that such entertaining enriches the lives of subordinates, and motivates them to greater effort. Very rarely is this so.

"Then there are unnecessarily long lunch hours, unnecessary meetings, time-wasting discussions . . .

"Do you recognize these types among your associates? There are those who leave the office early, to play squash perhaps, or to attend meetings of a local dramatic society; they can always find time for these activities. But these are the people who complain that they can't find the time to dictate a letter, discuss a new marketing plan, or simply to sit down and discuss creative thinking. These are the people who will jump at the idea of a blockbusting diary, when all they need do is to cut down on those extraneous, time-wasting activities which have little bearing on their work.

"Of course they should take part in such activities – that is a part of life's enjoyment – but they can't have it both ways.

Something has to be cut down somewhere, if time is to be found to carry out the necessary duties satisfactorily. They should learn to stop misleading themselves, stop using such sentences as 'But I must do that . . .', 'I can't possibly cut out . . .', or 'I simply must go to that meeting . . .', which are typical responses to suggestions from their wives or friends to ease the pressure of their work and so enjoy their home lives.

"There's one further factor before we give you some concrete time-management principles: many managers work late because they don't want to arrive home before the children have been put to bed. It's as simple as that!

"They don't need time management diaries, all they need is to find a way of placating a guilty conscience.

"There are others who, for no reason at all, will travel to X or Y, because they enjoy staying at luxury hotels. Don't ever believe them when they tell you they hate it. I know I'm on dangerous ground now, but this course is designed to tell you the truth about management — the whole truth, and nothing but the truth. You have to decide what you want to do, but don't waste time considering ways and means of saving time when you know that the main cause is your own lack of self-discipline.

"But enough of this preaching. It sounds like a sermon, doesn't it? But sermon or not, I've told you the truth.

"Now you will want to hear some other effective ways of saving your time."

Ryder paused, took a deep breath and said to his directors, "That will be my opening. It will of course be subject to some alteration later, and it wil be followed by one of you detailing time-management principles."

Nina said, "Were you getting at any of us, Greg — about doing what we want to do, I mean?"

"No comment!" came the response. Then he added, "I've said nothing new, nothing you have not all heard before, but it may well be new to our delegates. So let's get on with the session, George."

Young said quickly, "Let's face it, Greg, we're all guilty on occasion of time-wasting, by doing something we want to do, whether it be travelling abroad or leaving the office early to attend some local council meeting, or anything else that is dear to our heart. This doesn't matter, so long as we don't then complain about lack of time to carry out some task, or worse still, ask for an additional assistant or secretary to help us cope, when it is within our scope to cope quite adequately.

"But Greg, when addressing delegates, we must, while painting a picture of the time-wasters doing what they *want* to do rather than what they *ought* to do, also – perhaps with a laugh – remember that on occasion, no matter what rules are laid down, human weaknesses will take over.

"All we can do is to ask them to be objective, so that they will know when they are misleading themselves rather than misleading others. So few managers seem to realize that the others know exactly why they are wasting their time. This should enable them to learn the truth about time management, which is that it is largely human weakness which causes time-wastage rather than the breaking of a set of rules or trying to detail every activity in a diary."

Young waited for a comment from Ryder. None came, so he continued: "Human weakness is so often the cause of time-wasting, so I suggest that Nina, who is so experienced in matters of personnel, sets out a list of rules."

There followed some discussion, then Ryder said, "It seems, Nina, that you have 45 minutes before lunch to give us the benefit of your experience in time management. So go to it!"

Nina, looking very becoming in a white silk blouse and pencil-slim blue skirt, stood up and said, "That, I think, would be boring, Greg. I have another suggestion to make. Before we tackle the main problems of time management – priority of work – delegating, etc. – let us each put forward some time-saving idea which could perhaps be linked with human weaknesses. There are many areas rarely touched upon by those who believe that all that is needed is a filing system. Most managers understand about setting priorities –

carrying out the difficult tasks first — although they may not keep to these precepts and do not take into account those areas of time-wasting which are possibly the main causes behind pressure of work."

Ryder said, "You obviously have something in mind, Nina, so let's have your views."

"Thank you. Please remember that I am not suggesting any order of priority. My first contribution I learned the hard way. You will remember, Greg, when you couldn't pass my desk without criticizing its untidiness. I was like an alcoholic, unable to admit that I was in any way at fault. I always believed that I could find anything at a moment's notice, that I could only work properly in such a mess. Those who have desk dustbins always comment in that manner. A few may reply that piles of papers and magazines create the impression that they are very busy people. They don't. In addition, untidy people completely mislead themselves by believing that they can find any piece of paper instantly. They cannot. A first lesson in time management is tidiness.

"I say to managers, file everything immediately — have a priority file, a correspondence file, a memo file. Pass last month's unread magazines on to someone else or throw them away. Never allow them to collect. End of my contribution!"

Greg said, "You do now have a tidy desk, Nina, I've noticed the difference. I'm old-fashioned enough to believe that a tidy desk shows a tidy mind, and . . ."

Mary interrupted. "It's all right for you, Greg. You pass everything over to your secretary. We have to share secretaries . . ."

"Right! But look at her desk. She has a tidy desk. How do you account for that? She can't pass anything on, she has to keep to the rule. She has the files . . .

"Next point, please."

George Young said, "I must revert to the diary. I think most of us will agree that a boxed diary system doesn't work — not for long anyway. Anyone who disagrees with me should have a word with Peter Bales, who is in charge of our management course. He told me that he had never met anyone who really completed diary cards for longer than perhaps 6 months. By then they have tired of the exercise. Furthermore, they rarely have a travelling case big enough to carry such bulky equipment. But of course a diary is essential and should be allied to a simple task sheet, which need only be a sheet of lined paper divided into five columns.

"The first column is for the date; the second to list outstanding tasks; the third is for the degree of priority for each task, and these should be numbered from one to ten; the fourth is to note if the task is to be delegated, and to whom; while the fifth is for the completion date of each task, either for the manager, or for the person to whom he has delegated the task. This simple form is as effective as the most detailed planning diary. It would be almost insulting the intelligence of the managers to suggest that they didn't know what a diary is for, so we need not elaborate on that.

"Finally, a good word for the super bulky diary and filing boxes. As was said earlier, we all need a boost to our ego sometimes, and to carry about a giant time-saver does create an impression. At board meetings I can well imagine a managing director thinking that John Bloggs with his impressive filing box and diary must really be highly competent, someone who organizes himself extremely well. That thought, passed on to the Bloggses of the world, does increase their egos, and that to them is their main reason for having such a system.

"So may I now simplify and explain to the managers that for managing their time effectively there is a hard way and a simple way, both achieving equally successful results. The message should be clear enough: the eradication of useless information, and the supply of enough information to carry out the task succesfully."

"I agree," said Ryder, "and that must be the final word on diaries. Now back to the mini time-savers.

"So far we have Nina's tidy desk. Next comes George's 'keep it simple' diary, and I'll give a third.

"This is something I had to learn by hard experience. No

manager can indulge in an 'open door' philosophy, dear to those people who believe it wins them many friends and shows how broad-minded they are. Often we have read in books how Tycoon X or Entrepreneur Y invites anyone to call on him at any time.

"What nonsense! There are times when executives are busily engaged, or telephoning, or even concentrating on a big problem. They do not want to be interrupted. It doesn't even create goodwill when, on a subordinate's arrival, the manager can't spare him more than a few minutes.

"To save wasting anyone's time, contact with a manager should always be made via secretary or by the intercom. Then an appointment can follow. In addition, to avoid time-wasting, if a subordinate wishes to discuss something with him, a manager should if possible arrange for the interview to be held in the office of the subordinate or colleague. Why? Because, without being discourteous, it is sometimes difficult to rid oneself of a visitor who wastes time by not keeping to facts, embellishing every story, reminiscing, etc. Human relations dictate, however, that such a person must still be listened to and not cut off too quickly. When you call upon that person, you can leave his or her office at any time without appearing discourteous by so doing.

"Now I think it's your turn, Peter."

Lewis said, "Nina mentioned untidy desks. Sometimes desks are untidy because top management insists on too much paperwork. The manager receives a flood of memos, and he in turn sends memos confirming everything. To show authority, he may institute controls on the number of telephone calls made, double check controls on stock control, insist on documentary evidence for everything . . .

"At one time our salesmen were expected to send us a daily report detailing their activities. Let's face it, they were hardly ever read – hours of work wasted for the salesmen, and time-consuming for a conscientious sales manager.

"Now we have a weekly report system which is more than adequate and, because it is also to the point, is carefully studied.

"Other sales managers, told of our action, responded that their sales effort is different from ours. It always is!

"I suggest you try it. It is sufficient, and a time-saver."

Lewis sank back in his chair, indicating that he had ended his contribution.

Nina said, "Shouldn't we cover work priorities now?"

Ryder disagreed. "If we can all contribute more time-savers, or mini time-savers, then much of the problem of finding time to tackle the important tasks will be solved. So on again with these minis, which, when totalled up, can save so many hours, especially for the person who insists that he or she has to do everything for themselves. Mary, over to you."

Mary Glynne said, "My suggestion is to travel by train whenever possible. Many managers drive to and from work because it is more comfortable, while all the time lamenting the stress of traffic jams, roadworks hindering progress, etc. Others adore long journeys by car, which enable them to show their prowess on the M-ways . . .

"I suggest they take the train more often, especially for long journeys, although even on some shorter ones it is possible to read a magazine or a book we claim we would like to read if only we had the time.

"You can't always use trains, but if used even 50 per cent of the time, it's amazing how much work can be got through while a train driver takes the strain."

"Good", said Ryder. "I personally enjoy train rides, and always get through a lot of work on long journeys.

"Here is my suggestion. Don't knock yourselves out by doing work which you are not qualified to do 100 per cent. Don't give yourselves sleepless nights because you haven't been able to draw up an advertisement, design a brochure, plan a direct mail campaign, produce computer graphics . . .

"Call in the specialists. Within most companies there is usually someone to whom you can turn for advice. Only pride, or a fear of showing inadequacies, stop a manager from seeking specialized help or outside guidance from consultants, PR groups, or staff selection organizations. It isn't weak to seek advice from others — which surely leads on to delegation?"

"That's right," said George Young.

"I'm glad you agree with me," said Ryder, "because you, George, can now address us as new managers, and tell us how we should delegate so that our time may be used more effectively."

Standing up, Young coughed to clear his throat, then said, "There are two types of managers who readily delegate. One does so for the right reason — to help develop staff, to assist in assessing staff for promotion, and to create time for the manager's higher priority tasks. The other does it for the wrong reasons — to rid himself of onerous duties or routine tasks which bore him, or of tasks for which he does not want to accept full responsibility.

"Irrespective of whom you delegate to, however, you must always remember that the manager is ultimately responsible for the satisfactory completion of the task. Your chief executive will not accept the excuse that you didn't have the time for a task, and so delegated to Miss X or Mr Y, who were incapable of completing that task successfully.

"A manager cannot delegate total responsibility; the task must be monitored, so that assistance may be given if necessary. The reason you delegate therefore is to enable you to carry out your priority tasks, while the less important ones can be completed satisfactorily by a subordinate. Delegation also allows subordinates to use their special skills. A subordinate may not have a manager's all-round qualifications, but he or she may specialize in a particular area. Such technically qualified people, who show an interest in certain areas, are highly motivated by being allowed to use their skills.

"Now for an oft-quoted opinion, 'It's quicker to do the job myself than to ask someone else to do it'. This statement is an admission of failure — failure to select the right staff, failure to train subordinates. It hardly seems possible that a manager of a department should employ people of such low calibre that they are unable to carry out even routine tasks. If such a situation should occur within a company, I cannot imagine how that company could succeed.

"Here are some simple rules:

- One, before delegating, make certain that the subordinate is not only capable of undertaking the task, but can do so without stress.
- Two, teach your subordinates and assistant managers to delegate. But they must be trained in delegation, otherwise they will undoubtedly pass on routine work which they dislike, and that will demotivate their subordinates.
- Three, when asking a subordinate to undertake an assignment, explain the benefits to yourself, the company, and the subordinate, if the task is carried out efficiently.
- Four, make certain that your subordinate fully understands every aspect of the assignment, and knows the objectives to be reached, step by step. Check and recheck his or her understanding of them.
- Five, clearly indicate the parameters of the authority handed over to the subordinate, especially when money has to be spent. Watch out that the subordinate does not attempt to usurp the authority of others by using you as leverage. If this is not fully understood, the act of delegating is sometimes not worthwhile, because of the friction it can cause.
- Six, set a date by which the task must be completed.
- Seven, point out to the subordinate that it is not a sign of weakness if problems he or she feels unable to solve are referred back to you.
- Eight, explain that while you are not attempting to control their every activity, you will guide them on occasion. If this has not been made clear they may well complain of interference.

"That, I think," said Young, "is enough from me. But I'm

sure that you, Greg, as chief delegator, can make another contribution."

Ryder nodded, and replied without hesitation:

- One, be sure you have adequate staff training programmes. In a very small company the managing director himself may be the one who has to carry out the training.
- Two, always show complete interest in the task handed over. Try to create the impression that it is something of great importance to you and the company. Make the subordinate feel important.
- Three, always give praise when it is due.
- Four, if possible, avoid strong criticism. Some mistakes are avoidable. Try to put them right yourself. Try not to apportion blame. If you are too heavy-handed with your criticism you will sap the confidence of the subordinate for future tasks.

Ryder paused, looked at Cooper and said, "It's your turn Philip."

Cooper started: "May I come in again on monitoring? Some delegated tasks don't need monitoring. For example, when you ask your secretary or assistant to sort your mail properly, so that you will know what is most important and what is not so important, that doesn't need monitoring. When you ask someone to make a series of appointments for you, that doesn't need monitoring. But if you have a request from your managing director for a report on your customers' reactions to your salesmen, or your customers' reactions to a certain product, then you, who are perhaps the sales manager or the marketing manager, may decide to delegate that work to an assistant manager. That is the type of task which needs monitoring. You have to be quite certain that when you make your final report it covers the ground adequately. It is you, not your assistant, who will be judged on that final report."

Ryder said, "We're being repetitive," then added hastily,

"I'm not criticizing you, Philip, just making a general comment. Now it's over to you, Peter."

Lewis said, "Everyone has heard of test marketing. Say you are considering the launch of a large direct mail campaign. No matter how good the general opinion of the complete mailing shot, there should always be a test campaign to see whether your judgement is right or at fault in any way.

"You, as managers, can only find out if a subordinate can carry out the task by first giving him or her a simple task to perform. For example, new desks are required. Ask him or her to find out what will best meet needs, and to let you have a report with alternative quotations. This kind of simple procedure is the way to test whether you can trust a subordinate with a job. You will find that the act of delegating often brings out hidden talents in a subordinate."

Ryder interrupted, "On that inspiring note I think we can say that we've finished with delegation, and we can carry on with further steps in time management."

Nina said, "If you like, Greg, I'll continue now by covering the standard formula – 'What *must* I do?', 'What *should* I do?', 'What should I *like* to do?'"

Ryder nodded his agreement and Nina continued:

- One, under the *must* heading will come the important tasks, the priority tasks, and possibly the difficult tasks. These should never be put off until later in the day, but should be tackled as soon as possible after arrival at the office. So once more we're back to finding the time for priorities.

  Use time-fillers. These are the minutes spent between the end of one meeting and the beginning of another, perhaps while awaiting the arrival of someone who has an appointment with you.

  When making appointments, try to avoid 2 o'clock, 3 o'clock, 4.30 etc. Rather fix the time at 4.10 explaining, 'I hope this won't inconvenience you but I have appointments right up until that time, and starting again

at 4.30 or 5 o'clock.' Even a customer will not be upset at
not having to arrive at the standard time on the hour or
half-hour, but whoever is visiting you will know that the
time you have available is between 4.10 and, say, 5
o'clock. Strangely, when you make an appointment for an
odd time, people tend to be more punctual. Don't ask me
why! There must be some psychological reason, but our
records show that this is so. Now you have 10 minutes for
use as a time-filler in which to complete some of the minor
tasks which would normally eat into your day. During the
day there may be other periods useful as time-fillers; these
time-fillers, properly used, can save you as much as 2 or 3
weeks' work in a year. That's really something, isn't it?

- Two, there must be a routine for the completion of tasks,
  e.g. a set time for dictating, inspecting, or telephoning
  branch managers. Such tasks will of course be entered on
  the task sheets.
- Three, which outside visits are necessary? So many
  outside calls come more under the heading of *What I like
  doing:* for example, a PR exercise at a luxury hotel with
  free cocktails. If you must visit an exhibition, time it for
  early in the morning – say 8.30 till 10.00 – or after 4 p.m.
  If you pick the morning, you can return to the office early
  and carry out your set tasks; if the afternoon, you will
  almost have finished your day's work before having to
  leave the office.
- Four, meetings. All new managers like calling meetings,
  and many managers consider them as a part of the perks of
  management, the meeting allowing them to show their
  authority.

  Never call a meeting if a decision or message can be
  conveyed in any other way. As for outside meetings, could
  you not perhaps sometimes excuse yourself? You will not
  be thought less of if you back out of quite a few meetings.
  Remember, it's not only the meeting that will waste your
  time, it is accumulating all the facts necessary before
  holding that meeting, it is thinking about the speech you

will have to make. Meetings are great time-wasters.

- Five, another great time-saver is having the strength to say 'no'. If you haven't the time to tackle a job – your diary is absolutely full, in spite of all your time-saving activities – then it's best to be honest and not to accept a task you know you haven't the time to complete satisfactorily.

- Six, and my final point, refers to dictation. You will never know the truth of how good you are at dictating a memo or letter, either to a secretary or into a recorder, unless you ask for opinions. Even then, you may not be told the truth.

So much time can be saved by giving the subject matter thought before dictation. Are all the files available? Do you know all the facts relevant to the matter you are covering in the letter? Are the names and addresses correct? Have you ensured that there will be no interruptions by advising the telephone operator not to put any calls through and perhaps having a 'do not disturb' notice on your door?

When preparing to dictate a letter, have all these points clear in your mind:

(a) The message you want to convey.

(b) The sequence in which you intend to explain this message.

(c) How short a letter can you write which will still enable you to complete the message?

(d) If you have a competent secretary, you can leave the paragraphing and punctuation to her; but even the most efficient secretary will appreciate being given some detail about paragraphing, etc.

(e) Remember to spell out names included in the letter, or technical terms.

(f) Give instructions, if necessary, about any special layout or enclosures needed for the letter.

(g) If dictating to a secretary, no matter how efficient she may be, speak slowly and clearly. The same is equally applicable to talking into a tape recorder.

(h) Make certain that you have indicated who should receive copies of the letter.

Preparation is the key to successful letter or memo writing. A good manager will have a clear outline in his mind of the letter he intends writing, before his secretary arrives in the office or before switching on his dictating machine. Some managers waste a considerable time every day umming and ahing over their letters while a secretary sits idly by.

"That," concluded Nina, is my contribution to the session. Mary, I think it must be your turn."

Mary said, "I have only one point, which, although raised before, I want to stress, because it is such a big time-waster, and that is the constant nattering in shops, offices, and factories. It's difficult for managers to draw a line between building goodwill and listening to a bore explaining in detail an entire weekend's activities. One way in which the chat can be cut down is never to invite the 'chatterer' to sit down. Left standing, they don't go on for quite so long, but if allowed to sit down and become comfortable and relaxed, the chat becomes a long-distance monologue and a great time-waster. But hold on! Do you act that way? Be firm with yourself. If you meet an associate, decide exactly what you want to know from him or tell him, and complete that conversation as quickly as possible.

"In the same way, set an example of telephone usage. Keep conversation succinct, concentrate on making your point or points, and keep pleasantries to a minimum.

"I think that's enough from me," Mary concluded.

"Not true!" said Ryder. "We could listen to you for much longer."

"Very well," said Mary, "then I'll make one further point, or maybe it will be two.

"Use the telephone in preference to writing. You can get your message over more clearly by telephone than by dictating, reading, checking and then perhaps re-reading.

"Finally, and this is really finally, always rely on your three filing folders labelled *Priority, Urgent* and *Information* to be read at your leisure, and check those files two or three times a day.

"Oh, and one more final . . ."

"No," said Greg. "You're breaking all the rules."

"Yes, I enjoy doing that," said Mary. "Avoid writing memos – managers do so enjoy writing memos – and inform others that you don't want memos from them either. A few minutes' talk is preferable to dictating a memo, studying that memo, taking action on that memo – and it's time-saving. That definitely does end my contribution to the session."

Greg looked at his watch and said, "Just time for one more before lunch. It must be you again, Philip."

Cooper said, "I won't waste anyone's time. All I shall do is add a few quickies, so that when the lunch gong goes I shall have completed my contribution."

Mary said, "Philip, how can you make that promise? You know you never use one word when two will do. You can't make promises like that!"

"But that's where you're wrong, Mary. I have already learned from this session on time management that all of us waste time talking too much. Perhaps I'm one of the compulsive talkers mentioned, perhaps I overelaborate. As all of you know quite well, I have enjoyed calling a great many meetings to discuss the financial aspects of the group – it gives me so many opportunities perhaps to show how much I know about finance compared with the others. But no longer! If brevity is the soul of wit, as has been said, then it's witty for me from now on. No longer shall I visit you in your office and . . ."

"Philip," Ryder interrupted, "you're making a speech. That shows how hard it is to keep to time-management principles."

Cooper grinned. "It's the old actor that keeps coming out in me – but no more! Here are some additions to time-management principles:

- One, don't be a grasshopper. Complete one task at a time.
- Two, be objective about yourself. We all believe that what we do is important and therefore we have to work long hours, to take work home with us, while others, whose work is less important, can save time by keeping to time-management principles. I repeat, be objective about yourself and your actions.
- Three, advice is sometimes given when planning ahead that a half-day, or even a day, should be set aside for thinking and planning. This advice must surely be given by theorists, not practical people. It doesn't work! Anyone who can set aside a whole day for thinking and planning does not have a time-management problem, except perhaps one of his own making. But I know we are covering creative thinking in another session, so I won't elaborate.
- Four, if faced with an unpleasant task, give that task priority. Tackle it immediately. Never delegate such tasks.
- Five, the advice to take a rapid reading course is seldom taken, and I'm not sure that such a course is worth attending anyway. There may be little need for it if a manager learnes the art of skipping, and glancing, and delegating. When faced with a mass of literature to be waded through, ignore most of the small print and glance at the headlines − they will tell you whether or not an article is worth reading, or will be of interest to you. When studying textbooks, skip those parts which are not new to you.

  Most busy people do in fact skip through newspapers, but still manage to keep well abreast of the news. It's the same with advertising. We skip through advertisements until we spot a page which has some bearing on our lifestyle, business, hobby . . .

  Alternatively, delegate reading matter to a subordinate,

and ask him or her to underline those parts which he or she feels may be of interest to the manager. All subordinates are proud to be given this task. It makes them feel that they are a part of management – it's a motivator.

- Six, make sure that you have under your control a good filing system to enable you to check queries, a customer's balance, union problems, etc. quickly.
- Seven, keep all conversations short, unless you are counselling someone.
- Eight, don't take part in committees outside your work. Of course, you may take part if you are under no pressure and can easily cover your daily tasks. But if you complain that the day is never long enough for you, then don't become committed to committees; if you do, you will waste much of your working time on considering some future speech.

   Lets face it, most people join committees for the wrong reason – not because they want to help others, a most laudable reason, but because it boosts their ego to be on a committee, especially if they are elected chairman.
- Nine, if ever you have to speak in public, make the speech short – 5 minutes, perhaps. This will save preparation time, and it will also please your audience.
- Ten, a repeat, but it must be driven home hard: do try to avoid unscheduled interruptions.
- Eleven, never take work home to impress the family.
- Twelve, train your boss. A boss can waste so much of your time. No one can stop him walking into your office and interrupting your train of thought. He is allowed to send lengthy memos, and to demand lengthy memos in return. He can spoil a whole day's planning by calling a meeting, and no manager can refuse the call.

   How do you train your boss in time management? By simply talking about it, that's all. At every opportunity tell him how time management has helped you and your division, and give him some of the reasons. If he doesn't appreciate what you are telling him, then he is the one who should really be on this course.

Then, laughingly, he added, "None of this implies criticism of you, Greg."

Ryder shook his head. "That's where you're wrong! I shall watch my steps — or rather my meetings — in the future; so long as you don't worry me with problems which you as managers should be able to solve for yourselves. That comes under time management, too."

Then he laughed and added, "Don't look so worried, Philip, I do know that I'm not perfect."

Back came the chorus once more, "Oh yes you are, Greg!"

The mood changed, and, laughing heartily, the managers trooped off to lunch.

16 Decisions Postponed

Greg Ryder went straight to the registrars on the first floor. To him this was the focal point of the administrative offices. He believed that every director should visit the registrars at least once a day to hear how they were faring – which courses were fully booked, which courses needed a sales drive for extra delegates, how important customers were pacified when they demanded places on a fully booked course.

The registrars' task was not only to accept the bookings over the telephone, but also to retain the goodwill of clients making unreasonable demands. They also gave advice as to the type of course most suitable for a client's requirements. The telephone lines were always in use, many of the calls being requests for information. Queries about training programmes enabled the registrars to explain benefits and sometimes to make bookings over the telephone.

Ryder delighted, while in the registrar's office, in listening to their well conducted telephone interviews.

There were four registrars, and when Ryder arrived at their office, as usual, all were talking into telephone mouthpieces. He moved into the next office, where the telephone sales team was in action. Each member of the team was well qualified and so well trained that they were able to achieve almost as many bookings over the telephone as did the regional salesmen, and at a fraction of the cost. Ryder was aware, however, that without the groundwork of the regional salesmen, telephone selling would probably not obtain such spectacular results.

Ryder asked Julia Everett, in charge of the team, "How much this morning?"

"Well, er –"

"'Well, er' always means poor results," Ryder remarked.

"Yes, Mr Ryder, but it's only partly a 'Well, er' because a few minutes ago – remember you said 'this morning', and it is past midday now – Walter booked a £9000 in-company course."

Ryder patted Walter on the back and congratulated him.

Everett said, "I promise you we'll have a record period, Mr Ryder . . ."

Ryder said, "Highly efficient people like your team could never achieve anything else. My congratulations should go to whoever engaged you in the first place."

"You engaged me, Mr Ryder."

"So I did." He turned around, smiling broadly, "So now you can pat me on the back."

Julia obliged, and the laughter followed him out of the room.

He returned to the registrars to question them closely about the results.

Lewis and Cooper decided that during the break they would have coffee and sandwiches in Cooper's office. Cooper's secretary, used to changes of plan, quickly carried out her chief's request: "No butter, tomato and lettuce only, no salt". Lewis, the keep-fit fanatic, said "Not for me. Plenty of butter, chicken sandwiches, and an apple."

Cooper laughed. "You're the only one who continually preaches at us all to keep fit!"

Lewis responded, "My axiom is *break the diet rules occasionally – it has a good psychological effect*".

Cooper's secretary, who had left the room, reappeared quickly. "I forgot to tell you," she said, "a Mr Lyons telephoned. He wouldn't give me any information, and I didn't recollect the name as anyone we know, but he did say that the matter was urgent and would you call him back as soon as possible. Do you know him?"

"Yes, Jean, I do."

When Jean had left the room Lewis looked questioningly at Cooper. Cooper smiled, picked up his telephone, and dialled a number. When the call was answered, Cooper said, "I'd like to speak to Mr Standon, please" and a few moments later, "John, you wanted to speak to me".'

"Yes," came the reply, "I'll be brief. We must have a decision within 24 hours. An alternative has arisen – I don't like it but I could be outvoted."

"Well, John, I can't manage 24 hours. You will have a definite decision by 5 p.m. on Friday, and almost certainly it will be yes."

After replacing the receiver, Cooper said, "That was John Standon of Carter Lovell. I told him that if ever anyone of them telephoned me here they should use the name Lyons, and I would know who it was. It's decision time, Peter. Need we wait until Friday to tell them we accept the offer?"

Lewis thought for a few seconds, then said, "What's the urgency?"

"They obviously have an alternative applicant, or perhaps two applicants, but I should think they've given us priority, or they wouldn't have given us time to make our decision."

"Right," said Lewis. "They've given us until Friday, so let's wait till Friday, when we know the results of George's showdown with Greg. We've got to consider the fact that if we come to a decision and tell Greg we're leaving, there would be no compensation. But if he sells out and we don't want to work under the new regime, then I think we should be entitled to compensation – and a fairly substantial amount too. Either way, we mustn't resign. We've got to work it that we are sacked."

"Peter, you're wrong. No compensation could take the place of a first-class opportunity for both of us to build a new career."

"Maybe that's OK for you, but right now I could do with a lump sum. I won't go into details."

Cooper answered, "You needn't, I know your position very well. You never did take my advice about protecting your money. You spend too lavishly and you don't invest shrewdly; but I think you are in good company. To my knowledge, most marketing people are not safety-first people. We'll wait until Friday, then."

As the sandwiches arrived, Peter was wondering whether he could ever work closely and in harmony with such an unenthusiastic accountant as Philip Cooper.

Mary and Nina decided to join some of the course delegates for lunch. When they arrived in the restaurant, all the tables for six, eight, and ten people were full, so they sat down at a table for four, knowing that they would soon be joined by two delegates from a course that had not yet broken for lunch.

Nina said, "Mary, I'm quite excited about starting out on our own. I can't think of anything else."

Mary said, "Sorry, but I don't feel that kind of excitement. I think it's because I'm too concerned."

"What about?"

"Greg is acting out of character. I'm sure he wouldn't do anything which might harm any of us."

Nina said, "Everyone is talking about putting people first these days, but do tycoons ever really consider people's problems?"

"I believe Greg does."

"So do I," said Nina quickly, "but I'm so excited about our project. What are you hoping for?"

Mary replied, "Nina, you teach problem-solving, and you teach that problems are always solved step by step."

"Agreed," said Nina, "but we still haven't yet found the real cause of the problem, so making a decision is very difficult.

Why does Greg want to sell out? Is it solely because he is worried about his health? If so, then that's the cause of the problem."

"I disagree," said Mary strongly. "If he was really worried, he wouldn't have said a word to us about it. I'm sure of that."

"You know him that well?"

Mary made no response, so Nina carried on: "You won't back down on our pact though, will you?"

"No. But we must both reserve the right to make a final decision after George has spoken to Greg, because only then shall we know the real problem, and whether or not the solution, so far as we are concerned, is to move away into new fields."

At that moment two delegates from the Marketing course asked if they could join them. They both smiled their agreement, while Mary wondered whether she could work with Nina without the control of a Greg Ryder.

17 Problem-Solving

Ryder began the afternoon session. "We're having a record month, but I still believe that territories should be covered more intensely. How many have we in the sales force now, Peter?"

Lewis replied, "Twenty-three executive training advisers . . ."

Ryder interrupted, "Don't use your fancy titles to me, Peter, they're salesmen."

Lewis said calmly, "You may not like the title, Greg, but our clients do. They believe that training should be negotiated by liaison officers, not salesmen. They don't take to the idea that they might be persuaded to take any course."

"Rubbish! But I don't want to argue with you."

Lewis flushed, but did not continue the argument. He said, "I repeat, twenty-three training advisers, six regional managers, and one field sales manager — a total of thirty."

"Right. Then cut territories and increase the number to thirty-five."

"But . . ."

"No buts! You work it out, then we'll consider the implications. You can also step up the direct mailings, but keep within the budget. You can do that by cutting costs in other directions, and one of those is the cost of print. Our brochures are far too lavish, and they don't sell strongly enough."

Mary, smiling sweetly, said, "Didn't I hear you say just now, Greg, that we've had a record month? Are you sure you want to increase expenditure on marketing?"

"Yes. Now is the time to do it, for success begets success. Spend while the going's good, then eventually, when the depression comes, cut right across the board, except for marketing. Always spend on marketing.

"Now, let's get on with the next session – Problem-solving and Decision-making."

Young said, "You begin, Greg."

Greg's stern expression melted away and he said, "You are continually asking me to lay down the principles for the opening of sessions. I begin to think that you are enjoying flattering me."

"How can you say that, Greg," said Lewis, "when in every course in which we cover human relations, and that's most of them, we stress that justifiable praise and honest appreciation are always acceptable, as well as being great motivators? Flattery is not.

"We asked you to open two of the sessions because you disagreed with us. That wasn't flattery, it was praise for your objectives. If George asks you to open again, it is because you have had more experience in decision-making than the rest of us put together. That is fact, not flattery."

"Then your offer is accepted," said Ryder, "but I won't open, because you seem to have forgotten that this course is for new managers. Most of my decisions, covering strategy and investment, are in a different category from those of our delegates."

"That doesn't matter," said Nina. "The basic principles are the same, whatever the problem, whatever the decision has to be. I believe that the opening should generalize, and a lead from you for the others to follow would be most helpful. Then someone else can lay down the basic principles."

"Well, if you insist", said Ryder. "Here, then, is my message, which you know by heart, anyway: Problem-solving and Decision-making are as akin as Mercedes and Benz, Waldorf and Astoria, Rolls and Royce. You can hardly have one without the other. It's very difficult to think of a decision which has not been preceded by a problem, and when a solution for that problem is found, it is not usually in black and white, it offers alternatives, so that the decision-maker has to decide on which is the right alternative."

Ryder cleared his throat, then continued: "I will give typical problem areas: for example, interference by top management in the running of a manager's department."

Ryder stopped talking and looked sternly around before going on: "Did I see some lurking smiles at that indictment of a chief executive?"

"You never interfere," said Nina, emphasizing the *never*.

"Oh yes I do!"

"Oh no you don't!" came the childish chorus, and, again, general laughter. But unlike many chief executives, Ryder knew how to lessen tension, and that problem-solving and decision-making sometimes led him to tell his directors that they did not always practise what they preached.

Once more he began, as though addressing delegates: "Managers, it is essential in problem-solving and decision-making to keep to a standard set of principles − principles which have been practised and have proved their worth over many years.

"They are taught at all business schools, including Harvard and Columbia, Manchester and London. The principles never vary, and they should be adhered to every time a problem arises or a decision has to be made.

"Are there any golfers here? Ah, four of you − there should be more. Well, those of you who play the game may have read what Sandy Lyle, British Open champion of 1985, wrote for a magazine. He stated that one of the great faults of the high handicap player, and even some quite good players, is that they never set themselves up properly for a shot; and unless the setting up principles are adhered to, there is no chance of the ball being hit straight and true. He listed the actions he took before every drive: the positioning of the feet, the angle of the shoulders, the positioning of the ball, the mental picture of the result of the shot, and so on.

"Here you have a great player going through the fundamentals of shot-making hundreds and hundreds of times a week.

"Basic principles apply to managers as much as they do to sportsmen. There must be a conscious effort, however trivial the problem, however great the problem, to solve it in a standard, practical manner, step by step. That way leads to the greatest chance of success.

"The steps you should take will be given to you later, and should be seared on the memory bank in your mind. But there is a proviso. The first step in problem-solving is always to establish the true cause of the problem. The second is to call for all the facts relevant to that problem."

Cooper said, "Sorry, sir, to interrupt, but I thought you were not going to give the steps."

Ryder ignored the interruption and continued: "The one factor which could inhibit the problem-solver and decision-maker from arriving at the correct solution, after establishing the facts, is that even facts can be distorted to suit someone's purpose.

"I'll give you an example. When Ford's were fighting their great battles with General Motors and Chrysler during the 1950s, they decided to take on these giants by redesigning, to match the streamlined, glistening, radiator-snarling monsters being produced by their competitors. Fords therefore designed similar monsters, with chrome fins and grinning radiator grills. They then had to decide on a winning name, to match their rivals' Thunderbirds and Mercuries. After massive research, they invited newspaper editors and their readers to contribute their ideas. The originator of the prizewinning name would be awarded a Ford car. They also sought the help of such creative thinkers as poets and thriller writers. In all they received over 20,000 suggestions.

"But they were ignored by one executive who had already decided on a name — Edsel — after Henry Ford the Second's father. The fact that Edsel had never been a great success didn't matter. The originator of the idea believed that Henry Ford the Second would be delighted to commemorate his father's name by stamping it on a car.

"That executive became emotionally caught up with the name Edsel, which he believed would find favour with everyone. It didn't. Researchers told him that to most people Edsel was quite unknown, and to some it sounded like a detergent.

"What did the executive do? He told Henry the Second that he had vetted all the suggestions and a large percentage of those who wrote in believed that the best name would be Edsel. Henry the Second gave way reluctantly, believing that he was basing his decision on facts. He was not. The Edsel car, as we now know, failed to live up to expectations. The reasons given were many, but could one of them have been the name of the car?"

Lewis said, "That's a good story, Greg. But you're not going to deny, are you, that all the facts must be obtained before a problem can be solved or a decision made?"

"Of course not! What I intend to do is to drive home that irrespective of whatever steps may be used to solve a problem, if someone is emotionally caught up with that problem, that person can bend the facts and even sometimes cheat to get his own way. A manager must not always accept the facts at face value. Sometimes proof must be demanded.

"I shall remind managers that what we sometimes believe to be facts are no more that generalizations. We have touched on this before, but it is worth reminding managers of statements such as *Everyone thinks so; I spoke to X, the managing director, and he told me personally* . . .; and *The trade papers are full of the difficulties of obtaining Mishmash — we ought to get into that market.*

"The right response to such generalizations is 'You tell me you spoke to one managing director. Can you give me the names of half a dozen executives who have made similar statements?' or 'Will you give me all the cuttings you have regarding Mishmash?'

"Chief executives who analyse facts in this manner will annoy their subordinates, who will believe them to be reactionary for not appreciating the advice they are given. But a decision-maker should not seek popularity by accepting non-facts as facts.

"Here is another example. All works managers delight in buying new machines, spray booths, sheet metal benders and cutters. They mislead their bosses into believing that until such new equipment is purchased, there will be the risk of future problems caused by breakdowns, delivery dates being broken, etc.

"Once again, a manager is entitled to ask for precise facts – the number of breakdowns, the whys and whens of their occurrence, and whether or not other users have had similar experiences.

"Then, of course, there are the decisions based on the claims of public relations officers. It is strange that even very good managers, right up to chief executives, who employ their own PR people, believe the publicity that other PROs get away with in the press. A chief executive's wife may read in the papers about the tremendous demand for Itsy-Bitsy toys. She will tell her husband that their company should be manufacturing similar toys – all children want them. He too may have seen them boosted on television programmes, not realizing that this is the work of a very good PRO. Those most influenced by PR publicity are salesmen. They really do believe everything they read. Salesmen are most gullible people, and they often exaggerate. They will write to their sales manager making claims for a new product which cannot be substantiated by an analysis of the facts. Such facts should never be ignored, but they should be most carefully analysed.

"Now managers," continued Ryder, "I am afraid you have

to develop a little cynicism when listening to a subordinate, or a colleague, trying to prove that his is the only way to solve a problem. Advice from someone who has invested emotional capital in his solution is often disastrous.

"Be careful yourselves, managers, when you ask for a meeting with your managing director, to suggest a new development, to solve a problem, to suggest a new campaign or a new form of publicity to solve a problem, that you are not so emotionally committed to your idea that you are not so much seeking the advice of your managing director as his stamp of approval — which only means that if things don't work out you can at least apportion some of the blame to your chief.

"The first rule in problem-solving therefore is not only to collect the facts, or have the facts provided for you, but also, to check them by using other sources.

"Another point to remember, and again it concerns the emotions, is to use the more radical part of your mind when facing a problem — the part you would use when advising others to solve their problems. Why is it that we can always solve other people's problems more efficiently than we can solve our own? The answer is that we are not emotionally affected by many of the problems of others.

"Now to discover the steps which must be taken when faced with a problem. Any comments?"

Nina said, "Not at this stage. But Greg, you're the one who has to solve so many problems, and to make so many decisions. You don't hear about most of the problems faced by your managers. Often the first time is when you receive a letter beginning *Are you aware . . .?, I'm sure you don't know that . . ., Do you know the real reason why . . .?, I thought I ought to tell you that . . .* and so on."

Ryder smiled. "Yes, I get my fair share of those notes or letters. They don't necessarily mean that anyone's judgement is at fault, although obviously I have to investigate and ask for the facts. Mostly they seem to deal with people problems. The loser on such occasions will invariably disagree with the decisions made against him or her, and will attempt to have that decision overturned. This means solving problems twice; but with a team of good managers, a managing director should not receive too many of these notes. If he does, then the decision-making abilities of his managers is faulty.

"But enough on this subject. Please let us cover the steps, bearing in mind that we are addressing new managers, many of whose problems will be people problems.

"There is one further point which should have been, and will, I know, be made. On many occasions it is possible to pre-empt many of the problems which arise.

"Now I think you, George, should list the steps because you give this session so often in our leadership courses."

Without hesitation, Young began: "To repeat, when first faced with a problem, get the facts, and check those facts again and again. Next, identify the true cause of the problem. If you fail to do this, you will probably be dealing with symptoms.

"Here is an example. There was conflict within a typing pool between an audio typist and her supervisor. The supervisor had reported to her manager that no one could get on with Phyllis, the audio typist; her output was poor, she was always complaining that the room was too hot or too cold or too draughty, and when she felt like a shopping day, she would take time off and telephone in that she was unwell."

Young looked round. "Quite a typical situation you will agree, one which many managers would accept, considering, in line with the supervisor, that Phyllis should be dismissed. But the manager in this case decided to seek more facts, and try to discover why Phyllis, who had once been quite a reasonable worker, had suddenly become incompetent and lazy.

"The manager adopted the standard technique, that is, to look for deviation from the norm. Was Phyllis always difficult, lazy, and incompetent? Surely not, or she would not have lasted with the company more than a few months, and she had held her job for 3 years. He asked at what stage had she changed? When had the deviation from normal begun? A check back clarified the position.

"It had all happened 6 months earlier. Before then there had been no complaints.

"More checking back of facts.

"Phyllis had been moved away from working with two male buyers into another division, where she was working for two lady stock controllers.

"More research. Other workers in the pool were questioned in a most diplomatic way, and it transpired that Phyllis had been rather keen on Arnold, one of the buyers. Some 6 months earlier she had made the mistake of boasting to a colleague, and to the supervisor, that she thought Arnold was rather keen on her.

"No one believed her, but many were annoyed because they felt there might be some truth in it, and they didn't see why Phyllis should become a manager's favourite. The supervisor, a spinster of about 52, didn't appreciate the situation at all, and her decision – an instant one based on emotion rather than a study of the facts – was that Phyllis should immediately be moved to another department.

"The first step the manager took was to see Phyllis and explain to her in the nicest possible way that unless she improved her standards she could not expect to stay with the company. The supervisor was then told that although moving Phyllis was right at the time, she should be given the opportunity to prove whether or not the move was causing the problem. The supervisor agreed, and gave Phyllis a final warning, pointing out that in order to prove whether her work had deteriorated because of the move, she should return to work for Arnold for a short time. If her work remained below standard, then as she had received the first warning, there would be no alternative but to replace her in the pool.

"Arnold raised no objections. He was only concerned with having his work done efficiently, and Phyllis had always been efficient when she was working for him.

"The way the manager presented his case to the supervisor indicated that she had already come to the right decision, to determine the truth. The supervisor was pleased and told everyone that she was responsible for giving Phyllis a second chance. Phyllis reverted to type, and worked well, and the problem was solved."

Ryder said, "A good proof story, George. Who was Arnold? Was he with us?"

Young laughed. "Yes, he was with us, but I've forgotten the episode now, I can't remember any of the details." He continued: "Whenever you are faced with a problem, big or small, always look for any deviation from norm. If a production line breaks down and the cause is not obvious, seek the deviation. Were any components recently bought from a new supplier? Is there a new recruit on the production line? Has there been any report of some small change, a deviation from normal again, possibly referring to a shape, a colour, or a finish?"

Young stopped to drink some water, then went on: "When problem-solving, look for the obvious, because it is of little use considering all the steps to problem-solving when the cause of the problem is obvious. Next consider unlikely possible causes, which means more checking. Finally, check for an improbable cause.

"The wise manager," Young continued, "always attempts to identify possible future problems, so that these problems may be headed off.

"Now over to you, Nina, to list more steps in problem-solving."

Nina said, "You've covered most of them already, George, which means that there must be some repetition."

Once more Lewis interrupted, "Shouldn't it be made clear early that the problem-solver need not necessarily be the decision-maker?"

"A good point, that!" Young said. "We should make that clear. Most problems are solved by accountants, engineers, supervisors, local managers – and they may not be the ultimate decision-makers. In fact each of them can be working on the same problem, and each may provide a different solution. It is then the role of the decision-maker to decide on which solution is the most appropriate in solving the problem.

"Let us consider another problem, which occurred at Parret and Kilner. We had been called in to carry out a consultancy assignment, and while we were there, the problem arose. It makes a good case study.

"One day the works manager realized that his work-force had become discontented, which led to a stream of complaints, absenteeism, and a slowing down on the production line. The works manager thought the problem was the new bonus system; his assistant considered that the discontent was due to the food provided in the works' canteen; while one of the buyers said he thought it all stemmed from the dismissal of one of the militants, a paint sprayer who had been found smoking in a non-smoking area. We realized that these were all symptoms, and we had to find the true cause of the problem.

"It took some while to discover, because no one thought it was important. It concerned the car-parking system. More and more of the work-force were arriving by car, as the bus service was poor and the railway station some way away. There was therefore insufficient space for all those who came by car, and some of them had to be told that they could not use their cars to come to work. However, the chief executives, directors, and top managers had reserved parking spaces. The car-owners amongst the work-force objected strongly to the fact that someone like the marketing director, who was nearly always away from the works anyway, had a reserved space which could not be used by anyone else.

"The final straw came when the space allocated to one of the workers was withdrawn from him, so as to be made available for a newly appointed sales director.

"That, we discovered, after speaking to many of the employees, was the true cause of the problem. It brought out the *them and us* syndrome, which the directors had believed did not exist.

"Having discovered the cause of the problem, we had to find a solution. We sought information not only from all those who used cars, but also from those who arrived by public transport or walked. We accumulated the facts. We discovered that the bitterness was felt not so much towards the managing director as against those managers of the various departments who, the work-force felt, should not be treated any differently from themselves.

"The works committee offered their solution immediately – the company should build an additional car park on nearby ground. The managing director himself considered that the solution was to stop all reserved spaces, including his own. He thought that if badges were issued to those with cars, denoting perhaps the days on which a parking space could be used if the park was overfull – the managers also to use these badges – there could be a rota, so that all car-users in turn would have a space allotted to them. He maintained that if a concentrated effort was made to increase car-sharing, the problem would be completely solved.

"Another solution was put forward by the chief buyer. He suggested that the company should hire coaches to pick up personnel from two or three main points and take them home at night. It might, he said, be costly, but not nearly so costly as building a new car park."

Young paused, then said, "This case study covers the points you made, Peter, that usually the decision-maker is provided with a variety of solutions, often from different people.

"This is how I shall conclude the session. If you are a decision-maker, then, as in the case study we have just made, you will be offered a choice of solutions.

"On nearly every occasion when tackling a problem you will be given options, and you will then have to make a decision. How we choose the correct option will be covered in the next session on decision-making, when we shall take our case study of the car-parking problems to its conclusion."

Smiling at his colleagues, Ryder said, "Well done, George!"

They all agreed with Ryder who, once again using one of his standard remarks, said, "My decision now is that we break for tea."

18   Decision-Making

The tea break was a quick gulp, a hastily swallowed biscuit, then the directors went their different ways to check on departmental activities, telephone messages, and problems. It just gave time for a meeting with a secretary or other member of the team.

When they returned to the meeting room, there was a message from Ryder to the effect that he would be a few minutes' late for the next session.

Mary arrived carrying a newspaper. Closing the door behind her and looking conspiratorially around the room as if seeking bugging devices, she said, "Has anyone seen today's *Financial Times?*"

"What time have we had to look at papers?" retorted Lewis.

Mary ignored the remark and continued: "I must read you this snippet."

The snippet was a news item, stating that the marketing director of Dyson's had resigned. Neither the director nor the board would make any comment.

Putting the paper on the table, Mary asked, "What does this mean?"

No one could supply the answer.

At that moment Ryder arrived. "What's up?" he said immediately.

Young, furrowing his forehead to denote perplexity, asked, "What do you mean, Greg?"

"You're all looking puzzled."

They all knew that no one was more observant than Greg Ryder – he never missed a trick.

Young said, "We were talking about share prices."

Ryder answered, "You know my advice has always been to keep away from equities, but, on the other hand, if any of you ever has any inside information, let me know!"

There was some rather forced laughter, and Ryder went on: "Let's make a start with making decisions, and I'm not leading off this time. It must be your turn, Philip. After me, I think you're the main decision-maker, because hardly a day passes without somebody demanding extra cash to solve a particular problem. Isn't that right?"

Cooper nodded.

"Then carry on."

Cooper, imperturbable as ever, said, "Very well. Let me begin by covering some ground which was only touched on lightly in the previous session. We referred continually to the need to consider every fact before attempting to solve a problem, but there should have been constant reference also to more general information – information which might be given by any of those even remotely concerned with the problem or up-to-date information which could come from computers or mathematical models. So many problems can be pre-empted by seeking information from all concerned before the possible problem arises.

"A typical example was the rebuilding and refurbishing of the restaurant of a five-star hotel. After the work had been completed, problems arose with the wine-dispensing arrangements, with the space allocated to the bar, and with the table-seating arrangements, which led to too narrow gangways between the tables, making it difficult for the waiters to serve customers.

"Top management had played its part in the design, outside consultants had been acting as advisers, and a first-rate contractor employed, but as the head waiter said soulfully later when trouble arose, "No one asked my opinion, yet I have to control the restaurant, I have to make it pay, I have to satisfy the customers. I knew, from a practical point of view, what we should or should not have done, but nobody considered asking my opinion."

"Such a management attitude should not occur so often. All decision-makers, when they are planning a new move – a move to new premises, a new fire-prevention system, changing the offices around, buying various appliances – should seek advice from those concerned.

Cooper paused, then said, "Do you agree with that, Greg?"

Ryder laughed. "Don't ask me! Seek the opinions of those who are going to run the course."

More laughter, and Cooper went on: "Next, all managers, new and old, should ask themselves a question when asked to give a decision. *Am I the right person to make this decision?* Sometimes ego takes over when an office manager is asked, for example, whether a new sales brochure should be in colour or black and white, or which of three hotels to choose for the venue for the next conference. These decisions should be made by a marketing director, not a general office manager. His opinion may be sought, but the decision should not be his.

"In addition, the manager might not have the authority to make a decision, especially when high expenditure may result. But because it pleases his ego to do so, he may well give a decision which could lead to conflict subsequently, thus leading to further problems.

"To all managers I would say, ask yourself the question: *Have I the authority and knowledge to make a decision?* If not, don't.

"That's all for now," he said.

Nina was surprised. "I thought you were going to cover the car-park case study".

"We will," said Ryder, "but later. First we must continue to highlight more features of decision-making. It's your turn to take over, Nina."

Nina Westlake began, "I want to stress, for the umpteenth time, the emotional aspect. Most of those who offer solutions are keen to see them adopted. They know the choice they would make, and will try to influence the decision-maker to see their viewpoint – and only their viewpoint. They will slant opinions, facts, what have you, in that direction. They don't want a decision so much as a vindication of the option they have decided upon. Which leads me to my next point . . ."

As she was speaking, Ryder was appreciating the quality of her thinking. He heard Nina saying, "All managers must think an option through before coming to a decision. It's all very well to attempt to show quickness of mind, analytical ability, power, or strength of character by giving an instant decision, but why do it unless, for some reason, a decision must be made at that very moment? Most decisions should be delayed, and thought through.

"The decision-maker will meet subordinates and associates who will say something like this: 'If you don't decide now, we shan't be able to get delivery . . .', or 'We've got to sack him today or there'll be trouble . . .' All managers are faced, on occasion, with such decisions.

"*Never give way to them* is a good maxim. Estate agents have been using the fear close for years. There is hardly a house-buyer who is not urged to decide quickly, because someone else has made a good offer. Usually it's bluff, but it works almost every time, and it can be to the detriment of the buyer.

"Instant decisions do not always show someone's quick mind and authority, but often someone who lacks the experience of knowing that a quick decision can be a wrong decision.

"Having said that, I must add that there should always be a time limit for decision-making. It is no use explaining, 'I appreciate it's urgent. I'll let you know next month what I have decided'. If the person raising the issue believes it is urgent, then thought must be given to that decision immediately. A day or two should be enough to consider every fact and think the matter through."

Ryder thanked Nina, then asked Young to continue.

Young agreed, saying, "Every decision-maker should be cynical, difficult, argumentative, while seeking all the snags – snags which are not so obvious to those who are questioning the decision. Such people, be they subordinates or associates, will inevitably stress all the plus factors, and the decision-maker will often arouse resentment by asking pertinent questions to elicit the truth.

"The decision-maker must dig, dig, and dig again, to discover the snags, not because he or she wants to be difficult but because it is the only way to discover the answer. Too many decision-makers believe what they are told because it is the easiest way out, and don't dig deeply enough.

"May I refer to another basic – the *What if* technique – so rarely used now, although in all our teachings we repeat it over and over again.

"'It's bound to work well after all our research', the decision-maker is told. 'Our service department can handle it so easily; in any event, there won't be any breakdowns', or 'The managers are most agreeable to the move' are two other expressions of encouragement.

"Still the decision-maker must come back with, 'But *what if* service can't cope?', '*What if* some of the managers can't leave their homes because of the children's schooling, etc?', and continue with the *What ifs* right down the line."

After pausing to sip some water, he went on: "My next point is to warn you against a decision which may well lead to short-term profits but which, in the long term, may damage the company. A simple example would be to continue with a good selling unit, happy in the knowledge that high profits are being made, yet not considering what will happen when perhaps competitors infiltrate that market. The decision might well be a long-term one, of investing more in research and development.

"Thirdly, a manager must never be afraid to seek independent advice, which is not a sign of weakness, before arriving at a decision."

Young paused, and Ryder said, "I should like to give a case study which is allied to sport.

"Some years ago I was standing at the eighteenth green accompanied by one of the greatest golfers of all time, Henry Cotton. It was the final of the Captain's Cup. The finalists were all square at the seventeenth green, and at the eighteenth hole we watched the players from tee to green.

"On that green B was furthest away, but had an uphill putt. A was much nearer, but had a downhill putt. B, from the longer distance, took two putts, whereas A, from the shorter distance, playing downhill, found his ball ran well past the hole on the first putt, and he missed the return. So B won.

"I said to Henry Cotton, 'That was bad luck for A. He was much nearer the hole, missed his putt by a cat's whisker, and it ran 3 yards past.'

"Cotton replied, 'He didn't lose the game because of that missed putt. He lost because with his tee shot he aimed for the left-hand side of the fairway. It was the shortest way to the hole but there was rough to contend with. His ball finished in the rough, and it's difficult, if not impossible, to stop a ball dead on the green when playing from wet, rough grass. The ball therefore ran well past the hole, leaving a downhill putt – most difficult!' So A was punished, and lost the game, because he didn't think ahead. He didn't visualize what would happen from tee to green. If he had thought it through, he too would have taken the longer route, and been on the safe side. No, he didn't think it through."

"An excellent example," said Lewis. "I must remember that story."

Young said, "So will I."

Ryder laughed. "If I know our team, everyone will be using it! But we needn't make it a bone of contention now. Let's conclude the car-park study."

"Before we do," said Lewis, "may I raise another point?"

"Of course."

"If the decision demands that others undertake certain tasks, thought should be given to the ability of those others to carry out the decision. I remember a case where the decision was to buy another company — quite a small company. It was small because its management was poor. The decision was to buy, but the managing director who made that decision did not think through, or consider, who within his own team could move to that new company and take over the management. Actually there was no one available, and the acquisition proved a disaster."

Mary said, "Another example from me is that when a decision has been made, it must be communicated to whomever it may affect, however remotely concerned that person may be."

As no one else volunteered to add to the basics on decision-making, Ryder said, "So it's back to you, Nina. Will you now analyse the car-park case study, to show how it covers so many aspects of decision-making?"

Nina Westlake said, "A brief recap. The car-parking problem was caused by insufficient bays for the cars used by the work-force, the position being aggravated because many executives had reserved spaces which were often left vacant. The bad feeling caused had spin-off effects; although the work-force blamed management for a dismissal and a canteen problem, it was believed that the real problem was the *them and us* attitude adopted by management so far as car parking was concerned.

"Four solutions were put forward. I'll cover each of them, giving the pros and cons, while bringing out basic lessons in decision-making.

"The first decision was offered by the works committee, a committee elected by the work-force. The work-force was not union-minded and, if possible, preferred to settle matters through the works committee. Its solution was the obvious one: to build extra parking facilities on adjacent land. But what if that land were later needed for expansion? There was no other land available.

"Now we come to a decision-making lesson. Cost risk analysis is sometimes overlooked when decision-making.

"Building consultants, who were called in, studied the nature of the soil, and advised that before a foundation of any kind could be laid the soil would have to be dug out and replaced. This was on the assumption that there might later be a factory extension in place of a car park. But even cars themselves would cause subsidence, unless this work was carried out. The cost was high, which didn't bother the works committee, which believed that its solution to the problem was still sensible.

"The financial director was right against that solution. The cost was too high, but if it were possible to put a cash value on a dissatisfied work-force, would the risk in the long run be greater than money spent?"

Nina paused, then went on: "In cost risk analysis the first action to be taken should be to list both the benefits which might accrue from the expenditure and all the risks.

"The risks included the company being forced to build a factory elsewhere if there were no more space available, and, if a factory was eventually built on the site, greater dissatisfaction from the work-force at their car-parking facilities being taken away from them.

"We, as consultants, agreed with the financial director that this was not the right solution. Although temporarily pleasing the work force, it would be a bad management decision. The costs were too high, and the risks too great."

Nina paused again to sip water, before continuing: "I want to stress cost risk analysis, by giving another case study."

Ryder said, "Nina, you've made your point. Let us follow our own teaching in our Training the Trainer course. One case study or a proof story is sufficient. When a case has been made, there is no need for back-up stories. I'm sure you'll agree."

Nina, feeling extremely annoyed, did not agree, but nodded her head.

Ryder said, "To repeat, the first option was to consider building a new car park, but the costs did not justify the future risks. Carry on please, Nina, with the second option."

Nina, feeling even more annoyed than before, said tartly, "Thank you, Greg. The second option was suggested by the managing director, a share and share alike solution. No reservation spaces for anyone.

"Now comes another lesson in decision-making: contingency planning. What action can be taken if a decision is made to cover possible contingencies?

"An example was the miners' strike of 1984. The contingency planning to help in later decisions was bigger coal stocks, and use to be made of the nationwide co-operation between police forces, instead of just using the local police force.

"The contingencies arose, and they were successfully overcome because of the decisions made in advance.

"All decision-makers therefore should consider what contingency actions should be taken if their decision proves to be wrong, or partly wrong, or even if something occurs for which there could be no exact planning in advance.

"Contingency planning was essential if the managing director's solution was adopted. While his plan would please the work-force temporarily, it could lead to a highly dissatisfied managerial staff, unable to find parking space when they had to carry out priority tasks. We concluded that no contingency plans could be made to satisfy management need.

"The financial director, however, agreed with the managing director's views. As a cost-conscious person, he realized that the plan would cost nothing, and he could not put a figure on the cost of future dissatisfaction. Furthermore, he did not use a car. His wife drove him to work and collected him every evening – another case of emotion affecting decision-making.

"The managing director suggested a contingency plan. The commissionaire would be instructed to drive the managers' cars which could not be parked to a garage some 3 miles away, and take taxis back. The snag was that in the evenings it was very difficult to get taxis.

"Then the third solution was put forward by the works director, who had a reserved parking space. To remind you, it was the planned sharing of cars, organized by one of the company's administrators.

"There was a general feeling that this was the best of the options. We argued that it would be difficult to have contingency plans for such an arrangement. If a car-owner were taken ill one morning, those waiting at the pick-up point could go on waiting and waiting. Would they then be reprimanded for their late arrival at the factory? Car-owners would also expect passengers to share the expenses. There could be problems with insurance. How long should a car owner be expected to wait for anyone?

"We believed that this solution would be only partly successful, and the *them and us* syndrome would still be of concern to the work-force.

"The fourth solution, to hire coaches, was put forward by the chief buyer. It would be a costly exercise, but not nearly so costly as providing an additional parking area.

"It is a strange fact of life that people who will be late when being picked up by an associate will always try their best to be on time when the pick-up is by coach.

"This solution appealed to everyone except the financial director, who, again objected to the cost. Although a charge could be made for using the coaches, that charge would nowhere near cover the costs. There was also the risk of those who were not picked up by coach believing that the others were receiving a perk, and that they should have some reward for making their own way to the factory."

Ryder interrupted. "I know that you, Nina, came up with the ideal solution."

Nina blushed slightly. "That isn't strictly true. We had a brainstorming session that included the works committee, the main directors, and several managers. Options were discussed

222 *The New Manager*

and eventually there was complete agreement that the solution was number four. Again, the financial director was concerned about the costs, but it was Henry James, a steel worker, who said jokingly, 'If I were the boss, I'd buy up the coach company'. It's true that I took that up immediately and accumulated all the facts relative to a possible purchase.

"The coach was owned by quite a small company, which used six coaches altogether and made a profit. The coaches were hired out for weddings, holiday outings, parties, etc. and the profits from the company would more than cover the cost of transport, over and above the subsidy – even when the capital and the loss of interest from investm ents because of the purchase were taken into account.

That's the way it was organized. There would be a monthly draw for car-parking spaces, but the managers would still retain their rights to their own spaces. It was pointed out to the workers that without good management there could not be a successful company; and good management meant arriving at the works and departing from the works at various times, in order to meet the requirements of customers.

"A charge was made for using the coach, equivalent to a bus or train fare, to stop criticism from those who walked to the factory.

"The result – everyone happy. Car-users found that there was usually space available for them, others preferred travelling by coach and leaving their cars at home, and the company had a profit-making subsidiary in coach hire."

There was applause when Nina finished, which she acknowledged with a bob of her head and a smile.

Ryder said, "Now that's enough about problem-solving and decision-making. We've covered the ground adequately. There will, as always, be a brief summary at the conclusion session. I've made some notes. Here is the summary:

- One, the cause of a problem must be found before a decision can be reached.
- Two, alternative solutions to problems are always

provided by those other than decision-makers – engineers, office staff, research personnel, computer technicians, right down to the assistant handyman who believes he knows the reason why the plumbing is not working efficiently. The handyman doesn't make any decisions, but he does provide the evidence to back up the solution. Computers can provide so much information, and can even help in solving problems, but usually it is the decision-maker who has to make the final decision.

- Three, always obtain as many credible alternative solutions as possible, as we cannot accurately predict the future.
- Four, emotional intrusion is the greatest problem in decision-making, and this can lead to countless wrong decisions.
- Five, make contingency plans.
- Six, demand facts, not opinions.
- Seven, *what if.* Remember the sentence, *You may be right, but what if . . .?*
- Eight, don't make a quick decision unless you have prepared yourself for an 'apparent' quick decision, but never procrastinate. If you have all the information you require, you should not need more than 24 hours to come to your decision.
- Nine, *evaluate the risks.* Begin by asking the question: *What would happen at the very worst?* Remember, risk-taking can also be gambling. If a risk could lead either to riches or bankruptcy, that risk should not be taken. Calculated risks are being taken all the time, but always carry out risk analysis first. Think of the risks in terms of your product, your customers, the people who work with you and for you, and the company image.
- Ten, *think through.* Thinking through is very similar to the *what if* technique, but it entails going even deeper into problems which could arise in the future.
- Eleven, always communicate your decisions to everyone

who may be even remotely interested. Consider how others may react to your decisions.

"And that," said Ryder, "is definitely the conclusion of this session."

19   Staff Training

Awaiting the arrival of Greg Ryder on the Thursday morning, the team was much more relaxed than on previous occasions. The reason was the knowledge that on the following day George Young was confronting Ryder. Then Ryder's secretary arrived, looking most unlike her usual, calm self. "I'm so sorry," she said hurriedly, "I should have been here earlier, but I was held up . . ."

"That's all right," interrupted Young, "what's the problem?"

"It's Mr Ryder" − there was no Greg from her − "he's received a telephone call changing an important appointment from Friday to today. The call only came through about 8.50."

"What's so urgent?" asked Mary.

"I can't say."

"Then I'll tell you." Mary replied. "You know every one of Mr Ryder's appointments; therefore you know that he had an appointment with his cardiologist on Friday. I presume that's the one which has been brought forward?"

"Well − yes." Ryder's secretary hated to commit herself even when she knew that the others realized what was happening.

Young said, "You haven't divulged anything that we didn't already know. All I'm concerned about is whether or not he has been taken ill."

"Oh no. Mr Bartlett-Smith telephoned to say that he had to be away from home on Friday to attend a consultation outside London. He wanted to change the appointment to today by cancelling Friday's appointments. Mr Ryder was only too pleased to agree and left immediately. He's driven into town and hopes to be back later today, but he'll join you tomorrow morning. In the meantime he asked me to suggest that you carry on with today's sessions without him." She hurried away before any more questions could be asked of her.

Nina said, "I wonder what the truth is. It seems a bit unusual to me for a specialist of such eminence to have to change appointments. Do you think Greg has had an overnight scare or something?"

"No," said Young, "accept the obvious. Mr Bartlett-Smith did have an out-of-town meeting with other consultants. It often happens with leading surgeons in these days of transplants."

After further discussions which led nowhere, Young finally said, "We're going round in circles. Concentrate on this morning's sessions on staff training. After lunch we'll cover creativity and situation-adaptable management, and finish by teatime, so that if Greg arrives early we can meet him this evening. We can keep to this timetable if we give outlines for each session. Who'll begin?"

The cry of "You" was unanimous, followed by Mary remarking, "You do supervise most of the staff training here."

Young replied, "No. While I have organized training, it has mainly been a matter of delegation. Others have structured the training for individuals, often on a one-to-one basis, while I have organized standard courses. You, Nina, when you were a full-time consultant before moving over to training, carried out several assignments on staff training. You therefore are more widely experienced than I, so you will conduct this session." He smiled impishly and said, "That's an order!"

"Yes sir, certainly sir," Nina responded, and as the laughter died down, she began the session.

"Other than opening the courses, it is usually a departmental manager who either carries out the act of training himself, or delegates that duty to a trustworthy subordinate. A telephone receptionist would train a new recruit for that department, the secretary may initially train typists, although not in typing but in the general nature of her work. A garage hand may advise newcomers, a bank clerk keeps an eye on the beginner at the next till, and so on. Provided guidelines are given and those who undertake the task of training are themselves trained, the staff training will be a success. If not, it could fail.

"If new staff are left to pick it all up as they go along, they may succeed in the end, but on the journey towards that success, many mistakes can have been made. Training is designed to obviate those mistakes."

Peter Lewis interrupted. "How right you are, Nina! Too often the star salesman is the one directed to train newcomers, and what does he do? He attempts to train them in his own image, and maybe his image cannot be copied. He may have a style of his own, one not generally adaptable to other people. One of the surest ways to fail is to allow unsuitable people, uninterested people, or even reluctant people to train others. Sorry for the interruption, Nina."

"Life wouldn't be the same if you never interrupted, Peter," she said. "You can't keep a good salesman down. However, on we go, interruptions or not.

"A supervisor is the person most likely to handle training, but has he the time to train others? If he or she is under pressure, training may well be undertaken, but it will certainly take second place to other routine tasks. The supervisor's manager must make sure that the subordinate does have time to carry out effective training. The supervisor delegated to training others will first impress on the trainee the importance of the work to be done – whether the trainee is a filing clerk, a

sweeper on the factory floor, or a management controller —
otherwise the trainee may feel he or she is just a cog in a big
wheel. It should be explained that every small routine task
must be carried out satisfactorily and in an orderly manner, or
else the whole cannot function effectively. Every aspect of
work, whether it be strategic planning or the manufacturing
process, is made up of many tiny parts, each most important in
itself.

"The only way to teach beginners is little by little, step by
step, move by move — and that is not overstating the case.
Never attempt to teach the whole concept in perhaps a 1-hour
session.

"With a telephone receptionist, for example, on the
assumption that the quality of her voice has been checked at
the interview, the first step obviously will be the job
specification, so that the newcomer will know exactly what is
expected, and the trainer will know his objectives. Next, the
newcomer must gain a complete company departmental
knowledge, coupled with the names of executives and those
most often likely to receive telephone calls. The receptionist
will be given a printed list, but will strive to memorize the
names of those to be contacted when an incoming call is
received. A continual study of the list will automatically bring
this about. Speed of response is all-important to the telephone
receptionist.

"Often when telephoning even a well known and efficient
company, the response is 'Hold on', and this seems to go on for
ever. Then, when contact is finally made, the wrong person is
found to be at the other end of the line.

"Recently I wanted to make enquiries about certain aspects
of a car telephone. I was actually put through to seven
different people before finally making the right contact — and
this general knowledge factor is so often overlooked by
supervisors giving training. However, if there are many
departments to cover, even this step should be broken down
into perhaps four stages, rather than attempt to overload the
mind of the new receptionist by asking her to memorize some

fifty or sixty functions. No further training should be given until these first few steps have been mastered, and this may take several days.

"The next step is for the receptionist to acquire a full understanding of the switchboard, if it is new to him or her. There should be no move from this step until the supervisor is satisfied that the new receptionist's reactions to whatever signalling system is used is instantaneous.

"When the supervisor is confident that the receptionist is handling the switchboard effectively, then a check must be made as to the trainee's skills as a telephone receptionist. I won't go into details, as this is not a telephone receptionist's course, only an example of step-by-step teaching. But during the first 4 weeks there should be continual monitoring by the supervisor. There can be as many as twenty steps in teaching someone to become a highly efficient telephone receptionist: method of greeting, handling difficult customers, keeping calm, etc. If possible, always allow the trainee to practise what has been learned, step by step, before progressing.

"The emphasis, however, must be on training the trainer in this step-by-step method. It isn't good enough for a supervisor to delegate the job to someone who may be an efficient operator but not a patient trainer. Often when a newcomer arrives, a supervisor will say, 'Jean, this is Mary. She has a first-class background. I'm sure you will be able to put her in the picture', and leave it at that. It may be the same in a workshop, when the words used might be, 'Bert, this is Henry, our new mechanic. Show him the ropes, will you?'

"This is a certain way to perpetuate inefficiency and customer dissatisfaction.

"Obviously such tasks have to be delegated on occasion, but there cannot be delegation without responsibility. The supervisor who delegates must still maintain control, and be certain that the Jeans and the Berts have first been trained in training others. The person handed the task must be given, if not a training manual, then certainly a list of all the points that the newcomer must be taught before being able to tackle his or her task efficiently."

Nina paused for a drink, then went on: "Whatever the task may be, the basis of training must be an analysis of (a) what that person already knows, and (b) what that person is required to know.

"Underlying the training there must always be confidence building. The supervisor must never be anyone who is even slightly antagonistic towards the employers, otherwise the newcomer is likely to be hearing such statements as 'You mustn't take any notice of him', or 'She does go on a bit, doesn't she — just do it your way.'

"The newcomer wants to know that he or she is working for a first-class, caring organization, and that the job is of importance. Oh yes," Nina went on as an afterthought, "if there is a machine to be used — a typewriter, computer, duplicator, or photocopier — the trainer must ensure that before any training commences, the machine is operating satisfactorily. If this check is not made, often the training will be ruined because of the time taken to put the machine right, and the operator's confidence will be sapped."

Nina daintily selected a paper handkerchief from her bag, more as a form of ritual than necessity, and said, "I have referred to the trainee's previous knowledge and experience. This is a reminder to all supervisors that it is not good enough to judge purely on an interviewer's report. Statements made at interviews may not be strictly accurate. Another aspect of training is that the newcomer's personality and character should be evaluated, to some extent, while the training is taking place. Is he or she the nervous type, a quick learner, bombastic, aggressive, perhaps a know-all? Instant decisions must not be made because sometimes these characteristics only show up under stress, and there is always stress in a learning situation. A trainee may agree that a task is fully understood, which may not be true. It may be that he or she feels that it is a sign of weakness to admit 'I still don't understand'.

"Anyone who has tried to use a word processor for the first

time by studying the training manual will know the difficulties, and will also know how easy it is to tell a supervisor, 'Yes, I understand', when in fact there is no understanding.

"If a clerical worker is to be trained, there should be some examination to ensure that the person understands all the forms which have to be completed, reports annotated, and procedures carried out. Again, the trainer must never ridicule forms, no matter how much he dislikes them. Saying 'You needn't bother too much about this one' will lead to the trainee not bothering at all.

"In the retail trade one-to-one training is essential, even though the company may operate a standard procedure course. The newcomer to a cash till, for example, does need the trainer by his or her side. Most of us at some time have arrived at a cash till to be met with the cashier ringing a bell to attract the attention of the manager. She doesn't perhaps know how to complete a transaction or how to fill out a credit card form."

Lewis broke in. "The problem is always the time factor. In a busy office or factory no one ever seems to be able to find the time to help others. In a busy shop, assistants can become annoyed when asked by a newcomer for advice. Advice, however, should never have to be sought if the training is effective. In a department run by a highly efficient manager time will always be found for training. If staff cannot be available for such training, then the manager himself must carry out the tasks. Staff training is a number one priority if there is to be customer satisfaction."

Young said, "May I come in now?" Not waiting for a reply, he continued: "As you all know, I'm a fairly slow talker. I won't mention the names of those here whose speed of speech is something to be marvelled at. All who train, whether from a platform, sitting beside a newcomer in office, shop, or factory, or overlooking the work of a mechanic, must ask themselves the question: *Am I going too fast to enable the newcomer to retain knowledge?*

"May I suggest that the emphasis must be on slowing things down? Probably the worst feature of the speed merchants is that they believe they are being understood, and do not subsequently carry out tests. In my opinion the secret of successful training is to keep questioning the trainee to ensure that the teaching messages are being understood; and in order to enhance the chances of those messages being understood, the quality of voice, and the slowness of enunciation are the roads to success."

Cooper said, "I agree with you, and I'd like to add a point: too many trainers are too happy operating the machines themselves, like fathers with their children's toys. A trainer must give trainees continual opportunities to prove to themselves that they understand the intricacies of the machines."

Mary said, "I think it must be my turn now, as we all seem to be joining in. I want to refer back to our session on human relations. So much depends on the trainer's personality. No trainer should be appointed on a one-to-one basis if he is apt to shout, remonstrate, shrug his shoulders, implying that the trainee is a moron, or look appealingly at a colleague, conveying the impression that the task is far beyond the ability of the trainee to grasp. The word for all trainers to remember, whether they be on a platform, or supervising in shop, office, or factory, is *patience*. Without patience there can be no successful training.

Trainees also need encouragement, something they don't sometimes receive, because the wrong person has been appointed to train them. Too often they are thinking of their own problems, instead of the trainee. Shall I go on?" Mary looked at Nina.

"Why not? I'm going to sum up in a minute anyway."

Mary continued: "A trainer must make the trainee feel he or she belongs to the department, division, area or shop, and able to play their part in its success."

Nina interrupted. "Of course, finally, we all agree that trainers must always be congratulated when they have carried out their task in a satisfactory manner. That covers most of the ground. Can you add anything, George?"

"Not really," Young answered. "You mentioned that you will be summarizing. That's fair enough.

"However, perhaps there is one aspect of training that we haven't tackled, and that is jargon. In every organization, and especially of course in the electronic, engineering or scientific field, there is the trade jargon. Words which are used continually should be readily understood by a newcomer.

"Typical would be the typist, who has to type from a recording on which the manager has indulged in one of his favourite pastimes – using the technical phrases he knows so well to bamboozle others who may not be so well informed.

"One up for him! In the initial stages therefore may I suggest that where necessary a list of such jargon be provided for the newcomer, with the meaning of each word used alongside the word, phrase, or sentence."

"Sorry," said Lewis, "I must come in again now. We're all doing our usual interrupting act, aren't we?

"Throughout this session the need for asking questions must be mentioned to make sure that the trainee has understood the point or points being made. May I repeat what was said at an earlier session, that the closed question should be avoided.

"The open question technique is much more useful. For example:

- Tell me how you operate the plus and minus keys.
- Would you like to explain the techniques we use for sending out reminders when payments are due?
- What is the procedure for follow-up letters after enquiries?
- Explain how you would remove the binding . . .

Nina said, "We'll never get finished, never achieve our objective, unless we keep to our timetable. May I now sum up, so that we'll be on time for our final session after tea?

"Here's my checklist for training the trainer:

- One, prepare carefully.
- Two, put the trainee at ease.
- Three, explain how the trainee's task is part of the whole company plan.
- Four, explain the importance of the task.
- Five, go carefully through the job specification with the trainee, and agree each point.
- Six, teach section by section, step by step.
- Seven, teach in a logical sequence.
- Eight, talk slowly.
- Nine, emphasize the key points.
- Ten, prepare an information sheet relating to trade jargon.
- Eleven, build up the trainee's confidence in the company.
- Twelve, show interest in the trainee's private life.
- Thirteen, ask questions continually – open questions, whenever possible.
- Fourteen, ensure that all equipment to be used is in order.
- Fifteen, do not criticize.
- Sixteen, be patient.
- Seventeen, do not show boredom.
- Eighteen, give praise and encouragement, and this includes talking about opportunities for advancement which are open to the trainee.
- Nineteen, make certain the trainee reaches a high standard of performance; and even then, for the first week or so, make continual checks, rather than wait for mistakes to be made. The phrase 'Not bad for a beginner' is not good enough – it doesn't motivate.
- Twenty, be appreciative of the work being carried out by the trainee, when he or she is obviously trying very hard.
- Twenty-one, of great importance is to allow the trainee to learn by doing, rather than listening, although listening

will obviously have to take place before there can be
action.

Nina stopped, and Young had the last word. "To quote
Greg, we've made our case – let it rest at that."

20 Creativity

The lunch break was short. Everyone had been anxious to complete the final session that day, so as to leave Friday clear for the dénouement − as Nina had termed the agonizing over their future.

Again Young opened the session, saying, "I'm not certain that creativity can be taught."

Mary immediately interrupted. "That's not like you, George, it's more in line with someone on the verge of retirement, someone who has lost interest in what can be achieved by those who are enthusiastically willing to learn. You're not that someone, George. Your eyes light up at every suggestion that there might be a new concept in the office.

"Obviously some people are more creative than others, but all too many people can only associate the word creativity with the work of great writers, musicians and painters. We are considering creativity as it applies to a manager − how a new concept may improve the running of a department when the employees in that department are so rutbound that their heads rarely reach the top of the ruts.

"An eminent psychologist wrote in some magazine or other that we had a million − or was it a billion? − anyway, a very

236

large number of braincells, and we use only a fraction of them. He claims that if we exercised those redundant cells we could all be more creative. So let's start from there."

"Agreed," said Young. "I'd like to learn more about creativity myself, because you can't kid me, and I can't kid myself. I don't class myself as a creative person. But you're right, Mary, I do delight in the creativity of others."

Lewis said, "I should like to make the point that every manager should encourage, and be delighted in, the creativity of others. This is so often not the case. The creative ideas of subordinates need nurturing, or they will be lost amongst the thousands of unused ideas.

"The standard response, 'We did it before and it didn't work', can be a killer. On occasion, naturally, it may be the correct retort, but then proof should be given and a request made as to how the concept would be treated differently from before."

"Thank you," said George, half suppressing a smile at the inevitable interruption by the marketing director. Then he added, "Over to you then, Mary, to tell us how we can be more creative."

Mary's response was, "No, I'm going to ask Peter to continue. He's our most creative director. He's designed and written sales brochures, direct mail letters, exhibits for exhibitions, and has also helped many of our clients with their productivity problems. If any of us want advertisement copy written we always go to Peter. Rarely a week passes without him having a flash of inspiration." She paused, then with a perplexed look continued, "Isn't it strange, we run so many courses, and we have never included creativity and innovation in any of them. I wonder why?"

Young said, "Possibly because we ourselves work for a most creative organization and a most creative leader. We have initiated more new concepts in the training field than the rest of our competitors put together. In the industrial area our consultants have created so many ideas for improving relationships in work-forces, of instigating profit-sharing schemes, and novel ways of cutting production costs . . .

"Others in our field copy us – that we all know. In doing so, possibly they think themselves creative. They are not! They are plagiarists. It isn't being creative to copy others, but it is being creative to study the work of others and then seek improvements. It is seeking such improvements which needs creative skills, and – I've lost the point I was going to make."

Mary reminded him. "I suggested that Peter is our creative star, and then asked the question why we have not included creativity as a session in our courses."

Young scratched his chin. "Oh yes, that was it. We weren't being creative enough, were we? Now perhaps we can put that right."

Mary smiled. "That bit of decision-making is worthy of our dear Greg Ryder."

"Not so dear!" mumbled Nina, but no one commented.

Young continued, "I agree about your creativity, Peter. I suppose one has to be in marketing – so on you go."

Lewis began. "I believe that all of us in business can be creative within our own spheres of activity. Unfortunately there are too many people who, when set a difficult task which needs creative thinking, give up too quickly. There are others whose creativity consists of trying to discover easy ways of doing a job, when the easy way is not always the right way.

"The Eureka syndrome was OK for Archimedes, but it's not so available to modern business. We often have to plod our way towards a creative thought.

"Creative thinking begins with an appreciation of basics. For example, the basic principle when trying to create a job advertisement which will bring in applications from those with outstanding merit is to consider their point of view when they are reading such an advertisement, and to play down the company's viewpoint.

"Glance at a selection of advertisements these days and you will find that few copywriters show any sign of creative thinking. It is always 'I want this', 'I want that', 'We demand this', 'Are you qualified to join our star team?' etc. when of course the advertisement should be full of *you* appeal. '*You* will want', '*You* are seeking', '*You* will need', '*You* will know', – and the confidence builders, so far as the company is concerned, need only be the close to bring in the response.

"Anyone therefore who wants to be a creative copywriter of advertisements can only achieve this result by studying advertisements for days on end, and analysing the good and the bad. From this basic action, creativity will emerge. It's as simple as that!

"I'll guarantee that anyone with average intelligence will produce outstandingly good advertisements merely by practice, and practice, and practice. Creativity stems from a study of the work of others and then, as was said earlier, improving upon that work. If you take the field of writing, many people have said 'I'd like to write' but few ever make the effort. If a manager can communicate by the spoken word – and if he can't, then he is not an effective manager – he will be able to write effectively – yes, a letter, or even a book. Of course if that manager never reads other people's books, he cannot gain the experience to write himself. The emphasis again is on working hard at being creative.

"Instead of saying 'I wish I could be creative like you', think positively, and think to yourself, 'I can easily learn to be more creative, especially in the sphere of business, by, for example, looking more carefully at TV advertisements; and not then exclaiming, 'What the Hell is that all about?' but trying to discover what the objective of the advertisement was and how it could be improved.

"The problem in the advertising and design fields, as we know, is that too many creative people create for other creative people – their associates, their competitors – and forget about their customers' requirements. When next you watch a TV commercial, ask the questions, 'Does it sell?', 'Does it persuade you to change from one product to another?', and, even, 'Was it worth the cost?'

"Such thinking leads to creativity.

"To change the emphasis for a moment, however – and I

must remind myself that I am addressing new managers — creative thinking must be allied to cost-effectiveness. Every chief executive knows the upsets and hurts caused by a lukewarm reaction to some new concept, which, in itself, does indicate creative thinking but would cost too much to put into practice.

"In business, creative thinking must be assessed against all possible costs, as well as risks. How many films have failed, not because of lack of creative thinking but because the cost has eventually been too high to bring about that film's profitability. So remember that you, as managers, have to work very hard to be creative, but the effort is always well worthwhile. You will set yourself aside as a person to be watched and promoted.

"So few will make the effort to be creative; in spite of the demands on your time, you must read more, both textbooks and autobiographies by successful people. Remember that unless some indications, suggestions, thoughts, are programmed into the mind as if into a computer, no new ideas can emerge. Ideas, inspirations, don't arrive by sitting at a desk each day for 1 hour devoted to thinking time. This is sometimes suggested at time-management courses, and it is academic nonsense. The mind doesn't work that way. A creative idea can originate while you are watching television, driving the car, or walking the dog."

Peter hesitated, then asked, "Is that enough?"

Cooper replied, "No, we need a case study or two."

"Right," said Lewis, "then let Nina, our professional psychologist, give some case studies."

Nina responded. "Very well, but first let me continue on your theme, Peter, because at a course we shall get the inevitable answer when we suggest that managers should not only read more books, but certainly more business magazines and financial papers — 'I haven't the time'.

"We have covered this ground once, but let's go over it again. There are few people busier than Greg. He is not only deeply concerned in every aspect of our organization, but also serves on several government and charitable committees, yet he finds the time to read not only the British magazines on management but also those published in the USA. We all know this is true, because we are continually receiving clippings from such journals, annotated with suggestions for us to take action.

"We shall remind delegates of the time-management session, emphasizing again that possibly the biggest time-waster is that mostly we all do what we want to do, then try to justify ourselves for the time-wasting activity. Most managers can save an hour a day by following the rules of time-management. The old adage, *If you want a job done, ask a busy person*, is true. Why? Because usually the busy person is well organized and therefore can always find time. It is the disorganized person, whether it be a housewife or a road sweeper, whether it be a doctor or managing director, who can never find the time to help others to complete a task, or simply to read trade journals."

Young, thinking of a Ryder action, politely murmured, "Nina, we mustn't keep repeating sections of previous sessions."

"Sorry," apologized Nina, "you're right. But we all keep doing it, and reminders do help the learning process." Then, before Young could respond, she turned to Lewis and said, "I can't think of any applicable case studies, Peter."

"OK," said Lewis, "then I'll suggest some ways in which one can think creatively. The first is the rule of opposites. Activities, as well as designs and advertising formulas, reflect the fashion of the times. To increase creativity in whatever sphere always consider opposites. If the fashion is for angles, think of straight lines. If a catchphrase is popular, think of the opposite to the catchphrase. If a product is large, think about making one smaller – or vice versa. I'll give you a case study which I shall take straight from Greg Ryder's book of reminiscences. It hasn't been published yet, but it will be one day, and all his stories that we know so well will be included. This is how he used the rules of opposites:

"When he first decided to enter the training field, his company was small but an efficient marketing consultancy. There was a demand for training from his consultants, and therefore the decision was really made for him. He decided to visit the USA at that time the home of sales training. While there, he attended several courses, conferences and launches. It was the razamatazz era. The course would often open with an instructor first taking off his jacket, undoing his tie, then unbuttoning the top button of his shirt, and finally whisking away the tie. This style was adopted by nine out of ten instructors, supposedly to bring about a rapport with the audience – they would not feel uncomfortable if they took similar action.

"Greg also told us that in many courses the day started with a rousing song, and instructors believed that enthusiasm was engendered by such demands from the salesmen as 'Go out and get 'em!', 'Over the top and at 'em!', 'Fight, fight, and fight again!', as if they were engaged in a battle with their customers.

"Instructors ranted, instead of speaking quietly, concisely and effectively. There were the inevitable dancing girls when a new product was launched, leading to the audience concentrating their thoughts more on the girls than the product.

"When Greg returned to London he used the 'opposites' formula. His instructors wore dark suits and white shirts, and no jackets were to be removed. There would be no visual aids which would distract from the lessons. His instructors would teach selling as *the gentle art of giving other people your own way*. Then he introduced conversational selling, which has proved to be so successful, and has been copied by almost every training organization in the world.

"I shall tell the new managers that Greg Ryder believed that by using the 'opposite' technique he laid the foundations of the great success of our organization.

"Incidentally, if there are any budding journalists among you who would like to write for newspapers or magazines in your spare time, you will never succeed unless you use the rule of 'opposites'. The old saying that dog bites man is no use but man bites dog is news and is the basis of journalism.

"The next lesson in creative thinking is to forget all logical thoughts and think illogically. Fantasize, dream, think of the impossible, consider sheer nonsense, and from this nonsense thinking and fantasizing and dreaming, creative thoughts could evolve.

"All of us fantasize now and again. Instead of fantasizing about some dream holiday, fantasize about problems which need creative thinking to solve. If you are a sales manager, go beyond the circle, beyond the usual means of covering a territory. Is there any way? Dropping in by helicopter? Quite foolish, but an aerial view of the territory might give you a new concept.

"If you are a service manager, how can your service engineers help to obtain more business for you? Turn them into brilliant salesmen? We know that is rarely possible, but from somewhere in there a successful concept could emerge.

"There are few people willing to make these efforts to be more creative. As I said earlier, when a new manager does make the effort, it sets him aside immediately – above the others. But the manager must be prepared for rejections. Even successful creative authors sometimes have their books turned down. What do they do? They set to, and get to work on another book, or they try to put the first one right.

"In marketing, creativity can come about by studying our competitors – not to belittle them, not to write them off as of no consequence, but to discover how they win orders from us. Let the mind wander to create ideas, to improve upon those competitors' brochures, advertising, designs, products . . .

"You, as new managers, may think this is far beyond your job specification. You are not in marketing, perhaps you are an office manager. But the same rules operate. You have to think creatively on many occasions. Do please always remember that it is far better to put forward a stream of new ideas, the majority of which are turned down, than not to put forward any ideas at all.

"There it is," concluded Lewis, "my final plea for more creativity in management."

"Excellent!" said Cooper. "May I raise a point?"

Lewis said, "Philip, you have a way of saying excellent which seems to imply not too bad but I could have done better."

"Not at all," said Cooper. "I'm engrossed at the moment in thinking creatively about our accounts department. It seems to me that all my subordinates relate creativity to buying more and more computers; and that, as was said earlier, can be expensive without being creative. Have I made my point?"

Nina waited to hear if there were any other comments, then said, "May I suggest that those with rigid minds try to break the pattern, and those with closed minds open them up? Possibly that comes under the heading of useless advice. No one can really change the thoughts of such people. Fanatics, for example, never break away from their fanaticism, so forget that suggestion. In passing, however, it could be mentioned that the average manager who comes here for a course is willing to learn and will perhaps attempt to be not quite so set in his thinking in the future."

Looking slightly apologetic, Nina went on: "I have the feeling that I'm meandering, so let me sum up some of the points we have made so far:

- One, always think of change. What can be changed for the better? That should be the start of creative thinking.
- Two, forsake the obvious for the different.
- Three, don't always try to conform. Think of opposites.
- Four, ask if there is another way.
- Five, it is creative to discard that which is out of date for that which is more fashionable, particularly with regard to a range of products. No one ever likes to take anything out of a range, and can always put forward reasons why it must be remain. The creative manager must be adamant, otherwise, as so often happens, he will end up with an

obsolete range, ready to be taken apart by competitors. The creative person is always seeking to improve, and once that improvement has been effected, he is not satisfied but wants to continue improving.

- Six, pierce the circle. Try to think beyond the normal constraints.
- Seven, listen and listen intently, during discussions, to those who have a specialized knowledge or those who have greater experience than your own. Listen – don't interrupt, don't force your views on them, whatever position you may hold – and from that listening creative thoughts may emerge.
- Eight, about once every 3 months organize brainstorming sessions – these to include all members of the departments, from the most junior to the experienced manager.

Nina paused for breath, then went on: "I'm talked out. So now it's back to you, Peter, to close the session with an example of your own creative efforts."

Lewis nodded his agreement. He was never averse to talking about his own past success. He said, "I'll describe the thought processes which led to the production of a cover for one of our most successful leaflets; and also the compiling of a direct mail letter which, in its own way, was equally successful.

"All outside covers of leaflets or brochures should be designed to sell – to sell an idea, to sell confidence, to sell quality. We, as you know, decided to produce a leaflet that would emphasize the high quality of our training. We all decided that the front page should contain drawings, pictures or designs to highlight quality, and the word quality should be used. Most dynamic organizations seek quality in every aspect of their company – it is the 'in' word. Books on quality control pour forth from publishers. In the press there are regular advertisements for quality controllers. Managing directors extol the quality of their organization at annual meetings, there is quality in customer care . . . However, as we said earlier, one must be aware of bandwagons, because everyone is getting on to the quality bandwagon, and emphasizing their belief in quality. I felt that we had to move one step ahead.

"Thought process number one: think carefully before going along with the crowd.

"What would be the next in words following excellence and quality? I studied my thesaurus, and one word consolidated my thinking, *perfection,* a word not used extensively in leaflets, advertisements, etc., for it seems too wide a claim to make. But why shouldn't there be perfection in a business environment, as there is in the arts? My mind then circled the world, seeking perfection – a dream stage in creativity. My mind's roving stopped in India, visualizing the Taj Mahal; then in Paris, glorying in Leonardo da Vinci's 'Mona Lisa'. Rodin's marvellous statue of 'The Thinker' came to my mind, and, coming right home, Rolls Royce always means perfection in motoring.

"The front page of that leaflet almost designed itself – reproductions of these great creations.

"There was no caption. Anyone even glancing at the cover would be held by the image of perfection. The only words on the front cover, below the reproductions, were *We too are perfectionists in training.*"

Lewis looked around at his companions, smiled, and said, "That case study isn't new to you, but it will be to the delegates. I suggest we show them the leaflet."

Young said, "It was a brilliant concept, as we all agreed at the time. That's why we didn't applaud you just now. Of course we must show the finished product. Please carry on, Peter."

Lewis said, "This example of creativity is designed to show that the creative thinker must try to move ahead of a fashion. There are far too many average thinkers who believe that when they use an 'in' phrase they are up to date, modern, knowledgeable, and dynamic.

"Next time you want to create a new environment, a different schedule, a change in production, begin by thinking of one word to sum up your objective, and then seek a more descriptive word. Possibly that will set off a train of thought, and creative ideas will flash across the brain cells. Not quite 'Eureka' but very near it."

Although the directors had all heard the story of that perfect cover many times, they were still enthralled with Peter's enthusiasm and delight in explaining how the leaflet had been created. Peter also had the valuable asset of any instructor, that all those listening felt he was talking directly to them rather than to a group.

Lewis continued: "My next example of creative thinking concerns the direct mail letter designed to arouse interest in our Negotiating Course. Our previous DMA shot had not been too successful, but that's why we always have test campaigns.

"Greg asked me to be more original. Step one as always, when trying to compile or design a direct mail shot, is to think as the recipient will think on opening the envelope or seeing the letter on the in-tray. He or she undoubtedly receives many mail shots each week. The majority will be discarded through lack of interest. What then will concentrate the mind and interest of the recipient of a direct mail shot plugging a Negotiating Course – a course designed for those who have to negotiate on prices, products, discounts, quality, delivery, materials, etc?

"As you all know, negotiating always includes firstly the standard selling process. When the prospect has been told the standard benefits of course, the negotiating begins. He may want a lower price, he may demand a concession, a change of design, etc. That is when the good negotiator wins and the poor one fails.

"Next, still thinking as a managing director or marketing director thinks, I have to decide whether he or she is completely satisfied with the negotiating team – that there could be no improvement.

"Does such an executive exist? It's doubtful. Most believe that negotiators could do better, but how does an executive know whether his negotiator is good, bad, or indifferent?

"Maybe by results. But results are not always the most positive of tests, as we know. A company may consider itself most successful if, one year, it makes X million profits; but if the industry as a whole is achieving far better results than their organization, then they are not truly successful.

"Thinking as the recipient must think, I ask myself the question: How can I really discover the strengths or weaknesses of my negotiators? I read the reports of my field manager, but they are not always truly objective. So I fantasize – I try and dream up a solution to the problem of how a recipient, a director, could know what was going on during a negotiation.

"A possible solution would be to bug the room, but that suggestion leaves a nasty taste in the mouth. It would be a turn-off for the reader. Then one day I read a newspaper gossip columnist's comments, *I'd like to have been a fly on that ceiling,* in connection with a romantic affair.

"That set off a different train of thought. It would be ethical to write to a managing director and ask *If you could be a fly on that ceiling.* There was nothing underhand in it, unlike bugging or pocket tape recording, yet it was a phrase so readily understood.

"The DMA letter almost wrote itself. The right-hand corner depicted a fly. The copy said: Dear Mr Brown, if you could be that fly on the ceiling, what do you think you would learn about your negotiators? Would you find unnecessary concessions being granted, price reductions offered too early, negotiators giving way too quickly to the customer's bluff . . .?'

"'What you would like to hear is your negotiator not giving away any concession at all – or if any, very sparingly – and calling the customer's bluff when that customer states that a competitor delivers more quickly, is less expensive, or supplies better quality products.'

"'If you want to be sure that all your negotiators have star ratings, if you could oversee their work, you have only to send them to our Negotiating Course'".

Lewis smiled and said, "You all know that that letter was an outstanding success. The lesson to be learned when creating a DMA letter is to think as the recipient of the letter will think, react as he or she would react, and that will lead to your creating a winning idea.

"Think of the unusual, and try to make it usual."

There followed discussions as to whether those examples should complete the session, and Young said, "I think not. We need another case study, and I consider a very good one is the manner in which our clients Personnel Hygiene Services created a new plan for selling their pest control services."

Cooper interrupted. "One aspect of this session disturbs me. Our research shows that we expect newly appointed managers in the following spheres: sales office managers, service managers, departmental managers, shop managers, a variety of office managers, building society managers, hotel departmental managers, etc., but – and here is the but – also in our survey are factory managers, and those in charge of stores, transport, and productivity.

"All the sessions are suitable for nearly all managers, but we haven't emphasized creativity as regards to production. Will such managers arriving here expect to master product development, or how to improve their present range?"

Instantly, Nina replied, "Philip, the rules remain. Creativity is not restricted to one section of the business community more than another, except perhaps it is more prominent in advertising. Creativity always begins with constant thinking, until ideas form in the mind. The thought process is the same, whether one is in production or in any other aspect of management. We must emphasize that fact, otherwise we shall hear the same old story that we always hear, over and over again – 'It has nothing to do with me because . . .' What we are insisting upon is that creativity comes more easily when we use the techniques we are teaching. The point to remember is that brainwaves – flashes of inspiration, Eurekas – are not what they seem to be. They arrive on the instant, certainly, but that instant only comes about after days and weeks, perhaps months, of dreaming, thinking, fantasizing, reading, probing. It is by stretching our minds and continually stretching them that a creative thought suddenly materializes."

Cooper said, "You're right, Nina. I only raised the issue because I so enjoy listening to your response."

There was some flirtatious banter and Young said. "Greg wouldn't approve of this. It comes under the heading of bad time management. With your permission, Philip, I'll continue with my case study, the lesson of which is to consider carefully what the competition is offering and then try to move one step ahead.

"That is creativity. While we were acting as consultants to Personnel Hygiene Services, the firm was launching its Pest Control Division. Subsequently steady progress was made but not fast enough for the managing director — of course they were up against fierce competition.

"In the main the demand for pest control follows an infestation. Someone sees a cockroach, a mouse, or a line of ants, and a pest-control organization is called in. In almost every area there is a local organization, ready to step in when an enquiry arises, but not very forceful in marketing.

"The problem PHS had was how to be given priority when an infestation occurred. Better known companies were telephoned before newcomers.

"One day someone at PHS was reading a report on a new US early warning system being set up in Alaska. That engendered the flash of inspiration, but the flash followed many days and weeks of hard thinking to solve the problem.

"The company set up its own early warning system: it was a great success. The name did it. Leaflets were captioned *An Early Warning System*. Salesmen used the leaflets to explain that no proprietor, director, manager, should risk a health inspector's visit because a customer had perhaps seen a mouse or a cockroach. The early warning system comprised an expert, calling at regular intervals to look for infinitesimal signs of an infestation which would never ordinarily be noticed.

"No problem with the local health authority, no customers lost, and the client would only pay for the early warning system, not for unnecessary treatment. Treatment would only be charged for if there were the first signs of an infestation.

"It was a winner, and one which helped to put PHS well up the list of leading suppliers of pest-control systems. Again, this case study teaches us that by keeping our eyes open, our ears alert, our mind always at the ready, sometimes something totally inapplicable to the product or service we are selling it would seem will help our creative processes – will set alight an idea which, when finalized, will prove to be a success, as it did with PHS."

Young looked at his watch, and said, "That will be all, the session is concluded. Let us have tea, and then continue with the final session."

Everyone clapped enthusiastically. They knew their task was reaching its close.

21   Situation-Adaptable Management

During the tea break tension returned. They knew that next day they would learn the future for themselves and the company.

To break the tension, as usual, they related past experiences in the training field. The stories were embellished, some even apochryphal, but as always, they generated appreciation of each other, and aroused ready laughter. There were oft-repeated stories of difficult delegates, love affairs between delegates, affairs with colleagues, and of course the one about the delegate who fell asleep.

After tea Young began. "We will now cover our final session – Situation-adaptable Management. I should also include a summary of successful management techniques. At this stage I need only give a précis of situation-adaptable management. We know it so well, and it will only have to be changed slightly. Is that agreed?"

They all readily agreed.

Young continued: "Although we teach situation-adaptable leadership and situation-adaptable management at our courses for executive development, leadership in management, and executive leadership, it must be rewritten for our new managers' course.

"Let me open the session.

"How adaptable are you? The autocrat may claim 'I cannot change'. The structural manager may insist 'My rank gives me the authority to decide what is best for my team'. They, and others with set styles, are wrong – especially the paternalistic manager. He is only loved when he is being kind and giving. If he changes his style, he will see the affection in which he has basked dwindle. This doesn't mean that one must not be kind and paternalistic; it only means that one mustn't expect any gratitude for what has happened in the past.

"Situation-adaptable management entails thinking, planning, and adapting a management style according to the nature of the situation.

"Let me first cover the claim that we cannot change, and state that we do change, continually. We control our temper when what we want to do is give someone a piece of our mind. Say we intend being very tough with our bank manager – 'I've never asked you for anything during the 20 years I've been a customer here. I'll change my bank'. – don't we often end up being very adaptable and pleading for his help? We do adapt ourselves to varying situations, whatever our natural instincts.

"You decide to show structural authority, or more simply, pull rank, but quickly realize that you may well be obeyed so unwillingly that production, or good relations with others, will suffer. The rigid manager will continue to use his rank and give instructions. The situation-adaptable manager will change to a more charismatic form of authority, and that appeal of enthusiasm and calm explanation may be far more effective. It's all according to the other person's reactions or an unexpected change of circumstances.

"Situation-adaptable management encourages a manager to change his manner and attitude, in order to motivate others.

"Remember, inflexible management is the cause of jealousy and fear, leading to conflict. A manager must be flexible: one

day perhaps democratic, sometimes autocratic, and on other
occasions a dispenser of wisdom.

"Whenever there is situation-adaptable management, there
is a happy working relation between employer and employee
and even a better environment between personnel and union
officials, through the ability to adapt when one senses that a
wrong stance is being taken."

Young frowned thoughtfully, then continued: "Remember,
you new managers, don't be persuaded by anyone to be the
kind of manager you would like to be. It may make you feel
good to pretend that you are either democratic, paternalistic,
charismatic, or any of the rest of 'em, but you won't win that
way. It doesn't work in the long run when problems arise.

"Many union versus management problems are caused by a
manager believing he must be autocratic and maintain his
stance, rather than give way when right is on the side of the
unions. The same advice could be given to union officials.

"There is no substitute for situation-adaptable management
in today's environment. Policies change continually, and
leadership must adapt to the change."

Young paused briefly before winding up. "That is a précis
of situation-adaptable management, but we can include some
case studies in the full session. Now over to you, Mary, for
your summary of what successful management entails."

Mary, standing up to complete the session and the course,
said, as if addressing delegates:

- One, remember you are paid to be efficient managers. Do
  not therefore expect to receive acclaim and higher
  rewards because you achieve targets. You are paid to
  achieve results. Carrying out tasks satisfactorily is what is
  expected of all of us. Only by being outstanding will you
  deserve higher rewards or promotion.

- Two, never expect gratitude, loyalty, affection,
  devotion, from subordinates or associates. Devotion is
  ephemeral. Your aim is not affection, it is to win the
  respect of associates and subordinates by your objective

thinking, your interest in *them*, and the example of all-round efficiency that you set.

- Three, learn to accept defeat as well as victory. You won't win every argument, and you won't be right every time. Never try to justify mistakes.
- Four, nothing is more depressing than working for a confirmed pessimist, and nothing so exhausting as working for a bubbling, twitching, nervous wreck. Everyone likes working for the person who is an enthusiast, but an enthusiast for the suggestions of others as well as his own. That is the real test.
- Five, to get along with people you have to try to understand them. What we must not do is typecast people. Here are some examples:

> He's very deep, you can't get through to him.
> He's so humourless.
> She's bitchy.
> He's always calm.
> You can always rely on him.
> She would never leave, she loves her work too much.

The very deep person we can't get through to is maybe someone whose mind is a whirlpool of suppressed emotions. If it were possible to win the confidence of that person, we might find that he is not so deep after all, and that there could be common ground for understanding each other.

The humourless person may consider himself to be the epitome of wit, so don't misjudge him. It's just that his sense of humour doesn't line up with yours.

The bitchy lady may of course be a bitchy lady, but on many occasions she may be someone who considers that she has been unfairly treated by others. Investigation could be worthwhile. Find out if she is carrying burdens which should be borne by other members of the staff.

That calm person may be a 'two-ulcer' man. Why

should anyone want to be so calm all the time? It isn't natural. Try to find out what he is worried about.

The reliable person could be someone full of love for his work and employers, or it could be fear that has made him reliable.

Executives often imagine their secretary, for example, would never leave them, but this is rarely so. What that executive has to do is to make certain that he is not taking his secretary for granted, and make sure that her rewards are as great as she could obtain anywhere else.

We should always look behind the many faces of mankind therefore to try to achieve a better understanding and a better relationship. But more important, we can then make allowances for others, which will lead to a better work environment.

- Six, never be afraid of in-company competition from associates, and never keep a subordinate down.
- Seven, when someone tries to persuade you to adopt a new idea in which he is emotionally tied up, discount 50 per cent of what you are told. By research you may find that the facts presented are mere generalizations, and the proof not proof at all.
- Eight, win for yourself a name as a person who gets things done. Too many managers procrastinate.
- Nine, study to be a good administrator.
- Ten, take over the tasks others shirk, and never complain about doing so.
- Eleven, if you are disenchanted with your job or you have no faith in the executive management team, get out as quickly as you can; *but,* first check to make sure that *you* have succeeded in the tasks allotted to you. Far too often we hear the excuse that management has let someone down when in fact that person deserved no better treatment.
- Twelve, guard the company's money as if it were your own. Don't waste it. Management is quick to notice and typecast the manager who believes he can spend his way

to success.

- Thirteen, many managers are too self-centred. They continue to make plans which will accord with their own requirements, or will benefit *them*, rather than the company.
- Fourteen, this is what your managing director expects of you:

  1. Ability to get the most out of your team.
  2. Willingness to accept change.
  3. Ability to innovate.
  4. Not to be concerned about the overtime hours you work or keep telling others you are not appreciated for doing so.
  5. To ask for facts, but make your own decisions.
  6. To work well with others.
  7. To have staff who are willing to work hard for you.
  8. Not to act foolishly at conferences, meetings, project launches. This may occur through drinking too much, talking too much.
  9. Always to be profit-conscious.
  10. To have sound financial knowledge.

- Fifteen, to develop the right habits, make the following resolutions:

  1. I won't lose my temper over small matters.
  2. I won't put off for the future what I should do today.
  3. The decisions I make will be based on facts only, and not emotions.
  4. I shall manage my time effectively.
  5. I shall not be brusque, either on the telephone or in person, in an attempt to create the impression that I am a very busy, important person.
  6. I shall overlook small slips by members of the staff.
  7. I shall let no one get away with big mistakes because of fear of repercussions.

8. I shall try to work out the reasons why a chief executive makes decisions, before I condemn them. I shall think them through – maybe he is right.
9. I shall not allow badly typed letters to be posted.
10. I shall not send reprimand memos.
11. I shall not smile to everyone's face and then criticize them behind their back.
12. I shall not solve all problems, but will attempt to solve them to the best of my ability.
13. I shall give praise for work well done.
14. I shall not fight change because that change has been inaugurated by someone else.
15. I shall not overwork, but plan my day so that I do a full day's work and no more.
16. I shall enjoy what I am doing, whether it be routine work or attending meetings.
17. I shall try to create, rather than copy others.
18. I shall not get rid of the boring work I ought to do by delegating it to someone else.

- Sixteen, always strive to be an effective communicator.
- Seventeen, always remember that your most important tasks are to manage people, and solve problems. It doesn't matter how much you dislike someone, if he does his job well, do not penalize or criticize him because of your dislike.

You are bound to employ impolite and bad-tempered people, back-stabbing people, some very kind people, dictatorial people, and lazy people. There will be those who are argumentative and those who disagree with whatever you suggest on principle. Most people will act unfairly at some time or other, and very, very few will be grateful on a long-term basis for any kindness or rewards you may give them. But no matter. It is your job to give help and encouragement, to try to understand why your subordinate has taken certain lines of action. After all, you are the boss, so you can afford to be tolerant. If you manage people well, many problems will solve themselves.

- Eighteen, it is often an understanding of finance which separates the good manager from the poor one. When at a meeting a manager is obviously out of his depth during discussions relating to accounts, finance, cash flow, etc., the managing director may be concerned about that manager's future development. These days, without an awareness of what finance means to management, it is extremely difficult for a manager to come to terms with cost-cutting exercises, pricing policies, profit awareness, and the engaging or cutting down of staff, etc.

- Nineteen, never sell your own company short. The fact that you didn't get the rise you had been expecting or had been promised, or that you have been allocated a smaller office, is no reason for a manager to disparage his company to others. If it is not possible to discuss the matter sensibly and logically with a superior, or if it is not possible to get the grievance out of your system, then you should, both for your future and the future of your company, look elsewhere for a job.

- Twenty, I know I seem to have been sermonizing – demanding perfection when perfection is not possible – but my objective was to set out a series of steps leading to highly effective management.

"You are at the beginning of your careers. Remember, luck plays little part in management success. No company you work for will ever be perfect, no boss will please you all or even most of the time, and at times you will get the 'Why should I?' complex. But this I will guarantee: If you put into practice all the tried and tested management practices you have been evaluating this week, nothing can stop you being a successful – no, a highly successful – manager."

22 A New Beginning

At 9 am on the Friday morning the team assembled, awaiting the verdict. They were not in high spirits. In spite of the plans made by Mary, Nina, Peter and Philip, and George Young's determination that all would be well so long as they had faith in Greg, no one considered the future with any great enthusiasm.

The team had received a battering since the news of the Dyson takeover had been leaked to them, and they felt deeply hurt because Greg had not confided in them. Grudgingly, they admitted – if only to themselves – that life at Management Skills International had always been enjoyable and exciting. They were a winning team, at conferences treated like film stars, and they even received grudging admiration from their competitors. No one at the top likes to step down, and few want to risk going it alone. They were about to learn the worst, the facts of the great sell-out.

Greg Ryder arrived looking a healthy, dynamic leader. He strode into the room and, for once, shook hands with each of his colleagues.

Was that a good sign, or not? They would soon learn.

Ryder said, "Please relax and be of good cheer, the news I

have to tell you will intrigue you."

Young's head sank. Intrigue? Why intrigue? What was there to be intrigued about? A sell-out?

Then he cheered up. Perhaps it had all fallen through. A moment later he was downcast again at the thought that if it had fallen through Greg Ryder wouldn't have called the meeting.

Mary wanted to hear that Greg was in good health, while Cooper was interested to learn how much Dysons had valued the business at.

Ryder said, "I shall as always be brief. My health is not too bad." He smiled happily. "After evaluating all the tests and carrying out more up-to-date ones, my heart specialist is satisfied with my progress. He no longer feels that a bypass operation is necessary. The pills he prescribed for me are evidently doing a good job. My blood pressure is down, my cholesterol is down, and the semi-blockages have been eased by the pills. After further consideration he now thinks that the first advice he gave me was perhaps incorrect, unless of course my condition should deteriorate. His advice had been based on the experiences he had had with other patients, most of whom suffered from stress. Subsequently he realized after several conversations and possibly some medical research into my past, that I am not a stressful person. If I had been, the pills would not have worked so well.

"He also now believes that if I were to ease off, I should become introspective – perhaps a hypochondriac. His advice then is simple: carry on as before, take the pills, don't overwork and don't get over-chilled . . ." Ryder paused, then said, "I'm glad he came round to my way of thinking."

Mary said, "That's nothing new, Greg. Most people do."

Ryder smiled, and said, "Well, I did harangue him a bit about my mental state, and I 'phoned him many times. As you know, I always emphasize the difference between enjoyable problem-solving and miserable worrying.

"Stress, I believe, is often caused by an inability to tackle a job satisfactorily or a feeling of inadequacy. You don't need me to tell you, and I said this to the doctor, that I have always been confident in my ability to overcome all problems. So at long last he did come to the right conclusion, that I am not a worrier, only a hard worker. All my efforts give me tremendous enjoyment, great pleasure, resulting in a better quality of life. It's of little use living longer if there is no quality in the extra time.

"However, I did tell him that I will no longer hold meetings which continue until 3 am. That will please all of you, I'm sure. And I won't go out in bitterly cold weather without a coat, just to impress others."

Ryder shrugged his shoulders, then continued: "I am not inviting any health discussions, but when considering the future of our company, I had to take my span of life into consideration. I hope I shall now have a few more years, and I have based the decision I have made on that assumption."

He paused for effect, then went on: "You all know the Dyson Group. Once it used to send most of its staff to us for training. I was always certain that one day it would decide to set up its own training division, which it did. I also felt that one day it might enter the management field, to compete with us.

"Dysons is a public company, answerable to its shareholders. Its profits have not been increasing at a reasonable rate, but its potential is very good indeed. Its backers, however, are concerned that Dyson himself, now 82, cannot carry on for much longer and there seems to be no obvious successor."

Again Ryder paused for effect, and the effect was a drop in spirits all round. Worse was to come. It was going to be a sellout, with Dyson taking over Marketing Skills International and using the team to bolster the management of his company.

The pause came to an end as they heard Ryder saying, "I have always believed that the greatest selling story we could tell our clients would be that we practised what we taught. No rival could compete with that. I've considered all the risks, and the growth possibilities . . ."

Perplexed, Cooper said, "I don't follow you, Greg."

"Of course not," came the reply, "and you may well ask why I haven't consulted you.

"Firstly, I own most of the MSI shares. Secondly, if I had put my proposal to you, with all the goodwill in the world you might not have agreed with my views, you might not have wanted to accept the challenge. I alone had to make that decision.

"Had I been advised that my health would deteriorate, that I was not given much time and I would not be able to function as a managing director, I would have suggested a management buy-out to you, because I did think of your interests. But that no longer applies. Ladies and gentlemen, here is the news for which you have been waiting.

"I have arranged for Management Skills International to buy out Dysons. We are going into industry for the first time."

Once more he paused for effect, and this time the effect was electric. Everyone, except Cooper, suddenly saw clearly what lay ahead. Suddenly they realized that the news leak had been completely incorrect. It wasn't that Greg was selling out to Dysons, but Dysons were selling out to Greg; and it had been Dysons who had been determined on secrecy, not wanting their staff to know that they were selling out.

Ryder said, this time very firmly, "We are all going to be put to the test. Each of us will play a part in the success of the new venture. I'll take over as chief executive for the time being, and Dyson will retire, leaving only the production team intact. Those of Dysons' managers who show ability will remain, and the others will be dismissed, made redundant, or retired. We intend to prove to the world that as consultants and trainers we can, by putting our teaching into practice, become internationally successful as an industrial group.

"You, George, will take control of personnel. You, Peter, will be our marketing director. Nina and Mary together will control our training activities and you, Philip, will be the financial director.

"But before you get too excited, I expect more of you than that. You will continue also to be instructors. I shan't accept the excuse that you haven't time to be a manager and an instructor. If you wish to take part in our new great venture, you will do both. Your rewards will be higher, because I shall instigate a share option scheme, which of course we could not do with our company, because it was a private company. Now, with a public company, that is possible.

"What a challenge! What a great opportunity for all of us!"'

Cooper said, "Greg, where does the cash come from for the takeover? It must be more than our resources can cover."

"Yes," said Ryder, "although we already have several million in investment, Dysons is a far better investment. I personally shall be buying shares. I have already spoken to our merchant bankers, who are delighted to find the balance we need. There will be no problem in arranging the finance, and we need not be concerned about gearing at this stage.

"I repeat, it's a great challenge! For so long we have been telling others what they should do; now we shall *show* others what we can do. Ultimate success does not depend solely on our management and leadership qualities, our enthusiasm, our dedication, our management reporting systems – our success will largely depend on every member of the Dyson Group. Customer care must become a byword with them, and that end can only be achieved by having good managers in every Dyson department.

"We can only direct. Managers have to carry out those directives. They have to inspire, they have to enthuse, they have to teach. Success depends on the managers, whether they be newly appointed or old-timers. What we have to do therefore is to ensure that every manager lives up to the standards that we have set in every session this week.

"And that is all."

For a moment there was near pandemonium. Mary kissed Greg, Peter kissed Nina, others were back-slapping, hand-shaking and finally, all were cheering Greg Ryder.

Printed and bound in Great Britain by
Biddles Ltd, Guildford and King's Lynn